The Philippine Islands
Vol.-46

by

Ed. Emma Helen Blair and
James Alexander Robertson

The Philippine Islands
Vol.-46
by Ed. Emma Helen Blair and James Alexander Robertson

ISBN: 978-93-59398-73-0

Published by

DOUBLE 9 BOOKS

2/13-B, Ansari Road
Daryaganj, New Delhi – 110002
info@double9books.com
www.double9books.com
Tel. 011-40042856

ABOUT THE EDITOR

Emma Helen Blair (1869-1951) was an American historian and author known for her significant contributions to Philippine history and also scholarship. Born on July 19, 1869, in Ohio, she pursued her education at Ohio Wesleyan University and later at Columbia University. Blair's passion for history and research led her to collaborate with James Alexander Robertson, an esteemed scholar, in editing and compiling "The Philippine Islands, 1493-1898" series. This monumental project spanned fifty-five volumes and covered the colonial history of the Philippines from the 16th to the 19th century. The comprehensive series showcased her expertise in meticulously examining and also presenting historical documents and narratives. Her work significantly contributed to a deeper understanding of the Philippines' complex past and its interactions with various colonial powers. Her commitment to historical accuracy and attention to detail earned her a reputation as a meticulous and reliable historian. Beyond her contributions to Philippine history, and main thing that Emma Helen Blair also authored "The Philippine Policy of Secretary Taft" and co-wrote "A History of the Philippine Islands" with Robertson. Both of these works further demonstrated her dedication to scholarship and the exploration of the Philippines' political and social developments.

James Alexander Robertson was born in Corry, Pennsylvania, in 1873. He was the sixth of eight children born to Canadian parents who became naturalized citizens of the United States after moving to Corry in 1866. His father, John McGregor Robertson, was a builder from Verulam, Ontario, close to Peterborough. His mother, Elizabeth Borrowman Robertson, immigrated to Canada as a child from her native Scotland. When Robertson was seven years old, his mother died. After three years, he and his family relocated to Cleveland, Ohio, where James finished his secondary education. In 1892, he enrolled in Adelbert College at Western Reserve University for graduate study. He studied in Romance languages, majoring in Old French, and received his Bachelor of Philosophy degree from Western Reserve University in 1896.

CONTENTS

PREFACE

Most of this volume consists of the educational appendix which is continued from the preceding volume. The only regular document presented shows the general history of the islands for the years 1721–1739 both politically and religiously. The greater interest in the volume centers about the appendix. For here we see the first systematic attempts at a universal education in the Philippines, the first real though rude awakening of the inert mass of a people to the facts of broader life by the government establishment of primary and normal schools. As might be expected the paternal element is chiefly discernible in the laws and regulations made by the government. The complexities of the educational question, a problem that Spain would have been many years in solving, are well shown by the two documents which give the friar side of the matter.

A brief summary of the principal events from 1721 to 1739 contains several matters of interest. The murder of Bustamante by a mob arouses much indignation at Madrid, but the attempts to ascertain and punish the guilty ones prove ineffectual, and the affair drops into oblivion. The islands are regularly harassed by the Moro pirates; punitive expeditions are sent against them, but these are often too late or too slow to accomplish any results. The coast villages are fortified, much of this being done by the priests in charge of the Indians. In 1733 the royal storehouses at Manila are destroyed by fire, causing great loss to the treasury. Two years later, a Dutch fleet demands satisfaction for the previous capture of a Dutch ship by a Spanish coastguard, but retires when the Spaniards pay the value of the prize. A controversy arises (1736) between the Recollects and Jesuits over certain missions in northern Mindanao, in which the Jesuits gain the upper hand. In 1737, one of the auditors makes an official visitation of several provinces in Luzón, and reforms many abuses therein. During 1738–39, a controversy rages in Manila over the complaint made by the mestizos of Santa Cruz regarding unjust exactions imposed on them by the Jesuits; the decision of the Audiencia (sustained by the home government) is against that order.

The remainder of this volume is occupied by the educational appendix, which is the continuance and conclusion of the review of education begun in VOL. XLV. The first document, which comprises the greater part of the appendix, treats of primary and normal instruction in the Philippines, after the government really took such education under its protection by special legislation. The subject is prefaced by extracts and synopses from Barrantes which show the earliest legislation, beginning with 1839 and culminating in the decree of December 20, 1863. Although the appointment of a commission is ordered in the former year to draft regulations for schools, such appointment is delayed until 1855, and a report is handed in only in 1861, the work of the commission being stimulated perhaps by the fact that the governor appoints an official in 1860 to draft regulations along the same line. The chief point of debate in the commission is the teaching of Spanish, the vice-rector of the university of Santo Tomás declaring against such teaching but being overruled. The decree of December 20, 1863 is the greatest result of the work of the commission. The normal school created by the decree is formally opened January 23, 1865, although in operation since May 17, 1864. Irregularity of attendance and vacations prove the greatest obstacles. Barrantes, who defends the friars, concludes that the backwardness of primary education is due rather to the laws of the Indies than to any class such as the religious corporations; that before 1865 primary education was only a shadow; and that the Filipinos have not yet sufficiently far advanced to be granted the electoral right that they ask. The remainder of the document is from Grifol y Aliaga's book on primary instruction. An extract from the preface of that author shows that with the decree of 1863, new life is put into education, and that all the many decrees and orders issued later by the government are harmonious in effect and purpose; although they were in large part inoperative. Next follows the royal decree of December 20, 1863, establishing a plan of primary instruction in the islands. Its first part consists of the exposition addressed to the queen by the minister José de la Concha, stating the need of greater efficiency in the teaching system for the natives, in order that they may develop spiritually and intellectually. The aim is to diffuse the Spanish language. It provides for a normal school under the immediate supervision of the priests. Following the exposition is the decree proper, which decrees schools for each sex in each village, and gives various details of such schools. The regulations for the normal school of teachers for primary instruction end Aliaga's book. They consist of twenty-eight articles which state the object of the school; and the rules governing the scholars in their manifold relations. Next come the regulations, dated December 20, 1863, for schools and teachers of primary instruction for native Filipinos, which consist of thirty-five articles. By these regulations, separate schools are established in all the villages for boys and girls; attendance is made compulsory for children between certain ages; instruction is to be in Spanish, and the knowledge of that language especially striven for; tuition is free to the poor, and equipment for all; religious and ethical teaching is in charge of the parish priests. Rules are given in regard to the teachers, and assistants, the textbooks, vacations, the establishment of Sunday schools for adults, and the supervision, which is put into the hands of laymen—that duty having thitherto been performed by the parish priests, in so far as it was performed at all. The interior regulations, consisting of fourteen articles, for native primary schools, follow, as the preceding, dated December 20, 1863. They include rules as to the size of buildings, equipment, duties of teachers, manner of keeping records, sending of monthly reports, pupils and conditions of their admittance, attendance, system of merits and demerits, examinations, etc. Religious exercises are found to fill a considerable portion of the day. A government decree of February 15, 1864, approving the regulations for a municipal girls' school in Manila, is followed by those regulations of the same date, which consist of twenty-six articles. The school is to be in charge of the sisters of charity. Religious and ethical training is given great prominence. The courses of study, comprising the elementary branches, and needle-work, is outlined. There are both required and optional studies. Girls are admitted at the age of five, and admission is in charge of a member of the city ayuntamiento. Rules are given governing the daily and term routine of the school in its manifold relations. Examinations are both public and private. Supervision is in charge of three women appointed by the governor of the islands. This is followed by a circular of the superior civil government, dated August 30, 1867, discussing, and giving rules concerning, school supervision—an important document, showing well the Spanish love of philosophizing. Commenting on the importance of the supervisory function, the circular states the duties of supervisors, for on them "depends the development and conservation of the improvements which are being introduced." Since the supervision is partly in the hands of the ecclesiastical government, the outcome can only be the best. A rather lengthy quotation is made from a book on supervision, in which the duties and qualifications of supervisors are outlined. Great stress is laid on temperateness of action. The most delicate power is the correction and suspension of teachers. Suspension must only be for ethical and religious lack, and neglect of duties. The parish priests in their duties as supervisors must see that the heads of families recognize their responsibility in regard to sending their children to school. Special privileges are to be given to those attending school and learning the Spanish language—in which all instruction is to be given. Primary instruction in the islands is in a backward state, because of the few buildings and teachers, and the want of uniformity among the children. Statistics of March 1, 1866 show the number of villages in provinces or districts, the population, school attendance, schools possible, and buildings. The government pledges its support of the efforts put forth by the parish priests and the provincial supervisors. The former are to hold annual examinations, and are to have the children review their work when they confess and take communion. The provincial supervision of the alcaldes is to be exercised with the aid of a board composed of the bishop, parish priest, and the administrator of the public finances. Reforms are needed in teaching and supervision, and the efforts of the parish priest must not be opposed. Boards not yet appointed must be appointed at once, and monthly reports submitted. The government decree of June 19, 1875, approving ad interim the regulations for the women's normal school for primary teachers in Nueva Cáceres, is followed by the regulations. These number fifty-two articles in all. The object of the school is to train good moral and religious women teachers and to make this school a model for other schools. The practice school attached to it is an integral part of the public school system, wherein an education is given free to poor girls. Those attending the normal school may or may not be candidates for a teacher's certificate. The program of studies shows elementary branches, and demands instruction in Spanish and includes needle-work. The course lasts three years, though an additional year may be allowed to graduates; and the schedule of studies is to be sent annually to the governor for his approval. The time spent in the practice school is not to exceed four months in each year. Teachers' certificates are to be given to those completing the course, and such graduates are to be given schools of the proper grades, the method of marking being given. The school is organized under charge of the sisters of charity, and the school of Santa Isabel is to be used. The staff and their duties are enumerated, among whom it is to be noted is a secular priest to administer to the ethical and religious needs of the pupils. Pupils shall be both day and resident, the requirements for admission being stated. Women teachers may be admitted to the institution, if not over the age of twenty-three. Instruction is free, and provided for from the local funds. In proportion as the public schools are placed in charge of normal graduates, the number of resident pupils supported from the local funds is to be decreased to twenty-five, from whom vacancies are to be filled. Resident pupils supported by local funds are to teach ten years in the schools of Nueva Cáceres, under penalty of making restitution of their expenses if they do not carry out their contract. General public examinations are to be held at the end of the term, when rewards are to be distributed. Various other data regarding the running of the school in its different relations are given. The moral and religious supervision belongs to the bishop of Nueva Cáceres; secular supervision is in charge of the alcalde-mayor, the bishop, and the administrator of public finances, and one member of this board is to have immediate supervision for three months. A royal decree dated March 11, 1892 creates in Manila a normal school for women teachers under charge of Augustinian nuns. It is needed as is proved by that of Nueva Cáceres. The study of Spanish is compulsory. Expenses are to be met from the regular budget for the islands. Among other data included in this decree, it is to be noted that the certificate for elementary teaching is given for three years' study and that for superior for four; and that a practice school, whose expenses are to be met by the municipality, is to be annexed to the normal school. This is followed by a royal order of May 19, 1892 approving the regulations for the above normal school, which is followed in turn by the regulations bearing the same date, and consisting of one hundred and fifty-four articles. This is a document of considerable interest, for it goes into much detail concerning the school in its relations to government, teachers, pupils, and public. It is divided into various sections designated as títulos, which are in turn divided into chapters. Título i states in the first chapter the object of the school, and the subjects taught, which are both required and optional. The expense of equipment is to be approved by the general government. Chapter ii relates to the teaching force, and enumerates their duties and names salaries. The total expenses are to be seven thousand nine hundred pesos annually. Chapter iii gives in detail the duties of the directress, which are mainly executive; and those of the instructresses. Chapters iv to vii treat of the duties of the secretary, the librarian, the assistants, and the necessary help. Chapter viii deals with the board of instructresses, which is composed of the regular teachers, and outlines its functions. Chapter ix treats of the disciplinary council, which must consist of five members at least, and is convoked by the directress. Título ii deals with the economic management—chapter i treating of the annual budget, and chapter ii of the collection, distribution, and payment of accounts. Título iii has as its main subject the teaching: of which chapter i deals with the opening of the school, and the term in general; chapter ii, of the order of classes and methods of teaching, etc.; and chapter iii, with the material equipment for teaching. Título iv discusses the scholars: chapter i, treating of their necessary qualifications, entrance examinations, payment of entrance fees, and age of entrance; chapter ii, concerning matriculation, in which there is much red tape; chapter iii, of the obligations of the pupils, mainly in deportment; chapter iv, of examinations—an important subject—which are divided into ordinary and extraordinary, according to the time taken, and are oral, written, and practical; chapter v, of rewards; chapter vi, of certificates and decisions, and conditions under which they are given; and chapter vii, of discipline and punishments. Título v, which is, like all this document, laden with red tape, outlines the conditions of the examination for degrees. The practice school annexed to the normal school has its expenses met by the municipality, and is a public school. For the present the normal school shall have only day pupils, but if necessary later, they may enrol resident pupils. The nuns in charge of the school have liberty to follow the institutes of their order. This document is followed by a governmental decree of November 1, 1893, elevating to the grade of superior the normal school for men teachers in Manila, and approving provisionally the new regulations of this school. This exposition by the reverend father director shows that this school, created as an elementary normal school by the decree of December 20, 1863, has been fulfilling its function since its creation, and has made progress in the process of better understanding between the Filipinos and Spanish authorities, has diffused the Spanish language wider than ever, and encouraged the arts and industries. It has had a difficult path, because of the condition of its students who are far from homogeneous in preparation and ability. It has been necessary to lessen the age limit at which men may enter, because, as the average Filipino leaves school at the age of twelve, he readily forgets what he has learned, and consequently when he enters at the age of sixteen into the normal school, he has to take a year in special preparation. The proposal to elevate the school to the rank of superior can be done without any extra expense, as it will be in charge of the same force as at present. The Manila normal school compares with the best in Spain. A petition by one A. Avilés, asking for the extension, and the decree proper, both dated November 10, 1893 follow. Certificates from this school are to have the same value and rights as certificates granted in Spain. The regulations for the extension above-mentioned dated also November 10, 1893, follow. They consist of thirty articles, a number of which are similar or analogous to those of the regulations of December 20, 1863, establishing the elementary school. These regulations discuss the manifold relations of the school in regard to pupils, teachers, supplies, examinations, etc. The selections from Grifol y Aliaga are closed by a list of all the decrees, circulars, orders, etc., in regard to primary and normal education in the Philippines from December 20, 1863 to July 20, 1894 — in all one hundred and seventy-one. This is of distinct value, as the course of legislation can be followed easily, and one may note the new ideas that leaders were attempting to work out in this period of Spanish unrest.

A series of short documents regarding the religious schools follows. The first is a summary of the Dominican institutions for 1896–1897. The university of Santo Tomás has a total enrolment in all courses of 3,059, and a total of 36 degrees are conferred. The college of San Juan de Letran has a total enrolment of 5,995, which includes professors, collegiates, day pupils, and servants; and has conferred in all 177 degrees. The college of San Alberto Magno in Dagupan, has an enrolment of 947, counting teachers. The school of Santa Catalina de Sená shows an enrolment of 223, including the teachers, who are nuns. A total enrolment of 83 is seen in the school of

Nuestra Señora del Rosario of Lingayén; while the school of the same name in Vigan has 79. The school of Santa Ymelda founded in 1892, completes the list, with an enrolment of 110. A report for the religious schools for 1897 gives various statistics of the following institutions: La Concordia, Santa Isabel, Santa Rosa, and Looban, the military hospital, the hospital of St. John of God, the municipal school [of secular foundation], and the hospice of San José, all in charge of the sisters of charity in Manila; and certain of the provincial schools. The third document in this series gives an account of the educational institutions of the Recollects, probably for the year 1897. These are the beaterio of Santa Rita in San Sebastian, in the suburbs of Manila; school of San José of Bacolod, Negros, opened in 1897, and under the auspices of the university of Santo Tomás; the seminary school of Vigan, of which the Recollects had charge during the years 1882–1895; school of Santa Rosa, of which the Recollects were in charge in 1891.

The friar side of the educational question of the Philippines is well set forth in two selections. The first is a chapter by Eduardo Navarro, O.S.A., who spent many years in the islands, and who is, perhaps, one of the best representative men of his order, and moreover, of scholarly tastes. He introduces his subject in a somewhat philosophical manner. Education and religion he declares to be synonymous terms when taken in their real signification. It is the duty of the government to choose the best educational method. The earliest laws passed by the Spanish government in regard to the education of the American Indians are extended later to the Philippines, but they prove most unsatisfactory and unsuited to the conditions of those islands. They provide for the teaching of Spanish to the aborigines, but in an inadequate manner. The theme of the present chapter is to prove that the friars are not responsible for the backward state of education in the islands. On the other hand they early pass laws that are more advanced than those passed by the government. Their laws have always been consistent and have had but one aim. They have not endeavored to retard the learning of Spanish, but they rather favored it. They have done their best with the useless laws of the government. They have founded and taught schools, paid the teachers, and have made the textbooks, notwithstanding their immense toil. They have also introduced many of the arts and crafts. The friars have gone farther than the laws for they provided for girls' schools before the famous decree of 1863. The passage of those regulations has robbed the parish priest unjustly of much of his supervisory power, which has been conferred except in so far as morality and religion are concerned, on the civil authorities. It belongs by right to the friars, who only use that power as it should be used. The parish priest knows the people thoroughly, and as no laymen do. The Filipino cannot be identified with the Spaniards notwithstanding all efforts of the Spanish government. Navarro enforces his arguments by quotations from Escosura, whom he criticises harshly for his expressions. While modern ideas from abroad have made better sea communication, internal communication has become worse. Good roads are especially needed and the small barrios ought to be merged together whenever possible. That the friars do not oppose education is shown by the many schools that they maintain in Manila and the provinces. They should be allowed to establish normal schools under their own direction. The parish priest can best overcome the evil introduced by the free masons. The studies chosen for the Filipinos must be fitted to their capacity. Our author suggests the personnel of the Superior Board of Public Instruction, in which he places a majority of ecclesiastics, and this Board should revise the school laws. The majority of the Filipino students return to their homes with plenty of vices but little learning, although looked up to greatly by their fellow townsmen. This horde brings disaster and ruin upon the people. The rector of the university should have more power over the life and morals of the students, for only thus can the Filipino students become really useful to Spain.

The second selection is a chapter written by Fr. Eladio Zamora, also an Augustinian. Almost the last friar writer on the matter, since he writes after American occupation, his remarks may be assumed to be the present friar attitude. He begins with a quotation from the preface of Grifol y Aliaga to the effect that until 1863 there had been no real legislation concerning education, for the many decrees, etc., were isolated. It is rather the friars, says Zamora, who are the first educators, teaching themselves or paying teachers from their own funds. After 1863, the friars continue to encourage education as supervisors. They build schools, and visit the distant barrios whenever possible. On Sundays it is their custom to inspect the copybooks, etc. The distance of barrios and villages from one another makes teaching difficult. Many of the priests become suspected as having a bad influence, for many criminals resort to the barrios. The government orders the fusion of barrios into villages, but the order is not obeyed. In 1863, the government takes control of the schools founded by the friars. Under the new regime, so long as the parish priest has supervisory action, the schools flourish, but when that action ceases, so does progress in the schools, and attendance becomes only nominal and a record on paper. The intention of the government to have all teaching in Spanish fails of its purpose, for the scholars can not understand it. The famous Maura decree of 1893 gives the local supervision to local municipalities, a law that soon gives rise to serious trouble. Many unjustly blame the parish priest for the ignorance of Spanish, but he has no time to teach Spanish amid the multiplicity of his duties. Besides, it is easier for the few Spaniards to learn the languages of the natives than for the Filipinos to learn Spanish. The friars have not shunned the teaching of Spanish, as is proved by a citation from Zúñiga. If the Tagálog actors are allowed to use their native language in the theater, because they do not know Spanish, is it consistent to demand that all sermons and teaching be in Spanish? In spite of the early laws requiring Spanish to be taught to the Filipinos, it is impossible for Spanish to supplant all the numerous dialects. Zamora reproduces portions of an open letter by W. E. Retana to Minister Becerra, in which Retana decries the intellect of the Filipino, and declares that it is absurd to think of teaching him in Spanish, but that the best way of teaching it would be to settle 500,000 Spanish families in the islands. Zamora gives a résumé of the history of the university of Santo Tomás and the college of San Juan de Letran. The religious corporations have kept abreast of the times in the manner in which they have fostered education from the earliest period, and many schools are due to them, some being founded by the tertiary order of the Dominicans. Zamora criticises the capacity of the Filipinos, asserting that they are teachable and quick in imitation, although they never attain excellence in anything, but that they are utterly devoid of originality. They have greater capacity than the American Indian, and make fine clerks and the like, but they are lazy, and do not strive to rise beyond a certain point. They learn vices but not virtues. The Augustinians are the last of the religious orders to take up superior education, by establishing an institute at Iloilo, because a secular institution was planned for that place by Minister Becerra in 1887–1888. Zamora emphasizes the importance of arts and crafts for the Filipinos.

The appendix to our volume is brought to a close with a very brief statement in regard to American education in the Philippines since 1898. A bibliographical list of works treating of education will enable the student to follow the course of American work. The statement is concluded by the abstract of a philosophical address by Dr. T. H. Pardo de Tavera before the American and Filipino teachers in Manila in May 1906, in which he points out the beneficent results of Anglo-Saxon teaching.

The Editors

November, 1906.

DOCUMENT OF 1721–1739

Events in Filipinas, 1721–1739. Compiled from various sources.

Source: This document consists of citations and synopses from various authors fully credited in the text.

Translation: The translations and synopses are made by Emma Helen Blair.

EVENTS IN FILIPINAS, 1721–1739

The Marqués de Torre-Campo "brought with him commission to take the residencia of Bustamante;1 and as it found him already dead, many were the charges that resulted against him—which it would not be difficult to prove, since the minds of the people were so inflamed against him, as we have seen. Some of his friends, it appeared, were accomplices in his delinquencies; some denied the charges, and, as these could not be proved against them, it was necessary to declare them innocent; others excused themselves by his violent proceedings, and by their fear that he would kill them if they did not obey him. Don Esteban Iñigo, who was charged, among other things, with the exportation of rice, which caused a great famine in the islands, replied that he had undertaken this trade with the governor because he could not resist the latter, and feared that if he did not do so he would lose the rice and all his property. Other persons alleged other [reasons for their] exemption [from legal process], always blaming the deceased—who, as he had no one to defend him, came out of this residencia the most wicked man that can be imagined."2 (Zúñiga, Hist. de Philipinas, p. 469.)

The Council of the Indias gave answer to the royal Audiencia [of Manila] that they had received the [papers in the] investigation of the death of the governor, and were giving the matter due attention; and at the same time came another order from the king to the Marqués de Torre-Campo, in which the latter was commanded to take cognizance of this affair and punish the culprits. The governor, who, it appears, had little inclination to plunge into this labyrinth, a second time consulted Father Totanes3 and the Jesuits—who told him that, just as he had before stayed the execution of the first order, he ought to do the same with this one, until his Majesty, advised of the governor's reply [to the first order], which had not yet been received, should make another decision. Father Totanes in his advisory statement exaggerated the ruin of the fortunes of the citizens of Manila, the arrears [in the incomes] of the charitable funds, the scarcity of rice, and the lack of those who might give alms (on account of which, he said, many died of hunger), the cause of all these evils being the mariscal. The father expatiated on his acts of violence, and the consternation of the city, with which he strove to exculpate the action of the Manila people, who had no other recourse, in order to escape from such a throng of calamities, than to depose the governor from his office. "But to what tribunal," he said, "were they to resort in order to deprive him of his office? He had suppressed the royal Audiencia, and held the archbishop and the ecclesiastics prisoners; and the city [council] was composed of an alcalde-in-ordinary who was a nephew of the governor, and two regidors who were his henchmen. Not having any one to resort to, they tried to arrest the governor, in order to free themselves from so many calamities; he resisted, turning his weapons against the citizens, who wounded him mortally in defense of their own lives; but this should be regarded as the misfortune of the mariscal rather than the fault of the citizens." This statement, which veritably is a seditious one, they presented to the king, in order to show him the erroneous opinions of the religious of Philipinas; but it was a calumny, for Father Totanes was not the oracle of the islands, and most of the regulars thought as did the Jesuit fathers—who, while condemning in their advisory report the act of the Manila people, said only that the latter were worthy of the royal clemency. With this came to a halt all the severity with which at first this process was undertaken, and, the minds of people gradually becoming cool, the prosecution entirely ceased, and all these who were inculpated remained unpunished; the archbishop alone, he who had taken least part in these commotions and disturbances, was chastised4—a worthy prelate, who in imitation of Christ carried on his own shoulders the sin of his people. (Zúñiga, Hist. de Philipinas, pp. 514–517.)

[As soon as the Spaniards abandoned the fort of Lábo in Paragua, the Moro pirates renewed their incursions. When Zamboanga was reestablished, they attempted to capture it, but were repulsed with loss. In 1721–23 expeditions were sent out against the Moros, but they failed to accomplish anything.5 The sultan of Joló sent an ambassador to Manila in 1725, to form a treaty of peace with the Spaniards; this was accomplished in the following year at Joló, the Spanish envoy being Miguel Arajón, the alcalde-mayor of the Parián at Manila. By this treaty, among other provisions, the island of Basilan was restored to Spain. Nevertheless, soon afterward the perfidious Moros made several raids against Indian villages, captured many vessels and burned them, and committed many acts of cruelty,—the worst probably being the case of a vessel from Cebú, whose crew were all killed by the pirates, who then tortured to death the Spanish captain. Later, letters were received from Radiamura (the son of Maulana) and other friendly chiefs in Mindanao, asking for prompt action by the Spaniards against the Moro pirates, who, they claimed, were threatening them with attack because of their friendship to the Spaniards. Governor Torre Campo organized a punitive expedition for this purpose, but the royal treasury was so depleted that the costs had to be met by donations from the citizens of Manila and Cavite. The armada was placed under command of Juan Angel de Leaño, with directions to surrender the vessels and men to General Juan de Mesa when they should reach Iloilo; and the governor gave the commanders definite instructions, and powers for forming a treaty with the "kings" of Joló and Mindanao. "The result of this expedition is not definitely stated, except that it was successful; the fort of La Sabanilla at Tuboc was taken, and a great number of the rabble [canalla] were slain, and among them some princes and datos (the remembrance of which still continues among them, to the honor of our arms); and a treaty for the cessation of hostilities was drawn up, which the Moros, well punished, asked for." (Concepción, Hist. de Philipinas, x, pp. 134–157, 184–198.)]

[On July 23, 1726, the galleon "Santo Christo de Burgos" was driven by a storm on the rocks at Ticao, a long, narrow island adjoining San Bernardino Strait, and so badly wrecked that it could not be repaired. The auditor Julian de Velasco was on board the vessel, on his way to Mexico; as the official of highest rank on the ship, he held a conference with the officers, pilots, seamen, and other persons of experience, and it was decided (after several vain efforts had been made to save part of the cargo) to burn the ship and its contents, great part of which were ruined by the water. This was a great loss to the citizens of Manila, as all their investments for this year were thus destroyed. (Concepción, *Hist. de Philipinas*, x, pp. 157–167.)]

[Torrubia enumerates the armed naval expeditions sent against the Moro pirates during 1721–34, as follows: (1) An armada commanded by Antonio de Roxas sailed from Manila on July 10, 1721; it seems to have accomplished little, but cost the treasury much. (2) Another was commanded by Andrés Garcia; he fought with a Moro fleet—date not given, but probably in 1722—at Negros Island, and won a notable victory. (3) In 1723 a fleet set out under command of Juan de la Mesa y Aponte, warden of Fort Santiago at Manila; they went to Mindanao and captured from the Moros the fort at La Sabanilla, "slaying an immense number of that rabble, and among them several princes and datos." (4) In February, 1731, four galleys were sent from Manila under command of Ignacio Irriberri; at Zamboanga they collected the vessels already there—two fragatas, four despatch-boats or champans, one taratana, one falua, eight caracoas of Bisayans and two others of Lutaos—and went to attack Joló, at which they found six forts defended by cannon. Here they had a fierce battle with the Moros, of whom many were slain, including two datos; then they ravaged the adjacent island of Talobo, destroying its salt-works ("which are the entire livelihood of that people"); and laid waste the district of the dato Salicaya, who, with many of his people, was slain. In the same year Captain Pedro Zacharias Villareal, with some vessels of the same fleet, attacked the island of Capual, near Joló, and burned three villages and many boats, and ravaged the fields, destroying their cattle and the salt-works there. (5) In November, 1731, Zacharias was sent by Valdés Tamon with a squadron from Manila to Zamboanga; at that very time, the sultan of Mindanao, Maulana Diafar Sadibsa, was asking aid from the Spaniards against his tributary Malinog, who had rebelled against him and had secured the support of more than thirty of the principal villages on the Rio Grande of Mindanao. This rebellion was caused by Malinog's refusal to obey Maulana's demand that he restore to the Spaniards the captives and spoil which Malinog, in conjunction with the Joloans, had carried away in 1722–23 from Negros and Panay. It was learned that Malinog was negotiating with the Dutch for succor, which they were inclined to grant him. At a council of war (in which the Jesuits were prominent) held in Zamboanga, it was decided to send Zacharias with a fleet to Tamontaca, to aid Maulana and punish Malinog. The latter's fort—which, like that in Joló, was constructed by a Dutch engineer—at the entrance to his river, was captured by the united forces and large amounts of military supplies were destroyed. Two leguas further up the river, they attacked Malinog's principal town, defended by six forts; many of the Moros (including their general, Tambul) were slain, three of their villages were burned, and their lands devastated. Returning to Zamboanga, the Spaniards harried the coasts of Joló and Basilan, so thoroughly that, later, "in order to terrify the Moros, it is only necessary to say, 'Here comes Zacharias.'" (6) In January, 1733, a fleet under Juan Antonio Jove went to aid Maulana; but Malinog made a sudden attack on Tamontaca, which he destroyed with fire and sword, and slew Maulana, whereupon the Spaniards, disheartened, returned to Manila. (7) Maulana's successor, Radiamura, asked aid from Manila, which was granted; the citizens subscribed more than nine thousand pesos in silver, and a fleet of forty-eight vessels was equipped. Under command of Francisco de Cardenas Pacheco and Captain (soon afterward made sargento-mayor) Zacharias, this fleet left Zamboanga on February 18, 1734, and went to Tamontaca. At Tuboc they attacked the sultan of Tawi-Tawi, but the Bisayan auxiliaries of the Spaniards fled, panic-stricken, and the Moro allies of the sultan swarmed in upon the Spaniards, compelling them to retreat. They then went against Malinog at Sulangan; at sight of the Spanish fleet, he set fire to his village and forts, and fled up the river to Libungang—a place which was strongly fortified by both nature and art. A fierce assault was made on this stronghold, but the Moros could not be dislodged; they killed many Spaniards with their unceasing discharge of balls and small weapons, and finally, by poisoning the water-supply, compelled the Spaniards to raise the siege. Then the latter went to Sulungan, and remained there until that place was well fortified, and the passage of the river securely closed to Malinog, who was thus shut in from his allies the Joloans and Camucones. On April 20, Radiamura was solemnly crowned as king by the Spaniards; and he agreed to allow the entrance of Christian missionaries, the building of churches, and the establishment of Spanish forts and garrisons, in his territories; also to acknowledge his vassalage to Spain by furnishing a quantity of wax, cacao, and other products of the country. Afterward, Zacharias made a raid on Basilan, devastated the lands, and seized much and rich booty; "so great was the spoil of the 'enchanted island' that, when the men had laden our armada and the captured vessels [which numbered over three hundred], they had to burn many articles because they could not carry them away." (Torrubia, Dissertacion, pp. 68–90.) Cf. Concepción's and Montero y Vidal's accounts of these expeditions.]

[The Marqués de Torre Campo, after eight years of clement and upright government, was succeeded by Fernando de Valdés y Tamón, a knight of the Order of Santiago, who took possession of his office on August 14, 1729. As an experienced and able soldier, he gave his first attention to the fortifications and military equipment of Manila, which had been sadly neglected. He tried to purchase 1,500 guns with bayonets, but the Dutch refused to sell him these firearms. In May, 1730, the pirates of Joló sent out a large expedition, with 3,000 men, against the islands of Palawan and Dumaran, where they plundered the villages and carried away many captives. They besieged the fort at Taytay (the principal town in that part of Palawan) during twenty days, but were obliged to retire with considerable loss, including some of their datos. As it was evident that the islands could have no peace or safety until severe punishment was inflicted on these pirates, an expedition with over 600 men was sent from Manila in February, 1731, under the command of General Ignacio de Iriberri. This force attacked the town of Joló, which was well defended with forts and artillery; and after a fierce contest the Spaniards captured the place, and burned the houses and boats of the Moros. They also ravaged the islands of Talobo and Capual, near Joló, and destroyed the salt-works there, from which the pirates obtained much wealth; and returned to Manila in the month of June. A prominent chief of Mindanao, named Malinog, had revolted against Maulana Diafar, sultan of Tamontaca, securing the aid of many datos on the Rio Grande, and negotiating with the Dutch for their aid; in November, 1731, a small squadron was sent from

Manila, in answer to Maulana's petition for aid against the rebels; with the aid of the Spaniards the rebels were routed, their forts destroyed, and their villages and plantations ravaged and burned. Malinog, however, kept up the contest, so that another Spanish expedition was sent (January, 1733) against him; but while his town was besieged by the Tamontacans and the Spaniards he slipped away with 300 pirogues and invaded Tamontaca, where Maulana was slain by his foes.6 His son Amuril asked Governor Valdés y Tamón for aid against Malinog, which was granted; and in February 1734 an expedition left Zamboanga under command of General Francisco Cárdenas Pacheco, who placed a detachment of the armada under Pedro Zacarías Villarreal. Their campaign against the Moros was bravely fought, but was only partially successful, on account of the fierceness and overwhelming numbers of the Moros. The latter committed numerous depredations wherever and whenever they could find opportunity, and the Manila government took measures for the erection of lookout towers and fortifications at the coast villages, and for sending coastguard galleys and other vessels to the points most likely to be menaced by the pirates, so as to be ready to meet or follow up any Moro vessels that might attack the Indian villages or Spanish forts. In 1735, 2,000 Joloans and Mindanaos attacked the fort at Taytay, but they were finally repulsed with great loss. In this conflict, as often on like occasions, the native soldiers in the garrison were encouraged and incited by the friars in whose spiritual charge they were, to resist the fierce foe who attacked them.7 In 1735, Mahamad Ali-Mudin was raised to the sultanate of Joló, in virtue of the abdication of his father Maulana. The latter plotted to obtain possession of the fort at Zamboanga by treason, but the scheme was unsuccessful; the news of this so angered Maulana (who was then ill) that he hastened his own death. The new sultan of Joló professed (1736) friendship to the Spaniards, and even joined them in a campaign against the Tiron pirates; but in secret he encouraged the latter, and sent them warning of the movements against them. (Montero y Vidal, Hist. de Filipinas, i, pp. 438–452; his account is largely taken from Concepción's Hist. de Philipinas, x, pp. 198–238, 337–375.)]

[On June 18, 1733, the royal magazines at Manila were destroyed by fire, with all their contents, which included the supplies for the two vessels which were soon to go to Acapulco. The royal treasury had not the funds to make good this loss, and the galleons must sail at a certain time, in order to secure favorable winds; the governor therefore appealed to the citizens and merchants for help to meet the expenses of equipping the vessels. They responded with a donation of 30,000 pesos, which the governor duly reported to the king, asking that in view of the zeal and loyalty thus displayed by the citizens their interest might be cared for in the pending dispute regarding the Manila-Acapulco commerce. The losses sustained in the above fire were estimated by the royal officials at 66,807 pesos. (Concepción, Hist. de Philipinas, x, pp. 226–230.)]

The governor, not finding any corrective for the injuries which the Moros were causing, held a conference of the principal citizens of Manila. It was resolved therein that, so far as the funds in the royal treasury would permit, some small armadas should be despatched against the Moros; and that the coast-dwellers should be gathered [into larger villages] at certain places, at the rate of five hundred tributes to each one, in order that they might be able to resist the pirates and build some little forts, which would inspire respect in the enemy.8 This precaution had already been taken by some of the religious in charge of doctrinas—who, not finding any other remedy, had built some fortifications around their churches, in order to guard these and that the Indians might take refuge there when the Moros came. Others had built some small forts on lofty places, in order to protect the villages from the affronts of those robbers; and at night the fathers would go to visit these posts, and watch lest the sentinels fall asleep, performing at the same time the duties of parish priest and military officer. As a consequence of this order [by the government], there was no coast village which did not build some fortification for its defense, but no aid was given to them from the royal treasury. But the religious ministers, out of their own stipends, paid the overseers and artisans; and by dint of entreaties, persuasions, and threats obliged the people to give the materials and the day-laborers [peones], expending much money and patient endeavor for the sake of building these little forts. When the alcaldes-mayor saw these fortifications, now completed, they began to wish to subject them to their own authority; and they secured that in every one should be stationed a warden subject to the alcalde's orders, and that a certain number of men for the service of the fort should be furnished to the warden by apportionment [from the respective villages]. The warden regularly sent these men to work on his own grain-fields, or compelled them to redeem the [compulsory] service with money. This they had to do, usually leaving the fort abandoned— which is, for this reason, very burdensome to the people; and here comes to be verified what Señor Solorzano says, that all which is decreed in favor of the Indians is converted into poison for them. (Zúñiga, Hist. de Philipinas, pp. 526–528.)

[In October, 1733, a Spanish coastguard vessel captured a Dutch ship near the southern coast of Mindanao, and seized its despatches and instructions, "among these, the turban and crown which they were carrying as a present for Malinog." When this event was learned at Batavia, great indignation was aroused among the Dutch, and they sent three warships, which anchored in Manila Bay (June, 1735) and demanded satisfaction; the Dutch would not allow any vessel to enter or leave the bay, and threatened to seize the patache "San Christoval," which was expected to arrive from Acapulco. Warning was immediately sent to the commander of the latter, at the Embocadero; but the ship was already wrecked on the shoals of Calantás. The silver on board, 745,000 pesos belonging to the merchants and 773,025 to the royal situado, was transported by boat to Sorsogón, and the men removed the cargo to land and erected fortifications for its defense in case of necessity; the hull was then destroyed by fire, to prevent its being used by enemies. The Manila government, seeing that it had no funds for defense against the Dutch, and that the Acapulco galleon imprisoned in the bay might lose the favorable winds for its departure, finally came to a settlement with the Dutch, paying 6,500 pesos as satisfaction for the captured Dutch vessel and its contents; the Dutch ships thereupon retired. (Concepción, Hist. de Philipinas, x, pp. 375–410.)]

[In 1736, a controversy arose between the Recollects and Jesuits in northern Mindanao. The Indians of Cagayan, and the Recollect minister in charge there, Fray Hipolito de San Agustín, maintained a close and friendly communication with the native chiefs of Lake Lanao, who finally asked the Recollects (1736) to send missionaries to Larapan, a Malanao village, in order to instruct and baptize their people. The Jesuits were jealous of the Recollects, according to Concepción, and incited a heathen chief named Dalabahan in the mountains of the Cagayan district to attack the Malanaos, thinking that the latter would blame their Cagayan friends for the hostilities; but the latter were able to exonerate themselves from this suspicion, and remained on amicable terms with the Malanaos. The demand of these for Recollect missionaries had to go to Manila; the Jesuits, hearing of it, opposed the request, alleging that the Lanao territory belonged to them. The governor allowed the Jesuit claim, and the Malanaos appealed to the king himself; but "this remonstrance had no result, these unfortunate people being left in their barbarism—from which resulted to us most serious damages, as will be seen in due time." (Concepción, Hist. de Philipinas, xi, pp. 54–66.)]

[In January, 1737, the new archbishop, Fray Juan Angel Rodriguez, took possession of his see; he belonged to the Order of Mercy, and was a native of Medina del Campo, Spain. "He began to govern like an angel" (Concepción; in allusion to his name). "He lessened the number of days for church processions, in order to give opportunity for the business of the courts, and for the necessary work of the people; he prohibited the processions at night, on account of the troubles which are wont to occur in them; he regularly attended the choir, and introduced the use of the Gregorian chant; he taught the sub-chanters plain-song, which they did not know," etc. (Zúñiga, Hist. de Philipinas, pp. 535–536.)]

In the year thirty-seven, Governor Tamon issued a commission and powers to the licentiate Don Joseph Ignacio de Arzadun y Revolledo, in order that he might, in accordance with the royal laws, which decree that the provinces shall be visited every three years, fulfil that duty in those of Pampanga, Pangasinan, and Ylocos. There he was to inspect the fortresses, and the arms, ammunition, gunpowder, balls, and other military supplies, also their condition and circumstances; and to review the troops in the garrisons. He must investigate the mode and form in which the wages due them were paid, and the fictitious enrolments of men in the garrisons. He must also make lists of the warrants which the alcaldes-mayor might have issued; and if he found that these had not been confirmed by the general government, he must annul them. He must abrogate the enjoyment of exemptions, proceeding against those who should be guilty, in such manner as he should find most convenient; he might allow claims, and render definitive judgment in those of less value and amount than twenty pesos, placing the others in a condition to be judicially decided. He received full commission for the exercise and office of the said visitation, being appointed deputy (and a warrant for his title thereto being issued) in the offices of governor and captain-general in the provinces which were entrusted to him, for whatever emergencies might arise or which he might encounter, with superintendence over the other deputies who might be in those provinces. It is true, this is the royal provision; but it also is a fact that the governors profit by their opportunities, when any auditor resists their unjust maxims, and the dread of this often constrains the auditors to unbecoming acts of compliance; and they live as parasites, dependents on that quarter, in order to secure a shameful liberty and an inactive sloth.

Señor Arzadun set out on his commission, which he fulfilled with integrity; he was an unassuming and affable man. Without causing injuries to individuals, he reformed many abuses; and by mild measures he added two reals to each whole tribute. This peaceable result ruffled some persons, and led to various disputes with the ecclesiastical judge, provisor, and vicar-general, which ended in favor of the said auditor. Nor did he fail to have noisy controversies with some other persons; but all this ended as peacefully as possible.

Another controversy, no less disagreeable, occurred at that time between the fathers of the Society [of Jesus] and the mestizos of Santa Cruz. The latter complained, in a petition presented to the royal Audiencia, that with occasion of undertaking to build a bridge across a lagoon which extends from their village to that of Quiapo the fathers had compelled them to sign an obligation for two hundred and fifty pesos in favor of the superintendent of the work, for its cost and materials; and, for the payment of this, assessments had been levied in their village among the mestizos, and various persons had been arrested for not making their payments for this sum, part of which was not yet collected. On examination of this complaint, it was ordered that the auditor who was on duty for that week should proceed to the investigation of these statements; and the completion of such bridge was placed in his charge—for which he was to employ the means and measures that would be mildest, these being entrusted to his good judgment. In virtue of this order, the licentiate Don Pedro Calderon Henriquez, auditor of this royal Audiencia, made the investigation and examined the witnesses, which resulted in verifying the complaint made. It appeared from the judicial inquiry that the land of that village belonged to the Society; and the auditor drew up a formal statement, saying that the inhabitants of that village, who possessed no landed property, were paying ground rents that were exorbitant. He declared that the money for the cost of that bridge ought not to have been levied among the Sangleys and mestizos, even though they belonged to that village; and that consequently the owner of the land ought to pay it—citing laws i and v of título xvi, book iv of the Recopilación. [Here follows a relation of the various legal proceedings in this controversy; after hearing all the evidence in the case the decision of the court was against the Jesuits. It was shown that part of the land in question did not belong to them, and they were ordered not to disturb the tenants of it in their possession, and not to collect rents from them. They proved their title to other lands, but were warned that they must no longer exact, as they had been doing, three and one-half pesos as ground-rent for the sites occupied by the huts which the colonists erected within the grain-fields so that they might more conveniently cultivate the lands. "By this sentence the Jesuits lost some three thousand pesos a year for the [rents of the] ground-plots of the houses; each married man had paid them three pesos, and each unmarried man and widow a peso and a half—and this, besides, for houses and lands which belonged to those people." The Jesuits pleaded ecclesiastical immunity, and claimed that they had a right to the rents in question. A long and clamorous dispute arose, in which manifestoes were issued on both sides; it appears to have lasted from March 28, 1738, to July 1, 1739. The Jesuits appealed to the king, but Auditor Calderon's sentence was sustained. (Concepción, Hist. de Philipinas, xi, pp. 79–89.)]

1 The following summary of events, sometimes in full translation and sometimes abridged, is obtained from the histories of Concepción, Zúñiga,

and Montero y Vidal, the source of each paragraph being indicated at the end.

2 "As the latter [i.e., Bustamante] could not defend himself, and it was for the interest of the religious orders and of the principal citizens of Manila that the blame for what had occurred should recoil upon Bustamante, they accumulated against him numberless charges—most of them formulated by his assassins, by the officials who had defrauded the exchequer, by those who were debtors to the treasury, and by all who, instead of making amends for their offences in a military post, had been replaced in their offices by Archbishop Cuesta" (Montero y Vidal, Hist. de Filipinas, i, pp. 430–431).

3 Sebastian de Totanes was a noted member of the Franciscan order in the islands. He was born in the village of Totanes in Spain, in 1687, and entered that order in 1706. After finishing his studies he gave instruction in the Toledo convent for several years, departing thence (1715) for the Filipinas missions, which he joined two years later. He held various high offices in the order there, among them being that of minister provincial (1738–41); he also administered the churches in Sampaloc (1721–29), Lilio (1732–35), and Pagsanhan (1735–38). In 1746 he went to Europe as procurator of his order to Roma and Madrid, and died at the latter city, on February 13, 1748. He left a grammar and manual of the Tagálog language, which is regarded as one of the beat works of its kind; it was published at Sampaloc in 1745. (See Huerta's Estado.)

4 "Although the archbishop had not, in strictness, any direct connection with the assassination of the head of government of the islands, his connivance with the seditious element, the fact that the authority was entrusted to him, and his tolerance and lenity in the investigation and punishment of the criminals, aroused against him the wrath of the [home] government; and, in spite of his advanced age, he was transferred to the bishopric of Mechoacan, in Nueva Espana" (Montero y Vidal, Hist. de Filipinas, i, p. 432).

5 "In order to curb these so bold and inhuman actions, it was necessary that the squadrons should sail from Manila; for if they should be permanently stationed at Samboangan the expenses would be insupportable in so barren a region. If this establishment had been fixed in Yloylo, a fertile and abundant land, and sufficiently near to the Moros, the consumption of provisions on the voyages would have been more endurable; while at the same time there might remain in Samboangan a regular garrison of thirty-five men, and it would be a landing-place sufficient for our vessels when on a cruise, which from that port could go more quickly for any emergency. Moreover, in Samboangan there is not an adequate number of boats, nor is there in Yloylo—enormous sums being spent on the walls [of those forts] alone,

without their being able to hinder the passage of the Moros, or prevent their infesting the provinces." (Concepción, Hist. de Philipinas, x, pp. 184, 185.)

6 This account does not agree with the historical sketch given by N. M. Saleeby in his Studies in Moro History, Law, and Religion (Manila, 1905) pp. 57–59; but this is not surprising, as Concepción probably had but inaccurate and second-hand information regarding the rulers of Joló and Mindanao. According to Saleeby, Manāmir, a great-grandson of Dipatwān Qudrat (the Corralat of the Spanish writers), was declared sultan after the death of his father Barahamān; but the government was usurped by his uncle Kuda, and civil war followed, which must have lasted more than thirty years. Kuda was finally murdered by some Sulus whom he had invited to aid him against Manāmir, who therefore obtained the ascendency for a time. But the Sulus fomented discord between Manāmir and his brother Anwār, which brought on even worse hostilities and murders, weakening both sides. Manāmir was assassinated by his nephew Malīnug, and his sons Pakīr Mawlāna and Pakāru-d-Dīn were obliged to leave Magindanao, and retired to Tamontaka; and the larger part of the towns of Magindanao and Slangan were destroyed by fire. Sultan Anwār died at Batawa and Malīnug assumed the sultanate after his father's death, and kept up the fight. "After a tedious, desultory war, Malīnug fled up the Pulangi to Bwayan. Pakīr Mawlāna then got possession of all the lands about Magindanao, and peace was made soon after. Malīnug died a natural death, and some time later his two sons visited Pakīr Mawlāna." This account is cited from Capt. Thomas Forrest's Voyage to New Guinea and the Moluccas (London, 1779), a voyage made in 1774–76; Forrest obtained his information directly from Pakīr Mawlāna himself. That ruler, however, could not have been the one mentioned in the text; Mawlāna is apparently an official or a hereditary title.

From Forrest's original account (pp. 201–206) we take the following items in regard to the above events: "The following short account of the history of Magindano, is drawn from original records, in the possession of Fakymolano, elder brother to Paharadine the present Sultan, and father to Kybad Zachariel, the present Rajah Moodo; they are wrote in the Magindano tongue, and Arabic character. I took it down from Fakymolano's own mouth, who dictated in Malay.

"Before the arrival of Serif Alli, the first Mahometan prince who came from Mecca to Magindano, the latter had kings of her own. For the towns of Magindano, Selangan, Catibtuan, and Semayanan had, or assumed, the right of taking from the banks of the Dano, that portion of earth, on which the sovereigns were to be consecrated. The towns of Malampyan and Lusuden, are said to have been the first who joined Serif Alli: the other four soon acceded. Serif married a daughter of the last king of the royal line, and on this marriage founded his title to the crown. About the time that Kabansuan son of Serif Alli reigned, a person named Budiman, was Pangaran (a title much used in Sumatra, and inferior to Sultan or Rajah) of Sooloo. Budiman had a grandson, who became his successor; his name was Bonsoo, and he was related to the family that governed at Borneo: which family came also from Mecca, and the head of it was brother to Serif Alli. Bonsoo had two children; a daughter, Potely, by a wife; and a son, Bakliol, by a sandle or concubine. Bakliol, the bastard, robbed his sister Potely (a name which signifies princess) of her right, threw off his dependence on Magindano, and assumed the title of Sultan, his fathers having been only Pangarans of Sooloo. [Potely's daughter, Panianamby, married Kudarat (the Corralat of Spanish writers), who was succeeded by his son Tidoly; the latter had two sons, Abdaraman and Kuddy. Abdaraman was succeeded by his son Seid Moffat]; but, being an infant, Kuddy his uncle usurped the government, and went to Semoy, carrying with him the effects of the deceased Sultan. Thence he invited the Sooloos to support him against the lawful heir. [They, however, treacherously slew Kuddy, and plundered his camp, seizing therein many pieces of heavy cannon. Seid Moffat's party then obtained control, but the country was torn by dissensions and civil war. Finally, Seid Moffat was assassinated by his nephew Molenu, but left two sons, Fakymolano and Paharadine; they were obliged to leave Magindano, which town and Selangan were nearly destroyed by fire, and the country was laid waste. After several years of petty war, Molenu was driven up the Palangy to Boyan.] Fakymolano then got possession of all the lands about Magindano, and peace was made soon after, about thirty years ago. Molenu died a natural death, leaving by concubines, two sons, Topang and Uku, also a natural daughter Myong. Fakymolano had about this time given up the Sultanship to his younger brother Paharadine, on condition that Kybad Zachariel, his own son, should be elected Rajah Moodo. Topang and Uku, for some time after the peace, visited Fakymolano and his son; but afterwards, on Paharadine's marriage with Myong, their sister, they grew shy, as the Sultan took them greatly into his favour. Topang had from his father large possessions, which made him formidable to Rajah Moodo; he was also closely connected with the Sooloos, and had married Gulaludines, daughter of Bantillan, once Sultan of Sooloo. By this time Rajah Moodo had got himself well fortified at Coto-Intang, which is within musket shot of the Sultan's palace, and within cannon shot of the strong wooden castle of Topang; both of which lie on the south side of the Pelangy. The Sultan Paharadine has no children by his consort Myong; but had by a concubine, a son named Chartow, now arrived at maturity. Whether Myong, who is said to have entirely governed the Sultan, favoured Chartow, or her elder brother Topang, is uncertain; but she was believed the cause of the coolness that prevailed between the Sultan and Rajah Moodo; who, though duly elected, and acknowledged lawful successor, yet, when I came to Magindano, in May, 1775, had not visited his uncle for above a year. Fakymolano, Rajah Moodo's father, lived at that time, just without the gate of his son's fort." Some of the allusions in this account need explanation, which is partly obtained elsewhere in Forrest's pages. "The town, that goes properly by the name of Magindano, consists at present, of scarce more than twenty houses. They stand close to, and just above where a little creek, about eighteen foot broad, runs perpendicular into the Pelangy, from a small lake about one mile distant, and about half a mile in circumference. This small lake is called the Dano; the creek I have just mentioned, is the Rawass (or river) Magindano; and from the banks of the lake or Dano, a little earth is taken, upon which the Raiah Moodo (that is young king) must stand when he is consecrated Sultan. The Rajah Moodo is elected by the states, and succeeds the Sultan; similar to the king of the Romans succeeding the emperors of Germany. A Watamama (that is, male child) is also elected, who becomes Rajah Moodo, when Rajah Moodo becomes Sultan." "The town of Selangan may be said to make one town with Magindano, as communicating with it by several bridges over the Rawass; it extends about one mile down the south side of the Pelangy, forming a decent street for one-half of the distance. In the lower part the town extends about half a mile, in several irregular streets; where many Chinese reside. In the town of Selangan altogether, may be about two hundred houses; below the Sultan's palace, about twenty yards, is a brick and mortar foundation remaining of a Spanish chapel." The spelling of proper names in Forrest's remarks is more or less phonetic and Anglicized; the reader may compare them with the accurate spelling furnished above by Dr. Saleeby. In VOL. XLI of this series (pp. 280, 281) will be seen a map of the valley of the Pulangui River, with the towns on its banks and its tributaries; the original is in the British Museum, and is evidently the basis for two maps which Forrest published in his *Voyage* (at p. 200). (Cf. these, and the map of the Rio Grande in *U. S. Gazetteer*, p. 662.) The date given in VOL. XLI was furnished at the Museum as approximately correct; but Mawlāna's map was given to Forrest in 1775, and the latter says (p. 186) that it was deposited in the British Museum. The sultan of Mindanao ceded to the English, at Forrest's request, the island of Bunwoot, now called Bonga; it forms the shelter to Polloc harbor. The town of Mindanao or Magindano was at or near the site of the present Cotabato—"population, 3,000. The Chinese control the commerce of the place." (*U. S. Gazetteer*, p. 475.) Forrest says (p. 185): "The Chinese settled at Magindano are not permitted to trade higher [up the river] than Boyan; the Mindanoers being jealous of their superior abilities in trade."

7 The pay of native auxiliaries from Bohol was (in 1733) reckoned at a monthly wage for each man of "thirty gantas of rice, four silver reals, a span [mano] of tobacco, and one chinanta of salt." (Concepción, Hist. de Philipinas, x, p. 311.)

"The Indian's largest unit of weight is a chinanta, which they divide into 10 cates of the province, which are 20 of standard weight [de romana]; the cate contains 8 taels of the province, which are 16 of standard weight." (Encina and Bermejo's Arte Cebuano, Tambobong, 1894, p. 159.)

8 The governor sent orders to the alcaldes-mayor that "all the rancherías or visitas close to the coast should be compulsorily united, either to the larger villages or to each other, so that even the smallest village should exceed, if possible, five hundred tributes—in consequence of which measure all should fortify themselves, as the lay of the land should permit.... All these measures were at that time admirable, and would have been thoroughly effective if the inclusion of the smaller villages in the larger ones, or their consolidation, had been carried out more energetically by those whose duty it was. For this undertaking, and to stir up the negligent and careless, the armadas were more necessary than for opposing and restraining the Moros; they gave but little attention to the latter, and still less to the former, and everything was left in the same necessity, and the same condition, [as before]." (Concepción, Hist. de Philipinas, x, pp. 364, 368.)

BIBLIOGRAPHICAL DATA

The matter in this volume is obtained from the following sources:

1. *Events in Filipinas*, 1721–1739.—From various sources, fully credited in the text.

2. *Primary instruction.*—In its various parts, as follows: I—from Vicente Barrantes's *La instrucción primaria en Filipinas* (Madrid, 1869), condensed from pp. 97, 98, 147–151, and 166–168 (from a copy belonging to the Library of Congress); II—from Daniel Grifol y Aliaga's *La instrucción primaria en Filipinas* (Manila, 1894), extract from preface (from a copy belonging to the Library of Congress); III-XVII—from the above book, pp. 1–7, 11–16, 117–132, 148–157, 132–136, 41–52, 61–100, and 425–445, 401–405.

3. *Dominican educational institutions, 1896–1897.*—From an unsigned and undated MS. belonging to Rev. T. C. Middleton, O.S.A.

4. *Report of religious schools, 1897.*—Same as no. 3.

5. *Educational institutions of the Recollects.*—Same as no. 3.

6. The friar viewpoint.—In two parts. I—from Estudio de algunos asuntos de actualidad (Valladolid, 1897), by Eduardo Navarro, O.S.A., chap. vii, pp. 123–165; II—from Las corporaciones religiosas en Filipinas (Valladolid, 1901), by Eladio Zamora, O.S.A., chap. v, pp. 235–273, from a copy belonging to Rev. T. C. Middleton, O.S.A.

7. Education since American occupation.—Editorial, and compiled from various sources, fully credited in text.

APPENDIX: EDUCATION IN THE PHILIPPINES

Sources: The above documents are obtained as follows: The first document is obtained in its various parts from the following: I—from Vicente Barrantes's *La instrucción primaria en Filipinas* (Madrid, 1869), condensed from pp. 97, 98, 147–151, and 166–168 (from a copy belonging to the Library of Congress); II—from Daniel Grifol y Aliaga's *La instrucción primaria en Filipinas* (Manila, 1894), extract from preface (from a copy belonging to the Library of Congress); III–XVII—from the above book, pp. 1–7, 11–16, 117–132, 148–157, 132–136, 41–52, 61–100, 425–445, and 401–405. The second, third, and fourth are obtained from MSS. belonging to Rev. T. C. Middleton, O.S.A., of Villanova College. The fifth is obtained from the following sources: I—from *Estudio de algunos asuntos de actualidad* (Valladolid, 1897), by Eduardo Navarro, O.S.A., chapter vii, pp. 123–165; II—from *Las corporaciones religiosas en Filipinas* (Valladolid, 1901), by Eladio Zamora, O.S.A., chapter v, pp. 235–273 (from a copy belonging to Rev. T. C. Middleton, O.S.A.). The last document is editorial and a compilation from sources fully indicated in the text.

Translations: These translations and compilations are made by James Alexander Robertson.

PRIMARY INSTRUCTION

FIRST GOVERNMENTAL ATTEMPTS

A royal order of November 3, 18391 prescribed that a committee be specially appointed to draft a set of regulations for the schools of the Philippines.2 The creation of this commission or board was delayed until 1855, being appointed by Governor Manuel Crespo, February 7, of that year. The re-admission into the archipelago of the Jesuits on March 21, 1852, had given a new impulse to the teaching of Spanish in the schools, that organization always having been greatly inclined to the teaching of that language.3 The instructions given to the commission appointed by Crespo, were as follows:

"1. To draft regulations establishing and making uniform the teaching in the schools; with expression of what is to be taught in schools of both sexes, paying especial attention in their measures to the encouragement of the Castilian language.

"2. To determine the number of men and women teachers who are to be appointed, this need to be regulated by the number of tributes of each village.

"3. To report on the advisability of establishing a school for teachers in this city, without neglecting at the same time to state whatever is of service for it, and appears advisable for the end and object to which the expediency of this matter is directed.

"The commission was also recommended 'to draft a plan and project for the establishment of a normal school in the city of Manila, from which teachers instructed and suitable for teaching in the provinces might graduate.'"

The report of this commission, March 7, 1861, shows but few meetings and but little accomplished, since its creation, until the year 1860. In the last months of that year and the first of 1861 their deliberations began to take form and were completed. Already on August 10, 1860, Governor Solano had commissioned an official of the secretary's office to draft a project for reform along similar lines to the one which the commission was to draft. He completed that draft on the twenty-first of the same month, and his results may have spurred on the commission to finish its work. The fundamental points given to the above-mentioned official are as follows:

"1. Establishment in Manila of a normal school, as a seminary for teachers.

"2. That the pupils of such school, who are candidates for teachers, proceed from the various provinces in the proportion of one to each 50,000 or 60,000 inhabitants, their expenses to be paid from the local funds.

"3. That in the normal teaching, the studies with application to industry and the arts predominate.

"4. That the certificate shall not be issued to any pupil at the end of his course, unless he can write and speak Castilian fluently.

"5. Regulation of schools in the villages, all of them to be supplied with well-endowed pupils from the normal school.

"6. Prohibition to teach to all who cannot prove their ability by the proper certificate and good deportment.

"7. That the supervision in teaching belong to the provincial chiefs; and in regard to the moral and religious to the parish priests.

"8. That the normal school have a practice school for boys, under the charge of the pupils."

Doubtless the commission was influenced by the work of the above-mentioned official. The chief point of debate in the meetings held by the commission was that of the teaching of the Spanish language. One of the most influential and active members of the commission was Fray Francisco Gainza, then vice-rector of the university of Santo Tomás. He voted against the teaching of Spanish in the schools on the grounds that a unified language might open the door to Protestantism in the islands, but he was overruled by the votes of all the rest, even Fray Domingo Treserra, a Dominican. Governor Lemery, who took charge of the islands in the early part of 1861, also charged the Jesuit José Fernandez Cuevas to draw up a project for educational reform.

The next step and the greatest one yet attained in the matter of primary education was the decree of December 20, 1863,4 with its attendant regulations (q.v., post). The normal school provided for by this decree was formally opened January 23, 1865, although it had been in operation since May 17, 1864. As might be expected it was found that there were more scholars from the island of Luzón, who took advantage of this normal school, than from the Visayas and Mindanao, on account of the distance. On this account Barrantes advocates the founding of another school in Cebú. Teachers from the normal schools were placed in charge of their schools with great ceremony, in accordance with an order of the government, July 18, 1868. The most serious obstacles against which the Board of Education had to struggle were irregularity of attendance and the matter of vacations, as it was necessary to designate a distinct period in each province, and it was utterly impossible to follow the regulations. Also the management and supervision fails in great measure because it is diverted from the direct oversight into the hands of secondary officials.

In 1836 there was but one school of primary instruction in Manila, which was attended by 80 pupils. In 1867, there were 25 schools, with an attendance of 1,940 children, a number which advanced by 1868 to 30 schools with 3,389 children. The results in the provinces were also remarkable for the same period. In 1867, thirty-eight provinces showed 593 schools and in 1868, 684, with 25 more in course of construction. (Pp. 147–151.)

Barrantes's conclusions (pp. 166–168) are interesting. Among them are the following:

"We believe that we have demonstrated that the backwardness of primary instruction in Filipinas is purely relative, and cannot be imputed to the country or to any class, and much less to the ecclesiastical corporations, but to the spirit and letter of the laws of Indias and the royal decrees, which did not succeed in giving legal life in that colony to a service which did not exist, or was not at that time understood, in the mother-country.

"We have demonstrated that before 1865, primary instruction, properly so-called, was a vain shadow in the archipelago, since all the duties, all the administrative responsibilities of the department weighed upon public officials incompatible in purity with those duties and responsibilities; upon public officials, who, not being administrative, could and ought to drive out that imposition; upon public officials to whom no element or aid was given, while they were loaded with a leonine contract of an absurd and inconceivable character. And we have demonstrated this with the proof that the true responsibilities, in spite of the express text of the law, have not been exacted, because it was impossible to exact them or even the administrative public officials subject to them.

"We have demonstrated that this confusion of principles could and ought to engender a struggle between classes in the eighteenth century, prejudicial at the bottom to primary instruction, whenever, in order to unburden itself mutually of unjust responsibilities, the administrative element threw the responsibilities upon the ecclesiastical element, accusing it of being hostile to the teaching of Castilian; and this element not being able, in its turn, to investigate the accusation, acted in such wise that it appeared to accept it."

There are not schools in almost every village, and the identification of the Filipinos with the Spaniards has not progressed so far as has been declared, especially in the matter of intelligence; and "it is not certain that the condition of the institutions of teaching authorizes one to believe the Filipinos capable of making use of political rights so grave and so dangerous as the electoral right, in the form that they ask."5

ORGANIZED EFFORT OF LEGISLATION

[In his preface to his book *La instrucción primaria en Filipinas* (Manila, 1894) Daniel Grifol y Aliaga, who occupied an official post in the department of public instruction in the General Division of Civil Administration, and was secretary of the administrative board on school questions in the Philippine Islands, speaks as follows.]

Until the end of the year 1863,6 when the memorable royal decree, which established a plan of primary education in Filipinas, arranged for the creation of schools of primary instruction in all the villages of the islands, and the creation of a normal school in Manila whence should graduate educated and religious teachers, who should take charge of those institutions, was dictated, it can be said that there had been no legislation in regard to primary instruction in these islands; for, although it is certain that orders directed for the purpose of obtaining the instruction of the natives, and very especially, the teaching of the beautiful Spanish language, are not lacking, some of those orders being contained in the Leyes de Indias and in the edicts of good government [Bandos de Buen Gobierno], it is a fact that those orders are isolated regulations, without connection, and the product of the good desire which has always animated the monarchs of España and their worthy representatives in the archipelago, for the advance and prosperity of the archipelago, but without resting on a fixed foundation, for lack of elements so that such foundation might exist.7

Before the above-mentioned epoch the reverend and devout8 parish priests came to fill in great part, and voluntarily, the noble ends of propagating primary instruction through these remote regions, with the aid of the most advanced of their scholars themselves, who devoted themselves to the teaching of their fellow citizens, receiving scarcely any remuneration for their work and trouble, and without being regarded as teachers or having any certificate which accredited them as such.

The above-mentioned royal decree of December 20, 1863, and the regulations of the same date, established and unfolded a true plan for primary instruction, which has served as a basis for the innumerable number of orders relative to the said department, which have been dictated from day to day, both by the government of the mother country and by the former superior civil government, by the general government, and by the General Division of Civil Administration of these islands, in order to attain the degree of perfection which this most important department of public administration—the foundation of the culture and the welfare of the villages—obtains in Filipinas today.

That same accumulation of orders,9 which have produced the rapid advancement of public instruction in this archipelago, has been the motive for a certain apparent confusion, which, in reality, does not exist, for there is observed in those orders an admirable harmony, which is explained if one bear in mind that they have all been dictated for one and the same end, with one desire, and for the same purpose: namely, that of obtaining the greatest advancement of education in this far-distant Spanish province, and that of benefiting the noble class of teachers.

The confusion to which we refer, which, we repeat, is in its essential no more than apparent, must disappear from that moment in which all the orders in regard to the matter are methodically compiled, arranging them so that they might give as a resultant that harmonious whole of which we spoke before.

So we understood it, when we had to occupy ourselves in its detailed study, when we took charge of the department of public instruction in the General Division of Civil Administration [Dirección de Administración civil]; and for the purpose of being able to fill the office which had been committed to us to the best of our ability, we undertook the work of compiling, arranging, and annotating all the orders relative to primary instruction in these islands. When we had made considerable progress in our task, it occurred to us that, by publishing the compilation which we were making for our own private use, we might, perhaps, be doing a good service to the teaching profession, to the local inspectors of primary instruction, and to all persons who are engaged in this department, by reason of their duty....

This book will also serve to make patent the very great interest with which the government of his Majesty and the worthy authorities of the archipelago have viewed this important department,10 dictating continuously orders inspired by the most genuine sentiments of patriotism, directed through obtaining the greatest degree of instruction and culture for the natives of this rich country, and above all, so that all of them might speak the harmonious Castilian language, in order that that language may be one more bond of union between these islands and the mother country.

ROYAL DECREE ESTABLISHING A PLAN OF PRIMARY INSTRUCTION IN FILIPINAS

Exposition

Madam:

The constant desire and permanent rule of conduct of the august predecessors of your Majesty have ever been to introduce into the territories under your glorious crown across seas, the light of evangelical truth, and with it the principles of a civilization suitable for their respective necessities. The governments and their delegated authorities, with the powerful aid of the missionaries, and of the clergy in general, both secular and regular, have tried to accommodate their policy in regard to the Philippine Archipelago to these principles. But the extent of so vast a territory, the character and customs of a portion of its population, and the lack of an organized system of primary instruction, have been the reason why the knowledge of the Castilian language, and in consequence of the ignorance of that language, the propagation of the most elementary ideas of education remain in a remarkable condition of imperfection and backwardness. It is unnecessary to explain the evils that such a condition occasions to the natives in the casualties of social life, in their relations to the public authority, in the exercise of those relations which are confided partly to the said natives, in the onward march and progress, in fine, of that country so fertile in the sources of wealth. It is reserved for your Majesty to bring to this condition of affairs the remedy suitable for it, which for some time the superior authorities of Filipinas have been demanding, and in regard to whose urgent application the royal commissary, appointed to study the administration of said islands, has lately called the attention of the government. For this object is directed the subjoined project of a decree and the regulations which accompany it. They have been formed by the aid of the documents submitted by said functionaries. They agree in spirit, in tendency, and even in the prime basis of the solutions which they propose. Said project setting forth from the necessity of broadening as much as possible the teaching of the holy Catholic faith, of the language of the fatherland, and of the elementary knowledge of life, of creating capable teachers for that purpose, the lack of whom is the principal cause of the above situation, and that the basis of all education is the solid diffusion of our holy religion, establishes by means of its ministers a normal school under the care of the fathers of the Society of Jesus, whose pupils will have the right and express obligation of filling the position of teachers in the schools for the natives with pay, advantages, and rights during the exercise of that duty, and later after its honorable discharge, and who shall be capable of attracting the youth of the country to this now humble class [of employes]. It provides the means for joining teachers of both sexes until they graduate as teachers from that institution, and until a normal school for women teachers respectively is organized. It creates in all the villages of the archipelago schools for elementary primary instruction of boys and girls, with the obligation of attendance on the part of such, and with Sunday classes for adults.11 It confers on the parish priests the immediate inspection of said schools, with powers suitable to make that inspection effective, and the exclusive direction of the teaching of the Christian doctrine and ethics is vested in the prelates. And as a complement to the system which it establishes, it demands for the future, although after the expiration of a suitable time, the knowledge of the Spanish language as a necessary requisite for the exercise of public charges and duties, and for the enjoyment of certain privileges inherent thereto.

The application of all progress in a country presupposes pecuniary sacrifices, and although not excessive, some are contained in the establishment of the projected plan. Nevertheless, if the expense which is produced is divided among the different villages of the archipelago, and charged to their local funds, it is to be expected that it will neither be felt very sensibly nor will the general budget of the island be obliged for the moment to contribute an advance, certainly difficult today, when the calamities which have happened recently in one part of the Filipino territory have caused so considerable and extraordinary an expense to bear down upon it.

The minister whose signature is affixed, taking as his fundamental the above reasons, the Council of State having been consulted, and with the concurrence of that of the minister, has the honor of submitting for your Majesty's approval the subjoined project of a decree. Madrid, December 20, 1863. Madam, at the royal feet of your Majesty,

José de la Concha

Royal decree

In view of the reasons which have been explained to me by my minister of the colonies, after having consulted with the Council of State and with the concurrence of the Council of the ministers, I therefore decree the following:

Article 1. A normal school for teachers of primary instruction is established in the city of Manila, in charge of and under the direction of the fathers of the Society of Jesus.

Said school shall have the organization prescribed by its regulations and the expenses caused therein shall be defrayed by the central treasury of ways and means.12

Art. 2. Spanish scholars, natives of the archipelago or of Europa, shall be admitted into said school under the conditions prescribed by the regulations. After the termination of the studies prescribed by the said regulations, such scholars shall obtain the title of teacher.

The pupils of the normal school, to the number and in the class designated by the regulations, shall receive a free education; and those who take advantage of such provision shall be obliged to exercise the duties of teacher in the native schools of the archipelago, for the space of ten years following their graduation from the institution.

Art. 3. In each one of the villages of those provinces, there shall be at least one school of primary instruction for males, and another for females, in which education shall be given to the native children and Chinese of both sexes.

The regulations shall determine the proportion of the increase in the number of schools for each village in proportion to its population.

In all the schools there shall be a Sunday class for adults.

Art. 4. The instruction given in said schools shall be free to the poor. Attendance on the part of the children shall be compulsory.

Art. 5. The schools for males shall consist of three classes; to wit: *entrada* [*i.e.*, entrance]; *ascenso* [*i.e.*, promotion, or intermediary]; and *termino* [*i.e.*, final], of the second class, and *termino* of the first class. They shall be supplied with teachers graduating from the normal school in accordance with the qualification which they shall have obtained at the conclusion of their studies, their promotions depending upon their seniority and merit combined.

The schools of termino of the first class, namely, those of Manila and its district, shall be supplied with teachers by competitive examination among the teachers, with the certificate from the normal school, with experience as teachers.

Art. 6. Classification of the schools, in accordance with the preceding article, shall be made by the superior civil governor,13 after consultation with the superior commission of primary instruction, and after the report of the chief of the province. Once the respective classification is fixed it can be changed only in the same manner.

Art. 7. The teachers shall enjoy the salary and other privileges prescribed by the regulations.14 Said salary, as well as the foundation of the school, acquisition, and conservation of school supplies and equipment, and the rent of the building where there shall be no public building, shall constitute an obligatory expense on the respective local budget.

Art. 8. In the villages where the superior civil governor so decrees, as its small population so allows, the teachers shall fulfil the duties of secretaries15 to the gobernadorcillos, enjoying for such duties [concepto] an additional pay proportioned to the local resources.

Art. 9. The teachers appointed from the normal school cannot be discharged except for legitimate cause and by resolution of the superior civil governor, after a governmental measure drawn up with the formality set forth in article 6, and after hearing the interested party.

Art. 10. Examinations shall be held in the normal school at periodic times, and in the manner determined by the regulations, in order to choose a person with the title of assistant teacher. Those who obtain such certificates shall manage the schools for the natives in the absence of teachers, and shall in all cases exercise the duties belonging to their class in the schools which are to have such assistants according to the regulations. Said assistants shall have the salary and perquisites prescribed by the regulations, the first being an obligatory expense on the local budget.

Art. 11. The mistresses of schools for native girls need the corresponding certificate for the exercise of their duties. Until a normal school for women teachers is established, that certificate shall be issued in the form prescribed with the fitness determined by the regulations. The salary and perquisites which they are to receive shall be fixed by the same regulations, the first being an obligatory expense on the local budget, as are the other expenses expressed in article 7 regarding the schools for males.

Art. 12. Teachers and assistants shall be exempt from the giving of personal services so long as they exercise their duties, and after ceasing to exercise them, if they have exercised them for fifteen years. After five years of duty, the teachers, and after ten, the assistants, shall enjoy distinction as principales.16

Art. 13. The teachers of both sexes and the assistants shall have the right, in case of disability for the discharge of their duties, of pension under the conditions prescribed by the regulations.

Art. 14. Teachers and assistants with certificates, who shall have exercised their duties suitably for ten and fifteen years respectively, shall be preferred in the provision of posts of the class of clerk, established by the decree of July 15 last, without the necessity of furnishing proofs of fitness, as well as in the provision of employments not subject to the abovesaid royal decree which are to be appointed by the superior civil governor,17 and do not demand conditions of special fitness in which the above are lacking.

Art. 15. The superior inspection of primary education shall be exercised by the superior civil governor of the islands, with the aid of a commission which shall be established in the capital under the name of "Superior Commission of Primary Instruction." Said commission shall be composed of the superior governor as president, of the right reverend archbishop of Manila, and of seven members of recognized ability appointed by the first named.18 The chiefs of the provinces shall be provincial inspectors, and shall exercise their duties with the aid of a commission composed of the chief, of the diocesan prelate, and in the latter's absence, of the parish priest of the chief city, and of the alcalde-mayor,19 or administrator of revenues.20

The parish priests shall be the local inspectors ex-officio and shall direct the teaching of the Christian doctrine and morals under the direction of the right reverend prelates.

The regulations shall designate the powers of the commissions and above-cited inspectors.

Art. 16. After a school has been established in any village for fifteen years, no natives who cannot talk, read and write the Castilian language shall form a part of the principalía unless they enjoy that distinction by right of inheritance. After the school has been established for thirty years, only those who possess the above-mentioned condition shall enjoy exemption from the personal service tax, except in case of sickness.

Art. 17. Five years after the publication of this decree, no one who does not possess the above-mentioned qualification, proved before the chief of the province, can be appointed to salaried posts in the Philippine Archipelago.

Art. 18. The superior civil governor, the chiefs of the provinces, and the local authorities, shall have special care in promoting the fulfilment of the requirements of this decree, adopting or proposing, according to circumstances, the necessary measures for their complete fulfilment.

Art. 19. Decrees [cedulas] of petition and request shall be sent to the right reverend archbishop and the reverend bishops of the Philippine Archipelago, in order that they may arouse the zeal of the parish priests for the exact fulfilment of the duties vested in them by this decree, in what relates to the supervision of the teaching of the natives, and very specially to that of the holy Catholic faith and the Castilian language.

Art. 20. Special regulations shall detail minutely the organization of the normal school and of the schools of primary instruction for the natives.

Given at the palace, December 20, 1863. It is rubricated in the royal hand. The minister of the colonies,

José de la Concha

REGULATIONS FOR THE NORMAL SCHOOL FOR TEACHERS OF PRIMARY INSTRUCTION FOR THE NATIVES OF THE FILIPINAS ISLANDS21

Of the object of the normal school

Article 1. The object of the normal school is to serve as a seminary for religious, obedient, and instructed teachers, for the management of schools of primary instruction for the natives throughout the whole archipelago.

Art. 2. The scholars shall be resident, and subject to one and the same rule and discipline. For the present the number of day pupils fixed by the superior civil governor may be admitted, provided that their antecedents give hope that they can pursue their studies with advantage, and that their deportment corresponds to the good name of the institution.

Art. 3. In the same locality of the normal school, although with the fitting independence and separation, there shall be a school of primary instruction for non-resident boys, whose classes shall be managed, under the supervision of a teacher of the normal school, by the pupils of the same.

Of the branches and duration of the studies

Art. 4. Education in the normal school shall comprise the following branches:

1. Religion, morals, and sacred history.

2. Theory and practice of reading.

3. Theory and practice of writing.

4. An extensive knowledge of the Castilian language with exercises in analysis, composition, and orthography.

5. Arithmetic, to ratio and proportion, elevation to powers, and extraction of roots, inclusive, together with the decimal metric system with its equivalent of local weights and measures.

6. Principles of Spanish geography and history.

7. *Idem* of Geometry.

8. Common acquaintance with physical and natural sciences.

9. Ideas of practical agriculture with reference to the cultivation of the products of the country.

10. Rules of courtesy.

11. Lessons in vocal and organ music.

12. Elements of pedagogy.

Art. 5. During the sessions of the normal school, the teachers shall speak only the Castilian language, and the scholars shall hold their classes and other literary acts in the same language. They shall be strictly prohibited from expressing themselves in any other language, even in their daily recreations and common intercourse within the precincts of the institution.

Art. 6. The studies mentioned in article 4 shall run for three years, and during the six months of the last term [curso], the scholars shall have practical exercise in teaching, by teaching in the classes of the primary school annexed to the normal school, which is established by article 3.

Scholars shall not pass from one course to another without proving their efficiency in the general examinations, which shall be held at the end of each year.

During the first four years of the installation of the school the studies shall be completed in two years.

Art. 7. The scholars of the normal school who shall have completed the courses of their studies and shall have obtained by their good deportment, application and knowledge, the mark of excellent [sobresaliente] in the final examinations for the three consecutive years shall receive a teacher's certificate, in which shall be expressed their creditable mark, and they shall be empowered to teach schools of ascenso. Those who shall not have obtained the mark of excellent, but that of good [bueno], or fair [regular] in the above-mentioned examinations, shall also receive a teacher's certificate with their corresponding mark expressed therein and they shall be able to teach schools of entrada. Finally, those who shall have failed in said examinations, if after they shall have repeated the exercise, shall have merited approval, shall only receive certificates as assistant teachers.

Art. 8. If any one of the scholars of the normal school shall desire to continue his studies for another year, in order to perfect himself therein, he may do so, on condition of paying from his own funds his annual board, if he shall be a resident student, and if, in the judgment of the director of the institution, no inconvenience arises from his remaining in it.

Of the scholars of the normal school

Art. 9. The resident scholars of the normal school shall be divided into regular [de número] and supernumerary22 resident pupils. Both those who aspire to the said classes and to the class of day scholars, so long as there shall be any of the latter, must have the following qualifications:

1. To be natives of the Spanish dominions.

2. To be fully sixteen years old, that requisite to be attested by certificate of baptism or any other equivalent public document.

3. To suffer from no contagious disease, and to enjoy sufficient health to fulfil the tasks suitable for the duties of teachers.

4. To have observed good deportment which shall be proved by certification of the chief of the province and the parish priest of the village of his birth or habitation.

5. To talk Castilian; to know the Christian doctrine and how to read and write well: proof of which shall be made in an examination held before the director and teacher of the school.

Art. 10. The regular resident scholars shall receive their education free, and shall pay nothing for their support, treatment, school equipment, and aid from the teaching force.23

Art. 11. The regular resident scholars shall be obliged to fulfil their duties for ten years as teachers in the schools of primary instruction for the natives, to which they shall be assigned by the superior civil government. In case of not fulfilling that obligation they shall be indebted to the state for the expenses incurred in their education and teaching. The same thing shall happen if they leave the normal school before the conclusion of their studies without legitimate cause and by their own will or that of their parents, or are expelled from it for lack of application, or bad conduct. The model for calculating the expenses caused by said scholars during a given period shall be the board paid during the same period by a resident supernumerary scholar.

Art. 12. Places as regular resident scholars shall be supplied by the superior civil government to natives of the provinces of the archipelago, in proportion to the respective census of the population. As the number of aspirants for the places of supernumerary resident scholars continues to increase, the class of regular resident scholars will continue to decrease, the reduction beginning with those belonging to the provinces nearest the capital. Said class shall be suppressed when it happens that there are among the supernumerary [resident] scholars enough teachers with whom to supply the schools of the archipelago. In any event, the regular [resident] scholar, who shall have entered the school, shall have the right to keep his place, and such place shall only be suppressed when his course shall have been ended.

Art. 13. The supernumerary resident scholars shall pay the institution eight pesos per month for their board, and their rank in the school and other things will be equal to that of the regular scholars.

Art. 14. Only those young men shall be admitted as day scholars who, besides possessing the requirements demanded from the resident scholars, shall live in Manila or in its neighborhood, under the charge of their parents or in charge of a guardian and under such conditions that it can be assumed that they will find in their domestic hearth examples of virtue and morality. Such class of scholars shall receive school equipment free, and if they are poor, their textbooks.

Of the director, teachers, and dependents of the normal school

Art. 15. The normal school shall be directed and governed by the fathers of the Society of Jesus. At the head of the same there shall be a director to whose authority shall be subordinate the teachers, scholars, and inferior employes, and such director shall have the duty of directing the education and teaching, presiding at the literary ceremonies, visiting the rooms, watching over order and domestic discipline, correcting those who infringe the rules, and expelling pupils in the cases and under the conditions expressed in the interior regulations of the school, and he shall inform the suitable authority of the extraordinary measures and determinations of a serious nature which he believes it necessary to take.

Art. 16. Under the director's authority there shall be at least four teachers, one of whom must be at the same time spiritual prefect of the school, charged with directing the consciences of the scholars, with presiding at religious ceremonies, and with distributing the food of the divine word. Under his peculiar charge also shall be lessons in sacred history, morals, and religion. Another of the teachers shall fill the special post of prefect of customs, and his principal occupation will be to accompany the scholars and to have care of them in the ceremonies of the inner life of the institution. The other two teachers shall be occupied principally in the teaching of other matters.

Besides the director and teachers, the school shall have the brother coadjutors who shall be considered necessary. There shall also be one porter, and the other indispensable subordinates.

Art. 17. The salaries to be received by directors, professors, coadjutors, and subordinates, as well as the allowance for expenses of materials, shall be fixed by the superior civil governor by agreement with the right reverend archbishop of Manila, information of which shall be given to the government for its approval.

Of examinations

Art. 18. At the end of each month in each one of the classes of the normal school, there shall be a private examination in all the subjects studied during that period. A like exercise shall be held at the end of the first semester each year, in regard to the branches studied during that time. At the end of the course, a general examination shall be held. This exercise shall be public and in the presence of the authorities and persons of distinction in the capital, and shall be terminated with the announcement and distribution of prizes.

Of holidays and vacations

Art. 19. The holidays of the normal school shall be Sundays, feast days, Ash Wednesday, the day set aside for the commemoration of the faithful dead,24 and also the saint's days and birthday anniversaries of their Majesties and the prince of Asturias, and the saint's day of the superior civil governor.

The shorter vacations shall extend from Christmas eve to Twelfth-night, during the three carnival days,25 and from Holy Wednesday until Easter. During said vacations, the resident scholars shall remain in the institution.

The longer vacations shall last one and one-half months, and shall be during the time of the greatest heat. The resident scholars may pass to the bosom of their families for the period of the longer vacations.

The scholars may go once a month to the house of their parents or guardians.

Of rewards and punishments

Art. 20. The degree of excellence of the scholars shall be recompensed by honorable marks, which shall be kept in the book of the institution; and by annual prizes, whose solemn distribution shall take place at the termination of the public examinations.

Art. 21. Punishments shall be: public censure; deprivation from recreation and the walk; banishment and separation from the other scholars; and if these are not sufficient, the definitive punishment shall be expulsion from the school. Expulsion shall irremissibly take place because of any contagious disease, for notable laziness and lack of application, for serious lack of respect to the teachers, and for bad conduct or depraved morals.

Art. 22. As a reward shall also be the public reading of the marks of good deportment, application and progress; and as punishment the reading of the contrary marks. That shall be done monthly for that purpose, assembling in one place all the scholars with their teachers, in the presence of the director.

Of the interior regulations of the school

Art. 23. An interior regulation for the school shall be made, which shall specify the daily distribution of time on the part of the scholars, the order of their studies, and the division of classes, religious and literary exercises, conduct, food, and clothing, as well as the duties of the scholars respecting the teachers, and those of their parents and guardians in respect to the institution.

Of textbooks

Art. 24. The director of the normal school shall propose at the approval of the superior civil government, a list of books which can be used as textbooks by the scholars, to which the masters shall subject their explanation. Such list shall be revised according as is advised by circumstances.

The teachers shall give their lessons in the courses of which it is advisable for this system to make use, under the authority of the director.

Of special examinations to obtain certificates as assistant teacher

Art. 25. Examinations shall be held in the normal school every six months, to choose those who shall be given certificates as assistants. Those who present themselves at said examinations shall have the qualifications described in article 9, for those who aspire to enter the school. They shall be conversant with the matters prescribed in article 4; and their examinations shall be public and held before the director and teachers of the normal school.

Art. 26. There shall be no other mark in such examinations than those of passed or failed.

Of the issuance of teachers' and assistant teachers' certificates

Art. 27. The superior civil governor shall have the right to issue certificates as teacher and assistant at the proposal of the director of the normal school.

Art. 28. Certificates as teachers shall contain the mark which shall have been obtained and the class of schools for which such persons are qualified.

Madrid, December 20, 1863. Approved by her Majesty.26

CONCHA

REGULATIONS FOR THE SCHOOLS AND TEACHERS OF PRIMARY INSTRUCTION FOR THE NATIVES OF THE PHILIPPINE ARCHIPELAGO

Article 1. The teaching in the schools for natives shall be reduced for the present to the elementary primary grade, and shall comprise:

1. The Christian doctrine and principles of morality and sacred history suitable for children.

2. Reading.27

3. Writing.

4. Practical teaching of the Castilian language, principles of Castilian grammar, with extension of orthography.

5. Principles of arithmetic, which shall include the four rules for integers, common fractions, decimals, and denominate numbers, with principles of the decimal metric system, and its equivalents in the usual weights and measures.

6. Principles of general geography and Spanish history.

7. Principles of practical agriculture, with application to the products of the country.

8. Rules of courtesy.

9. Vocal music.

The primary teaching of girls will include the matters expressed by numbers 1, 2, 3, 4, 5, 8, and 9, of the present article, and the needle-work suitable to their sex.

Art. 2. Primary instruction is obligatory for all the natives. The parents, guardians, or agents of the children shall send them to the public schools from the age of seven to the age of twelve, unless they prove that they are giving them sufficient instruction at home or in private school. Those who do not observe this duty, if there is a school in the village at such distance that the children can attend it comfortably, will be warned and compelled to do so by the authority with a fine of from one-half to two reals.28

The parents or guardians of the children may also send them to school from the age of six years and from that of twelve to fourteen.

Art. 3. The teachers shall have special care that the scholars have practical exercise in speaking the Castilian language. In proportion as they become conversant with it, explanations shall be made to them in that language, and they shall be forbidden to communicate with one another during class in their own language.

Art. 4. Primary instruction shall be free for children whose parents are not known to be wealthy. That shall be proved by certification of the gobernadorcillo of the village, visoed by the parish priest.

Paper, copybooks, ink, and pens, will be free to all the children.

The parents, and for lack of these, the children who shall be well known to be wealthy, in the judgment of the gobernadorcillo of the village, with the confirmation of the parish priest, shall pay a moderate sum monthly, which shall be assigned by the governor of each province after conferring with the parish priest and the gobernadorcillo.

Art. 5. The parish priest shall direct the teaching of Christian doctrine and morality, and they shall be charged to give at least once a week the fitting explanations in the locality of the school, in the church, or any place which shall be assigned.

Art. 6. Schools shall have two months of vacation per year, during the time designated by the superior civil government, at the proposal of the chief of the province. The vacations may be continuous or divided into two or three periods.

Of textbooks

Art. 7. The Christian doctrine shall be taught by the catechism which is in use, and approved by ecclesiastical authorities. For reading, the syllabary prescribed by the superior civil governor, the Catechism of Astete, and the Catechism of Fleuri, shall be used. For writing, the Muestras de carácter español [i.e., Samples of Spanish characters] by Iturzaeta shall be used.29

As a text for the other matters included in the teaching, according to article 1, a book shall be compiled which shall contain them all as clearly and concisely as possible, and in addition, ideas on geometry and common knowledge of physical and natural sciences. Such book shall also serve for the last exercises in reading.30

Until the book mentioned in the preceding paragraph is compiled, teaching in matters not enumerated in the first paragraph of the present article shall be in the form prescribed by the superior civil governor.

Of the schools

Art. 8. In every village, if its population shall permit, there shall be a school for boys and another for girls.31 Those villages which have a population of 5,000, shall have two schools for boys and two others for girls. Those which have a population of 10,000, shall have three schools, and so on, increasing at the rate of one school for each sex for every 5,000 inhabitants, whenever an average of more than 150 children shall have attended all the existing schools during the last three months.32

In the visitas, very distant from the villages, whose population reaches 500 inhabitants, there shall also be a school for each sex, and if there is more than one visita, and together they have that number of souls, the schools shall be established in the most central.

If the number of children of one school exceeds eighty there shall be one assistant, and if it exceeds one hundred and fifty, two.

Art. 9. Schools shall be located in the most central part of the villages or barrios, and must be built well lighted and ventilated, with dwelling rooms for the teacher and his family; but such dwelling shall be independent [of the school] and have a special entrance.33

Art. 10. The schools shall conform to the classes fixed by article 5 of the royal decree of this date.

Of the teachers

Art. 11. The rank of teacher in the public schools of primary instruction belongs to the pupils of the normal school who are qualified with the suitable certificate, who shall be fully twenty years old, and possess the other requirements expressed in article 20.

Art. 12. Teachers shall enter the schools of entrada or ascenso, in accordance with the right which their respective certificates give them, according to the terms of article 7, of the regulations of the normal school for male teachers, approved by her Majesty on this date. After three years of teaching, the teachers may be promoted to the next class, whether of ascenso or término of the second class. When two or more teachers aspire to schools of higher rank, if their respective certificates are equal, he who has taught longer shall be preferred. If the certificates are not equal, he who possesses a certificate for a school of ascenso shall be preferred to him who has one for a school of entrada.

Art. 13. In case of the absolute lack of candidates with the necessary certificate, those who hold lower certificates may be appointed teachers for a school of the upper class, but it shall be ad interim, and they shall receive the pay belonging to the class of their certificate, until they complete the time of exercise with good mark, in which case they shall be appointed regularly.

Art. 14. For the lack of teachers with a certificate, those who are twenty years of age and have the other requirements prescribed in article 12, and have a certificate as assistant, may govern schools, and shall receive the pay of teachers of the third class.

Art. 15. For the lack of candidates possessing certificate as assistant, those who prove in the examination held before the provincial commission of primary instruction sufficient capacity and are of the abovesaid age, may govern ad interim the schools with the title of substitute, and shall receive the pay mentioned in the preceding article.

Art. 16. The position of teachers of the término schools of the first grade, namely, those of Manila and its district, shall be supplied in the manner determined by article 5 of the royal decree of this date, to wit, by competition among the teachers with certificate from the normal school, and practice in teaching. The time of such practice shall be at least one year. The competition shall be held with preceding edict for the term of three months, before a commission composed of the director, or, in his absence, of one of the teachers of the normal school, one of the individuals of the Superior Board of Primary Instruction, another of the provincial board, the senior parish priest as local supervisor, and one member of the ayuntamiento.

Art. 17. A graded list shall be formed of the assistants, in which, without prejudice to the right which is conferred on them by article 14, they shall be promoted according to seniority, commencing with the class of entrada, and continuing to those of ascenso, término of the second grade, and término of the first grade.

Art. 18. The appointment of teachers and assistants shall belong to the superior civil governor.

Art. 19. The issuing of certificates of regular teachers and assistants shall be attended to by the superior civil governor, in the manner prescribed by article 27 of the regulations of the normal school of this date.

The certificates of substitute teachers shall be issued by the same authority, at the proposal of the respective provincial commission, the examination papers of the party interested and the record of his examination first having been sent.

Art. 20. In order to be a teacher, assistant, or substitute, one must, in addition to the qualifications respectively expressed in the preceding articles:

1. Be a native of the Spanish domains.

2. Prove his good religious and moral deportment.

3. Be of suitable age.

The assistants may begin teaching in the capacity of such in the schools at the age of seventeen.

Art. 21. Positions as teachers or assistants cannot be exercised:

1. By those who suffer from any disease, or have any defects which incapacitate them for teaching.

2. By those who shall have been condemned to corporal punishments,34 or are incapacitated for exercising public duties.

Art. 22. Teachers of entrada shall receive from eight to twelve pesos per month; those of ascenso, from twelve to fifteen; those of término of the second grade, from fifteen to twenty.

The superior civil governor shall fix, by recommendation of the provincial commission and report of the superior, the sum to be received by the teacher between the greatest and least amount assigned, keeping in mind as an average the material cost of living and the number of pay children who attend the school.

Teachers of término of the first grade, or those of the schools of Manila, shall receive the pay prescribed in the municipal budget of that city. That pay must be at least equal to that which is assigned as a maximum to teachers of término of the second class.35

Art. 23. Teachers shall enjoy in addition the following advantages:

1. A dwelling apartment for themselves and family in the schoolhouse, or reimbursement if they rent one.

2. The fees paid by well-to-do children.

3. The privileges and exemptions mentioned in articles 12 and 14 of the royal decree of this date.36

Art. 24. Teachers shall have, in accordance with article 13 of the same royal decree, the right of pension and half pay after twenty years of service, and four-fifths' pay after thirty-five years of service, whenever in one or the other case they shall have reached the age of sixty years, or be incapacitated for the performance of the duties required by their profession.

Art. 25. Assistants, when they perform the duties of such, shall receive pay of four, six, or eight pesos per month, according as the school is entrada, ascenso, or término of the second grade, or the amount assigned in the municipal budget of Manila if the school is término of the first rank. They shall receive, in addition, the fourth part of the fees of well-to-do children; and shall enjoy the exemptions expressed by articles 12 and 14 of the royal decree of this date. They shall also have the right of pension in the same proportion and in the same manner as that prescribed for teachers.37

Of women teachers

Art. 26. Women teachers for girls shall be twenty-five years old at least, and shall possess the other qualifications that are demanded from the male teachers.

Art. 27. For the provision of schools, women teachers with certificates shall be preferred. That certificate, until the normal school for women teachers is established, shall be issued by the superior civil governor, on the recommendation of the commission established by article 16, associated with a woman teacher with certificate and examination in the matters which constitute the teaching of girls.

For the lack of women teachers with certificate, those who show sufficient ability before the respective provincial commission of primary instruction, shall be appointed as substitutes.

Art. 28. Women teachers shall receive monthly pay of eight pesos if they have a certificate, and six if the contrary be true, and all the fees of wealthy girls. They shall also have the right to live in the school, and in case they do not live there, to a reimbursement to pay their rent.

Of Sunday schools

Art. 29. Teachers shall be obliged to take care of the Sunday class which shall be established in each village for the teaching of adults. Said class will be free with the sole exception of the wealthy.

A special order of the superior civil governor, after a previous conference with the Superior Board of Primary Instruction, shall prescribe the duration and method of the above-mentioned classes.38

Of the supervision of the primary instruction among the natives

Art. 30. Superior supervision will be in charge of the superior civil government, with the aid of a commission composed of the diocesan prelate and six and seven members of recognized qualifications, appointed by the former. The director of the normal school shall be a member ex-officio.39

Art. 31. The chiefs of the provinces shall be provincial supervisors, and shall exercise their office with the aid of a commission presided over by the same and composed in addition of the diocesan prelate, or, in his absence, of the parish priest of the chief city, and of the alcalde-mayor, or administrator of finances. The respective reverend and learned parish priests shall be the local supervisors of primary instruction.40

Art. 32. The duties of the local supervisors shall be:

1. To visit the schools as frequently as possible, and see that the regulations are observed.

2. To admonish those teachers who commit any fault, and suspend them in case they commit any excess which, in their judgment, does not permit them to continue in charge of the school, and to give information thereof to the provincial supervisor.

3. To promote the attendance of the children at the schools.

4. To give in writing orders of admission into the schools, with expression as to whether the teaching shall be free or paid.

5. To propose, through the medium of the provincial supervisor, whatever they believe advisable for the progress or improvement of primary instruction.

6. To exercise, in regard to the teaching of Christian doctrine and morals, the direction expressed in article 4.

Art. 33. The provincial supervisors shall exercise, with the aid of the respective commission, their oversight over the schools of the province, and shall have authority, the said commission having been conferred with, to approve or disapprove the suspensions of teachers imposed by the local supervisors, giving account in both cases to the government, with remission of the record in the case.

Supervisors shall send to the above-mentioned authority monthly reports concerning the number of pupils of both sexes in each school on the last day of the month, with mention of those who pay, with the number of those who have entered and left, and the average attendance at the school during the month, with what remarks are deemed advisable.

Art. 34. The Superior Board of Primary Instruction shall consult the superior government of the islands:

1. In regard to the approval of textbooks.

2. On measures in regard to the dismissal of teachers, declarations of the grades of schools, and assignment of pay to the instructors.

3. In everything else concerning the execution of this plan, and especially concerning the doubts arising from the same.

Final resolution

Art. 35. Instructions shall be compiled comprising the principal ideas of pedagogy, and explaining minutely the duties of teachers, and the details of school organization and the progress of instruction. A printed copy of these instructions shall be given to every schoolteacher of the natives, of both sexes, and they shall be charged to learn them and observe them.

Another copy shall also be sent to every provincial chief and parish priest.

Madrid. December 20, 1863. Approved by her Majesty,

INTERIOR REGULATIONS OF THE SCHOOLS OF PRIMARY INSTRUCTION FOR THE NATIVES OF THE PHILIPPINE ARCHIPELAGO

Of the interior arrangement of the schools

Article 1. The edifice destined for a school must consist at least of a room proportioned in size to the number of children, an antehall, and a dwelling for the teacher and his family.

The furniture shall be composed of the following chattels: One table with drawers, one chair, one inkwell, and one bell for the teacher; desks with one lid, and benches for the children, one inkwell for each two children, one blackboard with an easel, one clock, and four chairs.

In the front of the hall, a crucifix shall be placed under a canopy, and under that the picture of the chief of the state.

The schools for girls shall have the same fixtures, and in addition, scissors, needles, thimbles, and sewing thread.

Of the teachers

Art. 2. Teachers and assistants must be in the school half an hour before classes begin, in order to prepare everything necessary for the teaching.

The teacher will daily look after the cleaning of the schoolrooms, and all the furniture in them.

He shall keep books entitled *Libro de Matricula* [*i.e.*, Matriculation book] and *Registro diario de asistencia* [*i.e.*, Daily register of attendance]. In the first he shall note: 1—the number of matriculations; 2—the names and surnames of the children; 3—their age; 4—the names and surnames of their parents; 5—the profession of the latter; 6—whether they pay and what sum; 7—the date of their entrance into the school; 8—the progress of their instruction; 9—the date when they leave school; 10—remarks on their character and deportment.

In the register of attendance he shall note daily the number of children absent and present, all in accordance with models which shall be drawn up.

He shall also keep a book with the list of those present, in order to note those children who are late at school morning and afternoon, in accordance with the corresponding model.

Art. 3. Before the fifth day of every month, the teacher shall send to the provincial chief a list of those children present in the school on the last day of the preceding month, in which shall be set down the names of those who pay for their education, as well as of those who have entered and left during the month, according to the respective model, and a copy of the *Registro diario de asistencia* for the same time. These documents must be visoed by the reverend or secular parish priest, for which purpose the teacher shall present to him the books referred to above.

Of the pupils

Art. 4. Children of both sexes will be admitted to the schools from the age of six to that of fourteen, but when they reach the latter age they shall cease to attend them.

Children shall attend school with clean faces, hands, and clothing, and shall not be received without fulfilling that requirement.

Art. 5. Children who suffer from any contagious disease shall not be admitted. As soon as the teacher shall observe any disease in anyone he shall advise his parents or guardians so that they may cease to send him to school until he is completely cured.

Art. 6. Every child who arrives at the school after the beginning of the class, without satisfactorily explaining the reason for his tardiness, shall be punished in proportion to the lateness of his arrival.

When any child is frequently absent from school, without his guardians giving the reason therefor, the teacher shall call it to the attention of such guardians, and if such child continues to be absent in the same manner, the teacher shall inform the religious or parish priest thereof.

Art. 7. Pay children shall meet their fees for the entire month, whatever be the day of their entrance and departure from the school.

Of school days and hours

Art. 8. School days shall be all those of the year except the following: 1—Sundays, and feast days marked in the calendar with two or three crosses; 2—All-Souls' day; 3—from Christmas until the day after Epiphany; 4—Ash Wednesday; 5—the six days of Holy Week; 6—the day of St. Joseph of Calasanz;41 7—the saint's day and the birthday anniversaries of their Majesties, the king and queen, and of his royal Highness, the prince of Asturias; 8—the feast day of the village; 9—the saint's day of the superior civil governor and of the bishop of the diocese.

Art. 9. Classes shall begin every season at seven in the morning, and shall conclude at ten; and in the afternoon they shall begin at half-past two, and end at five.

During the months of April, May, and June, there shall be no school in the afternoon, but the morning classes will last one hour longer, ending at eleven instead of ten.

Of the progress of education

Art. 10. In the morning at the hour assigned by the parish priest supervisor, the teachers, both for boys and girls, shall assemble with their pupils in the church and shall hear mass, during which they shall recite a part of the rosary. After the conclusion of mass, boys and girls shall go out separately, formed in two rows headed by their teachers and with the cross in front shall walk through various streets, whenever they may do so, to their respective schools. At seven, the children shall enter their class, salute the teacher, form into two ranks, and the teacher shall inspect the cleanliness of their bodies and clothing. Then they shall kneel down with their faces toward the front of the hall, and shall make the sign of the cross while repeating the prayers which the master shall say slowly. These prayers, as well as those which shall be said at the end of class, shall be those prescribed by the bishop of the diocese. The roll shall be called; the class in writing shall last until eight o'clock; the class in reading until nine; the grammar class until ten; prayers, as at entrance, and salutation; departure from the school whence they shall go to the church to leave the cross in the same manner as they took it. In the afternoon, the children shall also assemble at the church, and shall do the same as in the morning until reaching the school. At half-past two they shall enter, salute, have inspection of cleanliness, prayers, and roll call as in the morning; arithmetic class until half-past three, lessons in doctrine, ethics, and sacred history until half-past four; and what time is left they shall alternate day by day with rules of deportment, principles of geography and history, and principles of agriculture, until five. At the latter hour they shall leave the school, taking the cross back to the church, whence the children shall retire to their homes.

Sunday afternoon shall be exclusively employed in a general review of doctrine, ethics, and sacred history, lessons in vocal music, and in reciting a portion of the rosary, until the hour when the salve and the litanies are sung in the church, at which they shall be present accompanied by their teachers.

On Sundays and feast days marked with two or three crosses the children shall go to hear mass headed by their teacher, and then shall go to visit the regular or secular parish priest. Conferences in regard to Christian doctrine and ethics shall be at the hour that the latter prescribes.42

Every three months, on the day prescribed by the parish priest, the teacher shall take the children, who are ready for it, to confess and receive communion.

Of rewards and punishments

Art. 11. Ordinary rewards shall consist of *vales* [*i.e.*, merits], namely, a card or a bit of paper with the abovesaid word, and shall serve to liberate the scholars from the punishment which they deserve for slight faults. Extraordinary rewards shall consist of letters of advice to the parents of those who excel in application and good deportment; and a letter of recommendation of those who are excellent to the regular or secular parish priest.

Art. 12. Punishments will be in proportion to the degree of fault, and shall consist: 1—to remain standing or kneeling for the maximum time of one hour; 2—to do additional reading or writing; 3—to remain in the school writing or studying one hour after the end of the class; 4—in any other moderate and proportionate correction, at the judgment of the parish-priest supervisor, in accordance with the degree of the fault.

In no case shall any punishment not comprehended in the preceding article be imposed. The teacher who infringes this rule shall be admonished twice by the parish-priest supervisor, and if he does not correct himself shall be suspended from his employment.

Of examinations

Art. 13. Every year, at the time of election of justices for the villages, examinations shall be held in the schools. They shall be presided over in the chief provincial cities by the provincial commissions of primary instruction, and in the villages by the parish priest together with the gobernadorcillo and two persons appointed by the first.

A reward according to rank, which shall consist of books, samples, thimbles, scissors, or any other object analogous to the subject, shall be given at the judgment of the examiners to the child who excels in the exercises of the doctrine, reading, writing, arithmetic, and grammar. For this object each school shall contribute twenty reals per year.

Art. 14. The orders of these regulations may be modified by the superior civil governor, after the previous report of the superior commissions of primary instruction. The regular and secular parish priests shall inform that authority of their results and of the reforms which are necessary, especially in what refers to the duration of class hours and their distribution.

Madrid, December 20, 1863. Approved by her Majesty,

CONCHA

DECREE OF THE SUPERIOR CIVIL GOVERNMENT APPROVING THE REGULATIONS OF THE MUNICIPAL GIRLS' SCHOOL OF MANILA

Manila, February 15, 1864. Having examined the regulations made for the municipal girls' school created in this capital and in conformity with the modifications advised by the Government Section of the Council of Administration, said regulations are approved. Let it be communicated and proclaimed.

ECHAGÜE

REGULATIONS FOR THE MUNICIPAL GIRLS' SCHOOL PROPOSED BY THE EXALTED AYUNTAMIENTO OF MANILA

CHAPTER I

Object and character of the municipal school43

1. The object of this school in charge of the sisters of charity is to give the girls of this capital the inestimable benefit of a fine education and the elementary instruction, with all the solidity and amplitude advisable.

2. In their education is included the theoretical and practical teaching of Christian religion and ethics, which our own self respect, and our respect due to our fellows impose on us.

3. Therefore, so far as possible, the scholars shall hear mass and recite the rosary daily. They shall be obliged to confess and receive communion as soon as their age permits it, monthly, or at least every two months. They shall celebrate the act of communion on the day, and at the hour and place which shall be designated by the directress, after conferring with the superior. The feast of the Immaculate Conception and that of the Presentation of the most holy Virgin shall be celebrated in the school with all possible solemnity.

4. Instruction shall embrace two kinds of subjects: the first the necessary, to which all the girls must attend in their respective classes; the others optional, to which they shall apply themselves according to the wishes of their parents.

5. The [required] subjects are: Christian doctrine, politeness, reading, writing, Castilian grammar, arithmetic, the decimal metric system, and the needle-work suitable for their sex, such as sewing, darning, and cutting. On the other hand, the optional subjects are: geography; general history; special history of España; elements of natural history; embroidery in white, with silks, corded silk, beads, and gold, and other like needle-work.

6. To these subjects can be added any other subjects which experience shall advise in the future, and which is not outside the sphere of elementary knowledge.

CHAPTER II

Pupils of the municipal school

7. All the children who so solicit, within the number permitted by the size of the building, and according to the order of their presentation, whenever their moral condition does not make them unworthy the company and intercourse of those who are well brought up, shall be admitted without distinction, from the age of five years.

8. Permission to admit girls shall be in charge of a member of the exalted ayuntamiento, who, after having informed the corporation thereof, shall send for that purpose to the directress of the school a signed paper, in which will be noted the name and personal qualifications of the girl.

9. Teaching will be free for all pupils in all necessary and optional subjects named in these regulations, without prejudice of which, in case of enlarging the scope of teaching to other optional subjects, which occasion expense, the quota which must be paid by the girls who receive lessons in the said subjects shall be assigned.

10. The directress of the school, conferring with the superior and commission of supervision, created by article 26, is authorized to dismiss any girl who deserves it, informing the member of the ayuntamiento who is charged with the admission. Cases for expulsion shall consist of: a contagious disease, special laziness, and lack of application, stubbornness, and serious lack of respect toward the teachers, bad deportment, and morals harmful to the other scholars.

11. In case of a contagious disease, a medical examination at the wish and expense of the parents shall precede the resolution to dismiss the girl. For the cause of lack of application or stubbornness, the scholar who incurs these faults shall not be dismissed except after the attempt by reasonable means to correct her, and warnings, once, twice, and thrice, to the parents of the party interested. But when the deportment and irregular morals of any pupil concern the innocence of the other girls, she shall be dismissed without delay, with the advisable reservation. Nevertheless, both in such case and in the preceding, all due consideration shall be observed toward the girl and her parents.

12. Girls who, without any legitimate cause approved by the directress of the school, shall be absent from class thirty consecutive or interspersed times, in the same year, shall not receive a reward in their examinations. Sickness, necessary absence from this capital, and the bad weather which makes the streets impassable shall be a sufficient excuse.

13. For the admission of boarders and half-boarders, the resolutions drawn up in special regulations shall be observed. Until such regulations are published the directress of the school may admit half-boarders exactly in the manner in which pupils are received, namely, as arranged by articles 7 and 8 of this same chapter.

CHAPTER III

Classes and studies

14. Teaching in all the necessary subjects embraced in the municipal school is divided into three classes: lowest, intermediate, and upper.

15. In the lowest class shall be taught Christian doctrine and the beginnings of reading and sewing.

16. In the intermediate class shall be taught Christian doctrine, principles of sacred history, and the general history of España, reading, writing, principles of Castilian grammar, with practice in orthography, principles of arithmetic, and of the decimal metric system, overcasting, drawing threads, backstitching, gathering, and plaiting, darning, and sample work.

17. The upper class shall be taught writing, Castilian grammar, orthography, arithmetic, history of España, the decimal metric system, plaiting, making button-holes, crocheting, and cutting.

CHAPTER IV

Distribution of time for classes and studies

18. All classes shall begin in the morning at eight o'clock, and in the afternoon at two, and shall close at eleven in the morning and at five in the afternoon.

19. Girls of the lowest class shall employ the first hour of the morning in sewing, the second in praying and Christian doctrine, the third in reading; and the same in the afternoon.

20. Children of the intermediate and upper class shall employ the first hour of the morning in writing; the second, in praying, reading, Christian doctrine, and arithmetic; the third, in needle-work. In the afternoon of Mondays, Wednesdays, and Fridays, the first hour shall be employed

in grammar, general history, special history of España, and exercises in orthography; the second, in reciting the most holy rosary, and in hearing the explanation of Christian doctrine and sacred history; the third, in needle-work. Tuesdays, Thursdays, and Saturdays, in the morning, the same as on Mondays, etc.; but in the afternoon of Tuesdays and Saturdays, the first hour, in lessons in politeness, orthography, and the decimal metric system; the second, in reciting the holy rosary, and in hearing on Tuesdays the explanation of natural history, and on Saturdays that of the holy gospel; the third in needle-work.

CHAPTER V

Holidays and vacations

21. There shall be a holiday for all the classes on the afternoon of Thursdays in that week that shall have no feast day; and in the morning and afternoon, the feast day in commemoration of the deceased faithful, the saints' days, or anniversary of the birthdays of our sovereigns (whom may God preserve), and the feast of St. Vincent of Paul.

22. There shall be thirty days of general vacation after the examinations which shall take place at the end of May, but the last fortnight shall have only holidays in the afternoon.

CHAPTER VI

Rewards and punishments

23. There shall be a private examination in the classes at the end of each month, and some reward shall be given.

24. At the end of the course, after the public examinations, the solemn distribution of prizes shall take place. These prizes shall consist of silver, and gilded medals, and of rewards of merit and religious subjects, and other like objects.

25. The punishments which shall be imposed on the pupils shall consist of detention and remaining on the knees for a moderate time, loss of place of honor in the class, occupation of a seat separated from the other girls, and tagged with a card declaring the fault.

CHAPTER VII

Supervision and oversight

26. A commission composed of three women appointed by his Excellency, the superior civil governor, on recommendation of the ayuntamiento, one of whom shall be relieved annually, shall be created

for the supervision of the school. The functions of this commission shall be those only of supervision and oversight. In consequence of that they must inform the superior authority of any fault which is noted with the fitting remarks for its correction.

Approved by his Excellency, the superior civil governor, Manila, February 15, 1864.

CIRCULAR OF THE SUPERIOR CIVIL GOVERNMENT GIVING RULES FOR THE GOOD DISCHARGE OF SCHOOL SUPERVISION

The duties imposed by articles 30–33 of the regulations approved by her Majesty, December 20, 1863, for the schools and teachers of primary instruction in this archipelago, both on this superior government and on the chiefs of the provinces and the reverend and learned parish priests, charging them in their respective spheres with the supervision of so important a service, cannot be easily fulfilled without a preceding conference between this directive center and its delegates in regard to the transcendental points of doctrine, and of detail which the supervisions are called upon to resolve.

The briefest enunciation of the supervisory functions is sufficient to make its seriousness understood. The local functions especially, which are exercised in their villages by the reverend and learned parish priests, enclose the future of education. These are:

1. To visit the schools as often as possible, and see that the regulations are observed.

2. To admonish the teachers who commit any fault, and suspend them in case they incur any excess, which in their judgment does not allow such teachers to longer continue in charge of the schools, advising the provincial supervisor thereof.

3. To promote attendance at the schools by the children.

4. To give the orders of admission into the schools in writing with expression as to whether the education is to be free or paid.

5. To propose, through the medium of the provincial supervisor, whatever is thought to be advisable for the encouragement or improvement of primary instruction.

6. To exercise the direction which is expressed in article 4, in regard to the teaching of the Christian doctrine and ethics.

On the fulfilment of these sovereign requirements depends the development and conservation of the improvements which are being introduced into the department. Without a supervision, exercised with assiduity and intelligence, one cannot imagine, and never will there exist without doubt, good schools or intelligent teachers. The happy fact of her Majesty entrusting that supervision to the reverend and learned parish priests, assures its good outcome and shows well the foresight and practical spirit which shine forth throughout the regulations.

So deep is this conviction in me, that I do not hesitate to direct myself under this date to their Excellencies, the most illustrious prelates and the reverend father provincials of the religious orders, petitioning them in harmony with the request; and charge that her Majesty directs to them in article 19 of the organic royal decree of December 20, 1863, that they incite the zeal of the parish priests for the exact observance of their duties in what relates to the supervision of instruction. Besides this you, as chief and supervisor of that province, will please charge upon them the study of chapter ii, título vi, of the regulations dictated for the Peninsula, July 20, 1859, as a text or legal precedent; and as doctrine the wise observations which the author of the *Diccionario de educación y métodos de enseñanza* [*i.e.*, Dictionary of education, and methods of teaching] a very respectable authority in pedagogy, to whom the Peninsula owes in great measure the progress of its primary instruction. "Supervision," it says, "is one of the most efficacious means for the improvement of schools, and the acceleration of its onward progress toward perfection, but only when it is done with intelligence, faith, and perseverance, and at the same time, benevolent severity. The more serious are its consequences, the more difficult is the mission of the supervisor, and the more rare the qualities with which he ought to be adorned.

"It is necessary for him who shall exercise this duty to know how to examine things in their most minute details. He must see them at the same time in their make-up in order to judge of the harmony or unity existing between the means and the ends to which they are directed. Obliged to see and observe by himself whatever passes in the schools, he must for that reason descend to the level of the least intelligent teachers, and of the most dull and stupid scholars.

"The self-love of some, the ignorance of others, and the indifference and coldness of the majority of persons with whom he will have to do, are obstacles which can only be destroyed by a zeal, a strength of indefatigable will, and a constancy which, instead of becoming weak, increases its power in proportion to the resistance which is offered to it.

"The supervisor must have studied the schools and the legislation of this department very carefully, and further he must have a certain tact and delicacy in his intercourse with men, which can only be acquired by experience, and for lack of experience, by serious and profound thought. Without that, it will be difficult, if not impossible, to accomplish all the good that the supervision may produce, and attract all the party of the commissions and of the intelligent and influential persons, whom it is of great importance to interest in favor of and for the profit of education."44

So notable a synthesis of the honorable task charged upon the supervisors, and of the rules of deportment which must be presented, indicates at once the evolution which the requirements contained in article 32 of the regulations of December 20, 1863, will have to receive in practice. Nevertheless, this superior government will explain them to you, point by point, so that you may all be able to penetrate more and more into the delicate functions which you are going to perform.

I

Inspection of schools

The ocular supervision, to which the first part of these rules refer, is chiefly an act of policy and good internal system. The supervisor shall observe whether the school is clean and well taken care of, in order to inspire the children with ideas of order and personal neatness, which may have so great an influence on their future life; whether the interior regulations approved by her Majesty on the same date, and cited so often, are scrupulously observed; and whether the progress of the teaching is that prescribed by article 10. Such supervision must be frequent, at the least semi-annual, when, in accordance with article 5 of the school regulations, they give lessons in Christian doctrine and ethics to the children.

On one of these inspections, combined with the communications existing between the village and the chief city of the province or district, the supervisor shall devote himself to the examinations of the matriculation and record books referred to in article 2 of the interior regulations, in order to viso in fitting time the monthly report of entrances and departure, or the movement of the school, which, in accordance with article 3, the teacher must send before the fifth of each month to the provincial supervisor. This report is very important, as it must serve as data for the compiling of the general information of the province which must be published in the Gaceta de Manila [i.e., Manila Gazette],45 in accordance with the circulars of this superior government on the twelfth of the current month.

Lastly, if the supervisor is zealous, as is to be hoped, on the occasion of all inspections, in investigating thoroughly the progress of the children and the instruction of the teacher, he shall endeavor not to exact from either scholars or teacher things beyond their strength, and shall adjust his actions and words to the measure of good sense. He shall bear in mind that the result of his visit depends in that act on the impression which the supervisor produces on the teacher and on the children. In no case ought he to appear as a melancholy censor, or a too indulgent friend. His corrections must be mild when they are directed to the chief of the institution, in order that he may not become contemptuous in the eyes of his scholarship. If he merits an energetic correction, it shall be given with great reserve, bearing in mind that the second requirement of the above-mentioned article 32, places in his hand energetic means of action. In exchange, praises must be public, but not exaggerated, or told in such a manner that the teacher or the scholars shall grow arrogant. In a word, simplicity, prudence, and affability must rule these actions, the most transcendental of the supervisors' function, for they can render sterile in a moment the cares of the government, the sacrifices of the villages, and the lofty interests of the present and future, which the education of children represents for the country and for the families.

II

Correction and suspension of teachers

This is the most delicate power which the regulations give to the supervisors. From the last paragraph preceding is inferred the frugality with which it ought to be used. Faults of religion, public or private morals, or of zeal in the fulfilment of one's duties, will be the only things which authorize supervisors to initiate the governmental measure demanded by article 9 of the regulations for the discharge of teachers and assistants who have graduated from the normal school.

The abandonment of the Castilian language in the explanations or in the material ceremonies of the school, will also be considered as one of the most serious faults of the teacher, according to circumstances, in the tenor of law v, book i, título xiii, of Recopilación indiana, animated and reformed by the imposition of heavy penalties in the concluding requirements of chapters 25 and 26 of the Ordinances of good government of February 26, 1768, articles 5 of the regulations for normal school, and 3 for those of schools for primary instruction.

As it would scarcely be right that the authority of correcting and punishing be not accompanied by that of compensating, especially since the reverend and learned parish priests are authorized by the fifth clause of the above-cited article 32, to promote the progress or improvement of education, they will also be empowered to propose annually after the examinations justifiable recommendations for the granting of a prudent number of medals of civil merit to the teachers or assistants, who have most distinguished themselves. The supervisor, consulting with the commission of the department, shall remit the document with his report to this government, which, consulting in due time the superior commission, will grant or refuse the recompense within the maximum limit of two medals per province.

When extraordinary and excellent services are proved, the more honorable distinction may be obtained from the government of her Majesty. This shall all be without prejudice to the promotions and rewards of organic character, that is to say, those which are granted to teachers by articles 11 and 12 of their own regulations.

III

School attendance

Education is compulsory. This concluding requirement of the regulations exists in the laws of public instruction of almost all nations. Nevertheless, in its application, the governments pay attention to the social circumstances of the country. In our country parents incur a fine who do not send their children to school, the fine being from one-half to two reals, according to circumstances (art. 2, of school regulations).

Before having recourse to this coercive means, a zealous supervisor has other means of greater efficacy. The parish priest, venerated by his parishioners, ought to excite the consciences of the heads of the family, and make them comprehend their responsibility before God and men in depriving their children of education. If an instinctive duty counsels them to give their children bread, the duty to give them an education (the bread of the soul) is a sacred one, without which Christian man cannot live. The mothers of the family ought to be for the supervisor, under this point of view, the preferred object of their supplication, warnings, and tender and salutary counsels.

The goad of their own interests so powerful in the human heart ought also to be excited for this noble end. The law has considered them very carefully and it is fitting for the supervisor to unfold before the eyes of the parents so that their simple intelligence may well understand that *not only ought they*, but that *it is profitable for them to send their children to school*, for after the schools have been established for fifteen years in the village of their habitation those who cannot speak, read, or write Castilian:

Cannot be gobernadorcillos.
Nor lieutenants of justice.

Nor form part of the principalía; unless they enjoy that privilege because of heredity—a right which will continue to rapidly disappear, in proportion as the instruction develops, and as only those who possess an education become principales.

Lastly, after a school has been established in the village for thirty years, those who unite [in themselves] said circumstance can enjoy the enviable exemption of personal services.

Another more pressing thing must also be recalled to the attention of the parents daily and hourly if possible. Five years after the publication of the regulations, no one who cannot prove that he can talk, read, and write Castilian, can be appointed to any remunerative post in this archipelago.

So important requirements of articles 16 and 17 of the organic royal decree of December 20, 1863, recommended by article 18 to this superior government and the authorities of its dependency shall be fulfilled with all exactness. From December 20 of the last year, 1868, no one who cannot prove in the terms expressed in article 17 that he can talk, read, and write Castilian, shall be appointed in the archipelago, not even for the most insignificant and material posts of the offices of state or of the villages (such as agents, fagot-gatherers, tax assessors, collectors, etc., etc.).

If these inducements, or those which their religious and social zeal inspire in the parish priests, do not produce the desired result, then is the time when the supervisors must have recourse to the gobernadorcillos for the imposition of the fines authorized by article 2 of school regulations.

IV

Admission into the schools

Both clear and simple are the prescribed regulations in regard to this point. The supervisors perfectly understand the duties which are delegated to them and the best method of fulfilling them.

Without ever losing sight of the fact that education is free for poor children, they shall also bear in mind that this same principle of charity, which the state proclaims and which is imposed as an obligation, counsels them not to allow the admission of children under the term "poor" whose parents can and ought to bear some sacrifice. It is important for the gobernadorcillos to understand that if at any time they unduly issue certificates of poverty according to the tenor of article 4 of the regulations, the parish priests shall refuse to approve them, and the consequent permission for the child to enter the school. And in case this abuse is again committed they will inform the provincial supervisor.

V

Propositions for improvements

The just initiative conceded in this matter to supervisors by the regulations, must not be used without moderation, since innovations in public instruction are of great consequence. One single error is enough to lose a generation. Fortunately, as has already been said, the fact that the functions of supervisors are entrusted to the reverend and learned parish priests is a guarantee for the state and the heads of families, that, in religion and ethics, the cardinal basis of all solid instruction, reforms of principle or method shall not be introduced arbitrarily. In regard to the equipment, of which the experience and development of the respective institutions continue to advise the supervisors, it is to be hoped that they will harmonize with the general profit, which does not always build upon the best, but on what is good and possible.

A fertile field is offered by the lamentable condition of primary letters; by the scarcity of buildings for schools and teachers; by the grievous disproportion among the children who can and who cannot read; and between those who go and those who do not go to school, etc. Some data collected by this superior government, in consequence of the circular of March 1, 1866, show the following picture which is recommended by its very nature to the study of supervisors, although its accuracy must be a matter of doubt on all points.

Report of primary education of these islands with relation to the data of approximate accuracy which were sent to this superior civil government by the chiefs of the provinces and districts herein expressed, in observance of the circular of March 1, 1866.

Provinces or districts	Number of villages	Number of souls	School attendance		Number of schools possible		Buildings for	
			Boys	Girls	Boys	Girls	Schools	Teachers
Abra	8	23,140	876	569	10	10		
Albay	30	210,954	4,385	3,079			22	
Antique	19	88,243	1,930	1,663	21	21	16	
Bataán	12	45,177	1,005	704	16	16	10	
Batanes (Isla)	7	8,639	632	336	6	6	2	
Batangas	20	279,930	3,340	80	85	33	1	
Benguet	27	11,587	29				1	1

Provinces or districts	Number of villages	Number of souls	School attendance		Number of schools possible		Buildings for	
			Boys	Girls	Boys	Girls	Schools	Teachers
Bontoc		7,000						
Bohol	31	192,734	15,736	17,948	31	31	31	
Bulacan	23	241,698	6,485	2,162	47	55	17	
Burias	2	1,800	78	102	2	2	2	2
Cagayan	19	63,059	4,093	5,451	22	22	14	
Camarines Sur	33	95,630	1,176				6	36
Camarines Norte	9	26,499	480		9	9	8	
Capiz	31	191,818	5,072	4,436	35		28	
Cavite	6	65,225	2,045	713	16	16	16	1
Cebú	45	314,517	6,734	4,414			45	
Calamianes	5	13,851	718	298	6	6	6	
Cottabato	7	3,913	128	70	3	3		
Corregidor (Isla)	1	550	39	43				
Davao	2	937	107	81			1	
Ilocos Sur	23	163,758	4,603	1,993	20	22	23	
Ilocos Norte	15	135,868	2,440	1,056	30	30	20	
Iloilo	39	375,500	7,960	6,193	67	64	39	
Infanta	3	7,250	558		3		2	
Isla de Negros	41	144,594	1,829	1,776	30	24	29	
Isabela de Basilan	1	439			1	1		
Isabela de Luzón	10	29,674	3,199	2,820	16	16	9	
Laguna	28	129,064	4,689	1,438				
Lepanto	48	8,851			4	4		
Leite	40	154,530	5,107	3,156		89	40	
Manila	29	275,218	1,940	903			25	13
Marianas (Islas)	8	6,308	511	440	10	6	6	
Masbate y Ticao	9	11,716	425	425	56	56	9	

Provinces or districts	Number of villages	Number of souls	School attendance		Number of schools possible		Buildings for	
			Boys	Girls	Boys	Girls	Schools	Teachers
Mindoro	17	45,630	2,426				6	
Misamis	22	67,285	5,684	5,684	20	20	19	
Marong	12	49,859	934	558	12	12	9	
Nueva Ecija	18	80,463	2,561	1,408	36	34	16	8
Nueva Vizcaya	6	12,091	1,481	1,764	6	6	6	
Pampanga	28	188,694	1,580	517	52	52	21	
Pangasinan	29	171,503	13,228	11,685	40	40	23	
Porac	1	6,950	60	35	2	2	1	
Principe	3	2,080	239	174	6	6		
Romblón	5	21,992	2,594	2,319	6	5		
Samar	35	138,799	2,585		36	36	35	
Surigao	30	29,158	2,522	1,686	30	30	30	
Tayabas	17	94,509	3,211	624			14	
Unión	12	91,089	6,333	5,525	26	26	12	
Zambales	21	72,506	1,080	832	21	21	20	
Zamboanga	3	8,982	231	100	2	1		
Total	900	430,316	136,108	91,608	840	783	650	61

To study and remove the causes of that lamentable statistics; to cause all the children who ought to attend the schools; to promote the development of neglected institutions and the rebuilding of those destroyed; to establish schools in villages which have none; to persuade the justices to protect them, and the heads of families to visit them: beautiful and never-failing task for a supervisor of primary instruction! A thousand times more beautiful and more fertile, if a father of souls exercises it with his ardent charitable spirit, with his wide experience in the moral needs of the villages!

The fathers are also petitioned and requested to earnestly study and prepare for the installation of the Sunday schools, or the schools for adults established by article 29 of the regulations. In regard to that article, by the tenor of the same, this government shall confer with the superior commission of primary instruction, when the local supervisors, having been established and working in the proper manner, the danger of such innovation complicating their labors, disappears.

VI

In respect to the direction of moral and Christian teaching which that requirement fittingly gives to the reverend and learned parish priests subordinate to their respective prelates, this superior government limits itself to assuring them of its most decided support, and the support of the provincial supervisors of primary instruction. Thus educated there is no doubt that the new generations will respond to what is demanded of them by so wise a law, which is destined to unite purity of religious sentiments which form the heart of youth with the duties of patriotism, dignity, and intelligence, which form the civilized man.

I ought, lastly, to say a word on the transcendental act of the examinations, only in order to have the parish priests note that article 13 of the interior regulations did not take account of the royal order of August 28, 1862, which made biennial the period of the session of the ayuntamientos. They must then pay strict heed to the article in regard to holding examinations annually. It will be advisable for them to submit a short review to the children when they go to them every three months for confession and communion.

The provincial supervision entrusted to the alcaldes by article 15 of the organic royal decree, shall be exercised with the aid of a commission composed of the diocesan prelate, or in his absence, by the parish priest of the chief city, and the administrator of the public finances. Where the chief of the province is not the alcalde-mayor, he shall also form a part of the commission, but in the generality of cases, as is well known, he presides over it. Although the above-cited article 15 refers to regulations for schools and teachers for the organization of the provincial center, article 31 of this last order has been limited to a repetition of that precept, almost in the same terms, leaving the dictation of measures which regulate their supervisory action to the judgment of this government. This would be a most important task if the organization of the provincial governments in the archipelago corresponded to the necessities of public administration in all its branches. It would be, I repeat, a most important task, if this superior government could lay aside the difficulties which it would create for itself for the future, by dictating principles of which it is the first to doubt the application, and even recognizing, as it does, the most exquisite care in all the chiefs of the province. To this consideration of a practical nature answers perhaps the indicated vacuity of the regulations for schools.

On the other side, the organization initiated December 20, 1863, by its character of ad interim in so far as it refers to the directive centers of the provinces, seems now to feel the need of reform which afflicts those centers, when among other things it names repeatedly the provincial chiefs.

This superior government ought, then, to limit itself for the present to inciting their zeal, so that they may energetically aid it in the noble work undertaken by it, namely, to establish the primary instruction in these islands upon a solid foundation, without demanding from them an initiative incompatible with their occupations. It is enough that they do not render sterile the occupation of the parish priests. Enough on their part is the pure and simple observance of the royal decrees of December 20, 1863. The immediate installation of the provincial commissions, which has not been attended to at this date, will also permit the chiefs to delegate to the reverend parish priest of the chief city the functions which they cannot accomplish by their own efforts. Only they shall be very careful to send monthly statements to this superior government, in accordance with the circular of the twelfth of the current month, explained by the communication to the alcalde of Tayabas on the twenty-second of the same month; for this data will serve me in the exercise of the superior supervision with which the regulations have entrusted me. Nevertheless, it is to be hoped that the provincial chiefs will make compatible with their many attentions those things which are so grateful to an intelligent man that they engrave their indelible memory on the heart of new generations.

Although I am also told that the condition of the country and the humble organization which primary instruction has at present, advise us not to expect from the supervision all the fruit which it is called upon to produce, when, placed under the immediate direction of an initiative and responsive center, it may exercise in regard to the matters of the department the oversight which belongs to it by right, this consideration, although a powerful one, does not prevent me; and it is impossible, in a mediocre organization of public instruction, to renounce the establishment of general supervisors, considered in all countries as the key of the pedagogical edifice. The royal order of June 6, 1866, supplementary to the regulations of the civil professions of the colonies, opens the door or combinations which permit, without great sacrifices to the state, or to the villages, the appointment annually or for the period which her Majesty designs, of a public functionary of recognized ability to visit the provinces in the character of supervisor general and to promote, hasten, and give unity and scientific direction to the development which the institutions of primary instruction are acquiring. In this sense a respectful report will be sent to the government of her Majesty in a short time.

May God preserve your Excellency many years. Manila, August 30, 1867.

DECREE OF THE GENERAL GOVERNMENT APPROVING, WITH THE CHARACTER OF ad interim, THE REGULATIONS FOR THE NORMAL SCHOOL FOR WOMEN TEACHERS OF PRIMARY EDUCATION IN THE DIOCESE OF NUEVA-CACERES

Manila, June 19, 1875. In consequence of the provision of article 20 of the decree of this general government dated the ninth of the current month and at the recommendation of the General Division of Civil Administration, I have ordered the approval ad interim of the subjoined regulations for the normal school for women teachers in the diocese of Nueva-Cáceres.

Let it be communicated, published, and brought to the notice of the government of his Majesty for his approval.

MALCAMPO

REGULATIONS ad interim FOR THE NORMAL SCHOOL FOR WOMEN TEACHERS OF PRIMARY EDUCATION IN THE DIOCESE OF NUEVA-CACERES

CHAPTER I

Object of the school

Article 1. The normal school for women teachers in the diocese of Nueva-Cáceres has as its object:47

1. To turn out religious, moral, and intelligent women teachers for the schools of primary education in all the grades which are established in the villages comprised in the provinces and districts of the diocese of Nueva-Cáceres.

2. To offer, in the school of Santa Isabel, already destined as a girls' practice school of the normal school for women teachers, a model for all other public and private schools.

3. To serve those scholars who aspire to teaching, so that they may see and carry out for themselves in the said practice school, the application of the systems, methods, and processes of teaching.

Art. 2. The normal school for women teachers of the diocese of Nueva-Cáceres shall also serve to give to those young women, who do not wish to be teachers, the knowledge comprised in the program of the same.

Art. 3. The practice school shall form an integral part of the normal school for women teachers, and shall, at the same time, serve as a municipal public school for poor children of the capital of the province and the surrounding villages.

CHAPTER II

Subjects taught and duration of studies

Art. 4. The teaching of the normal school for women teachers in Nueva-Cáceres shall be divided:

1. In teaching for candidates to the teaching profession.

2. In teaching for the scholars who are not candidates for teachers.

3. In teaching for girls.

Art. 5. The teaching for those included in paragraph 1 of the preceding article shall include:

1. Religion, ethics, and sacred history.

2. Theory and practice in reading.

3. Theory and practice in writing.

4. Knowledge of the Castilian language, with exercises in analysis, composition, and orthography.

5. Arithmetic, with the metric system of weights and measures and their local equivalents.

6. Principles of geography, and history of España and Filipinas.

7. Principles of hygiene and domestic economy.

8. General principles of education and methods of teaching, and their practical application in the girls' model school.

9. Work of all kinds suitable for women, especially those of the most general utility and application to domestic life, such as sewing, weaving, embroidery, the cutting of garments, and ironing.

10. Useful knowledge.

Art. 6. Teaching for girls shall include the same courses with the exception of the general principles of education, and methods and processes of teaching, such processes extending to the elementary and superior grades.

Art. 7. In the lessons, exercises, and teaching practice, as well as during the hours of recreation, and in the common intercourse among the scholars within the school, only the Castilian language shall be used.

Art. 8. The studies mentioned in article 5 shall be pursued for three years, in accordance with the schedule which shall be made out by the instructresses of the school. That schedule, after having been reported to the board of supervision and oversight, shall be sent annually for the approval of the general government.

The course shall begin July 1, and end May fifteenth.

Art. 9. Every lesson given to the pupils of the normal school shall necessarily consist of an explanation by the teacher, and of intelligent recitation and practical application by the scholars.

Art. 10. The schedule of the school, and the distribution of time and work during the same, shall determine the necessary practice of those aspiring to become teachers in the girls' school, both as supervisors of order and class, and as assistants or teachers, but always under the direction of the head teacher.

The said schedule of the normal school shall determine the time which the pupils are to devote to the practice school, but such time shall never be less than four months for each term.

Art. 11. The scholars who are candidates for teachers may not pass from one grade to another without having proved their sufficiency in the general examination which shall be held at the end of every scholastic year.

Art. 12. When studies have been finished in the manner dictated by the schedule of the school, the scholars shall stand an examination in order to obtain the corresponding certificate, and for those exercises the fitting regulations shall be made.

Art. 13. If any one of the scholars who are candidates for teachers wishes to continue one year longer in the school in order to perfect and increase the knowledge which she has acquired, she may do so, but under condition of paying the annual board from her possessions, if she should be a boarder, and if it is not unadvisable in the opinion of the directress that she remain in the institution.

Art. 14. The scholars of the normal school who shall have completed the courses of their studies, and who shall have obtained for their good deportment, application, and knowledge, the mark of excellent in the final examinations of the three consecutive years, shall receive teachers' certificates, with expression in the certificate of their honorable mark. Such persons shall be empowered to take charge of ascenso schools. Those who shall not have obtained the mark of excellent, but that of good or fair in the above-mentioned examinations, shall also receive teachers' certificates, with the corresponding mark mentioned therein; and such persons may take charge of entrada schools. If those who shall not have passed in the said examinations, after the exercise has been repeated, shall deserve a passing mark, they shall receive assistant teachers' certificates.

CHAPTER III

Of the staff of the school

Art. 15. The normal school for women teachers in Nueva-Cáceres shall be organized under the direction of the sisters of charity, and shall make use of the elements of the staff and equipment of the school of Santa Isabel.

Art. 16. The staff of the normal school shall consist of the following:

1. A directress, who shall have charge of the teachers, scholars, and inferior employes of the institution. In her charge shall be the economic part, the direction, order, and discipline of the same, and the allowances which correspond to it, according to the schedule and regulations of the school.

The directress shall preside over the literary ceremonies of the school whenever the provincial chief, the reverend bishop of Nueva-Cáceres, or the board of supervision and oversight, does not attend them. She shall visit the classes and the practice school, in order to investigate the explanations of the teachers and the progress of the scholars. She shall correct those faults which she observes, and recommend to the board of supervision and oversight the expulsion of those pupils in the cases and conditions which are expressed in the interior regulations of the school, informing the above-mentioned board of the extraordinary measures which she believes it necessary to take.

2. A head teacher in the practice school, in charge of the communication of the teaching to the girls, responsible for their instruction, and for order and discipline in her department.

She must employ herself in the direction and management of the teaching of systems, methods, and processes determined upon in the board of instructresses, always with the approval and under the presidency and immediate authority of the directress.

The head teacher shall also have the duty of carrying out the orders of the schedule in reference to the practice of those scholars who are candidates for teachers, and shall explain the studies determined by paragraphs 2 and 3 of article 5.

3. Three teachers for the theoretical and practical teaching of the studies included in the school schedule, except those which the directress, the regent of the practice school, and the professor of religion and ethics have under their charge.

4. Two assistant teachers for the practice school, one for the upper section, and the other for the elementary section.

5. One virtuous and learned secular who shall be charged by the reverend diocesan bishop with the teaching of religion, ethics, and sacred history.

6. A sister to act as portress and the women servants or subordinates who are considered indispensable.

Art. 17. The interior regulations shall assign to each one of the teachers the duties which they shall have in charge for the moral and religious education of the scholars, whom they shall accompany, and watch during study hours, recreation hours, and during the other occupations prescribed by the same interior regulations.

CHAPTER IV

Of scholars and their admission

Art. 18. Scholars in the normal school shall be resident and day pupils, and shall be divided into the following classes:

1. Scholars who are candidates for teachers, and who are supported from the local funds.

2. Scholars who are candidates for teachers, and who are supported by their parents or benefactors.

3. Scholars who are not candidates for teachers, and who are supported by their parents or benefactors for the purpose of acquiring the education and teaching of the normal school, in order to apply them to the family and to the uses of domestic life.

4. Girls who attend the practice school.

Art. 19. The scholars included in paragraph 1 shall always be boarders.

Those included in paragraphs 2 and 3 may be boarders or day pupils, whenever they possess the qualifications which are prescribed in these regulations.

Art. 20. In order that any resident scholar sustained by the public funds may be admitted, the following requirements are necessary:

1. She must be a native of the diocese of Nueva-Cáceres.

2. She must be fully seventeen years old,48 and not past twenty-three. Those requirements shall be proved by her baptismal register, or by any other equivalent public document

3. She shall not have any contagious disease, or any chronic disease or any physical defect which makes her ridiculous whether because of lack of respect or because it incapacitates her for teaching.

4. She shall prove good moral deportment by means of a certification, issued by the gobernadorcillo, principalía, and parish priest, of the native village or habitation of the party interested, and investigated by the provincial chief.

5. She shall talk Castilian, know the Christian doctrine, how to read and write, the four rules of arithmetic for integers, and have some slight smattering of Castilian grammar, in order that she may pursue to good effect the lessons of the school schedule.

6. She shall be chosen by the provincial chief at the recommendation of the gobernadorcillo, of the parish priest, and of the principalía of the village in whose charge shall be the expense of her support in the school.

7. She shall be tested by an examination of the matters comprised in paragraph 5 of this article before the school tribunal formed by the instructresses of the same and necessarily presided over for this purpose by the reverend diocesan. The result of that examination shall be given to the president of the board of supervision and oversight, so that he may inform the provincial chief who has control of the village, for economic reasons.

Art. 21. The same requirements shall be exacted from resident scholars whose support is not taken care of from the local funds, except those included in paragraph 6 of the preceding article. These resident scholars shall pay to the institution a monthly board of six pesos, and shall receive the same teaching and the same treatment as those supported by the local funds.

Art. 22. Only those young women shall be admitted as day pupils who, besides possessing the qualifications demanded of the resident pupils, shall live in Nueva-Cáceres or in its environs, under the authority of their parents, or under the care of a person of the family, in such circumstances that it may be assumed that she will find at the domestic hearth the necessary examples of virtue and morality, so that her deportment may not be harmful to the other scholars.

Art. 23. If the villages let three months pass without proposing to the chief of the province the young woman who ought to enter the normal school as a resident pupil supported from the local funds, it will be understood that they renounce this right, and the vacancy, after such announcement, shall be filled by the board of supervision and oversight. It must be kept in mind that the young woman chosen must possess all the qualifications prescribed in article 20, and, all things being equal, she who is a native of the province, to which the village belongs, will be preferred.

Art. 24. The women teachers already established, who desire to improve their education, or who shall be obliged to do so, after a preceding investigation and by accord of the suitable authority, may be admitted as resident pupils in the normal school, under condition of paying the board of six pesos per month. In order to be admitted as resident pupils they must possess the qualification of being single and of not exceeding the age of twenty-three. In any other case, or the size of the institution not permitting, they shall be received as day pupils, shall receive their instruction free and must submit to the requirements of article 22.

Art. 25. As soon as all the villages of the diocese of Nueva-Cáceres have a public school for girls directed by a woman teacher from the normal school, the number of resident pupils supported from local funds shall be reduced to twenty-five. With this number the vacancies, occurring through the death of the teachers in charge, or for other causes, shall be filled.

Art. 26. The resident pupils sustained from the local funds shall be obliged to fulfil their duties for ten years in the girls' public school of their own village, or of any other school which the general government assigns to them in the diocese of Nueva-Cáceres. They can only become exempt from this obligation by returning to the local funds, after the fitting measure has been taken, the sums spent on their support, education, and instruction. The same thing will be true when they leave the normal school before finishing their studies, without legitimate cause, and by their own wish or that of their parents, or are expelled from it for lack of application, or bad deportment. The standard for calculating expenses caused during the given period shall be the board which the village has satisfied for this purpose, plus 6 per cent annually, as interest on the sums advanced.

CHAPTER V

Of the directress of the school and the teachers of the same

Art. 27. The directress shall have charge of the interior government and administration of the institution. She shall have special care and shall be responsible for the instructresses, scholars, and subordinates performing with exactness their respective obligations. She shall watch over the conduct of the scholars, both resident and day. She shall cause the fulfilment of the study schedule, shall impose the punishments which are authorized by the regulations, shall have charge of the effects of the house, shall keep the books, shall render the accounts, shall form the monthly and annual budgets, and shall carry on the correspondence with the board of supervision and oversight and with the parents or guardians of the scholars.

Art. 28. One of the teachers shall act as substitute during the sickness and absence of the directress, being approved beforehand by the general government. Another teacher shall exercise the duties of secretary.

Art. 29. The school teachers shall observe the class hours, the practical exercises, the conference, and the duties imposed on them by the regulations.

CHAPTER VI

Of examinations

Art. 30. At the end of each month, in each one of the classes of the normal school, there shall be a private examination in all the matters studied during that period. A like exercise shall be held at the end of the first semester, in regard to the matters studied during it. General examinations shall be held at the end of the course. This exercise shall always be public and presided over by the board of supervision and oversight. Persons of distinction and the parents and guardians of the scholars shall be invited to it. At the end of the general examination the distribution of rewards shall take place.

Art. 31. The examinations of all classes prescribed in these regulations, as well as of those which shall be prescribed in the future, and in which the board of supervision and oversight intervenes, shall always be held in the building of the normal school.

CHAPTER VII

Of holidays and vacations

Art. 32. Holidays in the normal school shall be Sundays, feast days, Ash Wednesday, day for the commemoration of the faithful dead, and also the saints' days, and birthday anniversaries of their Majesties and the princess of Asturias, the saint's day of the governor general and that of the diocesan bishop.

The short vacations shall extend from Christmas eve to Twelfth-night, the three carnival days, and from Holy Wednesday until Easter. During the said vacations the resident scholars shall remain in the institution.

The long vacations shall last one and one-half months, and shall be during the time of the greatest heat. The resident scholars may pass the long vacations in the bosom of their families.

CHAPTER VIII

Of rewards and punishments

Art. 33. The directress shall keep a register with as many columns as there are subjects taught, as contained in the school schedule. In it, she shall note the degree of progress of the pupils, and shall make the necessary remarks regarding their character, ability, application, and deportment. This register shall be presented to the board of supervision and oversight at the end of each month. That board shall examine it, and in view of that examination, shall take the advisable measures.

Art. 34. The deportment, application, and progress of the scholars, shall be rewarded with marks of honor, which shall be placed on their certificate of studies and in the school book; and further, with the annual prizes, whose solemn distribution shall take place after the termination of the examinations at the end of the course.

Art. 35. The punishments which shall be imposed on the scholars shall be:

1. Secret admonition.

2. Loss of recreation and the walk.

3. Censure in the presence of the scholars.

4. Seclusion and separation from the other scholars.

5. Strict suspension from course.

6. Loss of course.

7. Expulsion from the institution.

The punishments included under nos. 1, 2, 3, and 4, shall be imposed by the directress.

Those included under nos. 5 and 6 [shall be imposed] by the board of teachers presided over by the board of supervision and oversight.

That included under no. 7 shall be imposed by the general government on recommendation of the board of teachers, and after a report of the reverend diocesan bishop and of the board of supervision and oversight.

Art. 36. The rewards obtained and the punishments suffered by the scholars shall be noted in the school registers, and mention will be made of them in the certificates which are issued.

CHAPTER IX

Of textbooks

Art. 37. The board of supervision and oversight shall recommend, with the approval of the general government, a list of the books which may be used as textbooks by the scholars, and to which the teachers shall subordinate their explanations. This list shall be revised according as conditions warrant it.

CHAPTER X

Of the issuing of certificates

Art. 38. The General Division of Civil Administration has the power of issuing, in the name of the governor general and in the tenor of the order of article 8, of the decree of September 9, 1874, teachers' certificates at the recommendation of the board of supervision and oversight.49

Art. 39. The teachers' certificates shall contain the marks which they shall have obtained and the class of the school for which the certificates entitles them.

CHAPTER XI

Of the interior regulations of the school

Art. 40. In the daily distribution of time on the part of the scholars, the order of the studies, the division of the classes, the religious and literary exercises, the intercourse [*trato*], food, and clothing, as well as the duties of the scholars toward their teachers, and the duties of the parents and guardians in regard to the institution, the teachers and scholars shall obey the interior regulations of the school of Santa Isabel, which were enacted by the diocesan prelate and approved by the superior government in the year 1868, until the interior regulations of the normal school for women teachers shall be drawn up by the board of inspection and oversight, and approved by the general government.

CHAPTER XII

Of the supervision and oversight of the school

Art. 41. Besides the superior supervision which belongs to the general government, and to the superior board of public instruction in regard to the normal school for women teachers in Nueva-Cáceres, the reverend diocesan prelate shall exercise the moral and religious supervision which belong to him in accordance with the laws, and the literary supervision, and that of the internal organization, to which the fervent and evangelical zeal with which he has promoted the creation of the institution gives him a right. In this regard, he shall recommend whatever occurs to him for the prosperity and improvement of the same.

Art. 42. For the constant and active oversight and supervision of the school, there shall also be a board composed of the alcalde-mayor of the province of Camarines Sur,50 as president, of the reverend diocesan bishop, or in his absence of the ecclesiastical governor, and of the administrator of public finances.

Art. 43. For the relations of the board of supervision and oversight with the reverend diocesan bishop, article 1 of the circular of the superior government, dated May 17, 1864, shall be observed.51

Art. 44. The board shall observe and cause to be observed with all exactness whatever is prescribed in these regulations, as well as in the regulations which are to be drawn up for the interior management of the school, in the matter of examinations for obtaining a teacher's certificate, and in the schedules of teaching.

Art. 45. The board shall visit the normal school for women teachers in a body at least once each three months; shall examine the affairs of the same; shall ask or cause the instructors to ask questions of the scholars in regard to the teachings of the schedule, shall note and make the remarks which it judges advisable for taking or recommending, according to circumstances, the measures which it judges fitting for the prosperity and better organization of the institution.

Art. 46. The board shall designate its member who shall be charged, in his turn, with the exercise of immediate and efficient oversight of the school for each month.

Art. 47. The board, or the member of it who shall be so chosen, shall execute, and cause to be executed, the measures of the same; shall oversee the observance of the regulations; shall visit the school frequently; shall assist in the professorships and at the practice school; and in examinations shall have the authority determined by the regulations.

Art. 48. The board shall inform the general government concerning the condition of the school every three months, and at the end of each course shall make a detailed report in regard to the results obtained and the methods which it is advisable to adopt, so that they may be more satisfactory.

CHAPTER XIII

Of the bookkeeping of the school

Art. 49. The staff and equipment expenses of the normal school shall be met:

1. By the sums assigned at present in the provincial budgets for the staff expenses of the sisters of charity charged with the teaching in the school of Santa Isabel, and with those which are included for the increase of two teachers.

2. With the sums which shall be assigned in the municipal budgets for the support of the scholars and the equipment of the institution.

3. With the sums which are at present included in the municipal budgets of Nueva-Cáceres for the practice school since it is a girls' public school.

Art. 50. The board of supervision and oversight shall report annually the budgets of receipts and expenses of the school. That report shall be made by the directress, and shall be sent to the General Division of Civil Administration without prejudice to the obligation of the chiefs of the province to include in the municipal and provincial receipts and expenses the sums which belong to this object.

Art. 51. For the collection and distribution of funds as well as for the rendering and approval of accounts, the order prescribed by the laws in force and the special orders dictated by the General Division of Civil Administration shall be followed.

Transitory regulations

Art. 52. The board of supervision and oversight shall draw up a project of regulations for the examinations to which those who are candidates for teachers' certificates must submit themselves, as well as for the placing and promotion of the same.

Art. 53. Until the staff of the school is complete, the directress shall confer with the reverend diocesan prelate for the application in so far as may be possible, of article 16 of these regulations.

Manila, June 19, 1875. Approved.

MALCAMPO

ROYAL DECREE CREATING IN MANILA A NORMAL SCHOOL FOR WOMEN TEACHERS IN CHARGE OF THE AUGUSTINIAN NUNS OF THE ASSUMPTION ESTABLISHED IN THE ROYAL SCHOOL OF SANTA ISABEL OF MADRID

Exposition

Madam:

Primary instruction in the Philippine Archipelago demands reforms for its invigoration, and to assure, at the same time, the teaching of the Castilian language and the greatest facility possible for the religious education—the elements of culture which are the necessary basis for superior studies which are indispensable for the youth of that beautiful archipelago, without distinction of origin or of class.

Until prudent and meditated reforms, harmonized with the respect, which deep-rooted and traditional customs merit, succeed in establishing a complete organism in the management of public instruction, the undersigned minister esteems the creation of a superior normal school for women teachers in the city of Manila as an imperative necessity, since experience proves, by that formerly created in Nueva-Cáceres, the undeniable advantages of a like nature in that country.

Since the two principal objects of primary education in Filipinas is to inculcate in the heart of studious youth love for religion and the Castilian language, it is certainly beyond discussion that whatever attempts in this sense to improve the qualities of intelligence and of the religious character which distinguish the Filipino woman,52 must redound, in consequence, to the greater degree of culture and of the well-being of that society, so intimately bound up with the destinies of the most glorious Spanish traditions.

For the attainment of this proposition, the undersigned believes that the most efficient form for the ends of an education, suitable for the habits and traditions, perfectly compatible with the greatest progress of modern culture, is to confide the direction of the superior normal school for women teachers in Manila to instructors of well-known intelligence and excellent moral endowments, who give, together with testimonies of knowledge, examples of virtue and zeal in which that youth may be inspired. Therefore, there is nothing more in harmony with this aspiration than to give the direction of the Manila school to the congregation of the Augustinian nuns of the Assumption, who are established in this capital. Their efficiency is proved by the long and brilliant period of teaching to which they have devoted themselves in the school of Santa Isabel in Madrid.

Consequently, then, with personal fitness, adorned with the certificates which are requisite for teaching and of true ability for the same, the superior normal school for women teachers in Manila can be founded upon secure foundations of the most brilliant future, which assure and prove the noble aspirations of a culture which so much distinguishes that country, for whose destiny and prosperity the government of your Majesty is trying to the best of its ability to continue to establish as many beneficial institutions as necessity inspires.

The undersigned minister, relying on the preceding considerations, has the honor to submit the subjoined project of a decree for your Majesty's approval.

Madrid, March 11, 1892. Madam, at the royal feet of your Majesty,

Francisco Romero Robledo

Royal decree

At the recommendation of the minister of the colony, in the name of my august son, King Don Alfonso XIII, and as queen regent of the kingdom,

I decree the following:

Article 1. In order to attend to the necessities of primary education in the Philippine Archipelago, and with the object of turning out fitting women teachers, to whom to entrust the development, progress, and successful direction of the same, a superior normal school for women teachers is created which shall be established in Manila.

Art. 2. The direction and personal oversight of said centre of education shall be in charge of the congregation of the Augustinian nuns of the Assumption, established in the royal school of Santa Isabel of this capital.

Art. 3. The sums for the staff and equipment of the above-named school shall be assigned in the general budgets of expenses and receipts of Filipinas for the present year, and shall be distributed in the following manner: 7,900 pesos for the teaching force and management, and 4,500 pesos for equipment.

Art. 4. For the management of teaching in this school, there shall be five regular instructresses, two assistants—one of the department of letters, the other of sciences—one music and singing instructress, and another for hall gymnastics, and one professor of religion and ethics who shall also be the chaplain of the institution.

Art. 5. To obtain the post of regular instructress in the school created by this decree, the holding of a teacher's certificate of superior primary instruction shall be an indispensable condition. Such academical studies shall have been carried on in the national normal schools.

Art. 6. The directress and regular instructresses shall be appointed by royal order by the minister of the colonies, from the aspirants who solicit said posts from the above-mentioned congregation of the Augustinian nuns of the Assumption.

Art. 7. The teachers' certificate which shall be given in this school shall comprise two grades—elementary and superior.

The teaching corresponding to the first shall be in three courses. The second shall include one course more [than the first].

Art. 8. In the three years included in the elementary grade, studies shall consist of the Castilian language, expressive reading and caligraphy, religion and ethics, arithmetic and geometry, history, geography in general, and, in especial, that of España and Filipinas; principles of physics, chemistry, physiology, and natural history, principles of law in application to the common exercises of life, pedagogy, scholastic organization and legislation, special pedagogy applied to deaf mutes and the blind, principles of literature and the fine arts, general hygiene and domestic economy, French, English, drawing, and singing, gymnastics, needle-work, and practice in teaching. For the upper grade, the same studies shall be pursued, enlarged as may be advisable.

Art. 9. The division and extent to which the previous branches shall be studied, as well as the number of elections of each one, shall be prescribed in the regulations.

Art. 10. The conditions which shall be demanded from the scholars for entrance into this school, shall also be prescribed in the said regulations.

Art. 11. The courses shall commence on the first day of June of each year and close March 31 following.

Art. 12. To the normal school shall be annexed the corresponding school for girls supported by the municipality where candidates for teachers' certificates may acquire the practical knowledge indispensable to those who devote themselves to this profession.

Art. 13. All the orders which prevent the fulfilment of the contents of this decree shall be null and void; and the minister of the colonies shall be authorized to settle any doubts which may arise in the application of the same, as well as to dictate the measures which their observance demands.

Given in the palace, March eleventh, one thousand eight hundred and ninety-two.

MARIA CRISTINA

The minister of the colonies:

FRANCISCO ROMERO Y ROBLEDO

ROYAL ORDER 241 OF THE MINISTRY OF THE COLONIES APPROVING THE REGULATIONS FOR THE SUPERIOR NORMAL SCHOOL FOR WOMEN TEACHERS IN MANILA

Your Excellency:

In accordance with the order of article 13 of the royal decree, of the eleventh of the present month, by virtue of which a superior normal school for women teachers is created in Manila, and for the purpose of facilitating the institution of said school, and of regulating the exercise of its functions from the beginning:

His Majesty, the king (whom may God preserve) and in his name, the Queen Regent of the kingdom, has considered it advisable to approve the subjoined regulations by which the abovesaid teaching centre is to be ruled.

I inform your Excellency of this by royal order for your information, and for the following ends, it being at the same time the will of his Majesty that this resolution, as well as the regulations to which the same alludes, be published entire in the *Gaceta* of Madrid, and in that of Manila, in accordance with the rulings of the royal decree of October 5, 1888. May God preserve your Excellency many years. Madrid, March 31, 1892.

Romero

[*Addressed*: "Governor general of the Filipinas Islands."]

Cagayán de Misamis, May 19, 1892. Let it be fulfilled, published, and sent to the General Division of Civil Administration, for the purposes abovesaid.

DESPUJOL

REGULATIONS OF THE SUPERIOR NORMAL SCHOOL FOR WOMEN TEACHERS IN MANILA

TÍTULO FIRST

OF THE OBJECT OF THE NORMAL SCHOOL

CHAPTER I

Article 1. The normal school created by royal decree of the eleventh of the present month has as its object:

1. The turning out of suitable women teachers, who shall have charge afterward of the schools of primary instruction for girls, so that these will well and faithfully meet the necessities of the present time.

2. To serve as a model so that the scholars who attend it may acquire an exact knowledge of the methods, which must be employed with good results in directing and developing the intellectual, moral, and physical qualities of the girls who will later be entrusted to their direction and care; and in so far as possible also consider its establishment for good results in teaching according to the systems by which they may rule those girls who shall be entrusted to them at the end of their course.

Of the subjects to be taught

Art. 2. The subjects which must be the object of study for the pupils who attend this school shall be those described in article 8 of the above-cited royal decree, comprising the three courses for the elementary grade, and one additional course for the superior.

The subjects which shall be taught in the normal school of Manila are as follows:

1. Religion and ethics (this course will include the explanation of the catechism and sacred history).

2. Castilian grammar.

3. Expressive reading.

4. Arithmetic.

5. Caligraphy.

6. General geography and the geography of España and Filipinas.

7. History of España and Filipinas.

8. Hygiene and domestic economy.

9. Needle-work.

10. Geometry.

11. Room gymnastics.

12. Pedagogy.

13. Natural sciences.

14. Music and singing.

15. Practice in teaching.

16. Principles of literature.

17. Designing, with application to needle-work.

18. Principles of law and its application to the common exercise of life.

19. French.

20. English.

21. Pedagogy for deaf mutes and the blind.

22. Fine arts.

Elementary grade

The first and second year shall include studies from 1 to 11 inclusive, and the same instructress may unite the pupils of both years in one class.

The third year shall be an enlargement of the same studies, adding the studies from no. 12 to no. 15 inclusive.

Superior grade

For the superior grade of the fourth year, all the subjects of the preceding years shall be studied in an enlarged form, adding the studies of nos. 16 and 17, and substituting geometry for drawing.

From no. 18 to no. 22 the studies shall be optional, the study of all or any of them being at the desire of the pupil, after the conclusion of the studies of the fourth year.

Art. 3. Lessons shall be alternate, weekly or bi-weekly, according to the importance of the subjects with relation to the course.

Each election shall last in general one hour, more time being given to the lessons in needle-work, which shall be daily, and in the other lessons to that which is believed to be for the advantage of the pupil.

Of school equipment

Art. 4. Since the effort must be made to try to give to the teaching in this institution the greatest possible practical character, it shall be furnished with sufficient scientific equipment. Accordingly then, it must have:

1. The equipment for teaching suitable for each subject whose budget formed beforehand by the directress, shall be submitted to the approval of the governor general, in order that the sum assigned for this purpose may be annually expended on it.

2. Since the economic condition of some of the pupils of this center will not permit them to acquire a certain class of books, which it would be necessary for them to know, the governor general shall assign the said center a copy of the books, which have application to the school of which these regulations treat, and the ministry of the colonies shall send them for the encouragement of the public libraries.

The books shall be submitted to the approval of the directress, and her permission shall be necessary so that the pupils can make use of them. She shall also make the necessary rules in order for their consultation, whenever she considers it advisable.

CHAPTER II

Of the teaching force

Art. 5. The school shall have the teaching force prescribed in article 4 of the royal decree of the eleventh of the present month.

Art. 6. One of the regular instructresses shall exercise the duties of directress. Her appointment shall belong to the minister of the colony on recommendation of the reverend mother superior general of the congregation of the Augustinian nuns of the Assumption.

Art. 7. The duties of secretary and librarian shall be filled by the instructresses appointed by the directress.

Art. 8. The appointment of assistant instructresses shall be made by the directress.

Art. 9. The appointment of an assistant professor of religion and ethics, who shall also be chaplain of the institution, shall be made by the directress, with the consent of the diocesan.

Art. 10. The teaching force of the school will receive remuneration in the following manner:

	Pesos
Instructor-directress, with an annual salary of	1,000
Five regular instructresses [profesoras numerarias], with a salary of 700 pesos each	3,500
One instructress of music and singing with an annual salary of	475
One instructress of room gymnastics	400
Two a ssistant instructresses, one for the section of sciences, and the other for the section of letters, with an annual salary of 475 pesos each	950
One assistant instructor of religion and ethics, who shall also be the chaplain of the institution, with an annual salary of	475
Total	6,800

Administrative force

One secretary	250
One assistant clerk for secretary	200

One portress	200
Three serving women at 150 pesos each	450
Total	1,100

CHAPTER III

Of the directress

Art. 11. The duties of the directress of the school are as follows:

1. To observe and cause the laws, decrees, regulations, and other superior orders to be observed.

2. To adopt the measures advisable for the conservation of scholastic order and discipline.

3. To see that the instruction is given in the proper manner, for which purpose she shall frequently visit the different rooms and take care that the material aids which each subject demands are not lacking.

4. To call and preside over the board of instructresses and the disciplinary council, and to execute their decisions or send those decisions for superior approval if they require it.

5. To appoint the instructresses and the subordinates whose pay does not exceed five hundred pesos, after informing the governor general of said appointments.

6. To send the requests of the instructresses, employes, pupils, and dependants, to the governor general with her report; with the understanding that the course of instruction will not be granted to those who do not submit their conduct [to her], in order that there may be no complaint against her.

7. To represent the school in judicial matters in which the school may be a party, or to delegate someone else to represent it.

8. To recommend the measures which she believes conducive to the growth and improvement of the school, and which are not among her duties.

9. To see to it, with the greatest of zeal, that the instructresses observe all the duties which are prescribed for them in the regulations which are to be drawn up by the cloister for the interior management of the school.

10. To preside over all the meetings held by the cloister and to direct their discussions.

11. To direct the teaching, in accordance with the schedules presented by the instructresses and approved by the governor general.

12. The administration of the economic part of the institution, receiving the sums which are assigned for its support, and distributing them in accordance with the approved budget, whose preliminary project must be drawn up in due time.

13. The formation of the schedule of teaching hours, and the designation of the place where it is to be carried on, after conferring with the instructresses, so that the result may be more satisfactory. She shall send to the general government a copy of the schedule made out for each course.

14. To inform the governor general opportunely of the pupils who have entered for each course, and to draw up the *Memoria anuario* [*i.e.*, Annual report]. She shall send copies of these reports to the governor general and the minister of the colonies.

15. To form tribunals for the term examinations53 and revalida.54

16. She shall confer directly with the governor general and must act through the medium of the latter when she shall have communication with the supreme government.

17. When vacancies occur in the teaching force of the school, the directress shall take the necessary measures so that the teaching may not suffer the least loss, and shall immediately inform the ministry of the colonies, so that they may be advised as soon as possible.

18. The directress of the school shall take the necessary measures so that the pupils may not be deprived of the frequency of the sacraments, of the holy sacrifice of the mass, and of other religious acts.

Of the instructresses

Art. 12. The instructresses shall be under the immediate orders of the directress in whatever concerns school matters.

Art. 13. They shall lend their aid to whatever the directress of the institution demands, endeavoring constantly to attain the greatest aggrandizement and splendor of the same.

Art. 14. In the absence or sickness of the directress, the senior instructress shall fulfil her duties, and if there should be two or more instructresses appointed at the same time, she who shall be designated by the governor general.

Art. 15. That instructress who shall fulfil the duties of directress for any of the above-mentioned causes, shall not receive any remuneration therefor, and only in case of vacancy shall she receive the difference in pay.

Art. 16. Each one of the instructresses shall give a list to the secretary of the pupils who in her judgment may be admitted to the ordinary examinations, according to the number of failures, in the first fortnight of the month of March.

Art. 17. Regular instructresses may use as a distinctive mark in all the acts which concern the institution the professional medal suspended from the neck by a cord made of the colors scarlet, sky-blue, and turquoise blue.

Art. 18. The medals mentioned in the preceding article shall be—that of the directress, of gilded silver, and those of the instructresses, white of that metal.

CHAPTER IV

Of the secretary

Art. 19. The obligations of the secretary shall be:

1. To inform the directress of matters which occur in the government and administration of the school.

2. To draw up papers, and record the reports and communications which are offered, according to the instructions of the directress.

3. To make the entries of entrance examinations, and term examinations of the pupils.

4. To petition and despatch the necessary resolutions for the attestation of the documents presented by the pupils.

5. To superintend matters of receipts and disbursements.

6. To fulfil the duties of pay-mistress of the institution; to collect and distribute fees for inscription55 and academical fees.

7. To take charge of the archives, and of the classification of the documents under her charge.

8. To issue with the proper authorization and in accordance with the documents which are in her care, the certificates demanded by those interested or by those who legally represent them.

9. To record the minutes of the board of instructresses, and of the disciplinary council.

10. To keep all books and registers necessary for the successful progress of the institution.

11. To open a register in which shall be recorded both the merits acquired by each one of the scholars and the faults of any consideration

which the same ones may commit during the course of their studies, and according to those data their study certificates shall be made out.

12. To record and sign all the certificates ordered by the directress and on which the latter shall place her O.K.

Art. 20. The secretary shall receive as a remuneration for her services one per cent of the receipts of the institution, and for certificates, the fees assigned in these regulations, in addition to the one per cent of the academical fees as a compensation for the loss of money and of the responsibility which she has in the collection thereof.

Art. 21. The secretary shall always be responsible for the correct drawing up of papers, and for the accuracy of the documents which she issues.

Art. 22. The regular instructress appointed by the directress shall act as substitute for the secretary during the absence and sickness of the latter and during vacancies.

CHAPTER V

Of the librarian

Art. 23. The duties of the librarian shall be:

1. To make an inventory of the works existing in the library, to classify the volumes, and stamp them with the seal of the institution.

2. To name, after conferring with the directress the hours during which this subordinate department will be open, and to watch after the good preservation of the books which are committed to her care.

CHAPTER VI

Of the assistants

Art. 24. The assistant instructresses shall have the following duties in the institution:

1. To act as substitutes for the regular instructresses in their absence and sickness in their respective section.

2. To take care of the classes and whatever belongs to the duties of any regular instructress, in case of a vacancy, until that vacancy is filled in accordance with the royal decree of the eleventh of the present month.

3. To aid the secretary in the extraordinary labors, and those suitable for that office when she asks it. In this task the two assistants in the sciences and letters shall alternate in each course.

CHAPTER VII

Of the subordinates

Art. 25. The portress shall have charge of the principal door of the building, and both she and the servants shall execute whatever the directress orders them in regard to the order, arrangement, and cleanliness of the institution, and its furnishings.

Art. 26. The help cannot leave the edifice so long at it is open to the public without express orders from the directress.

Art. 27. The help of the school are prohibited under penalty of discharge to receive any tip from the pupils for the services which they give in fulfilment of their obligations.

CHAPTER VIII

Of the board of instructresses

Art. 28. The board of instructresses shall be composed of the regular teachers of the institution.

Art. 29. The directress shall consult the board of instructresses:

1. In the compiling of the annual and monthly budgets of the school.

2. In the making of the list of studies mentioned in these regulations.

3. In any other matters, both concerning the teaching force and the government and management of the school, in which she believes it advisable to hear their opinion.

Art. 30. She shall also convoke them:

1. For the annual opening of the studies.

2. When any matter is held in the school which in the opinion of the directress merits the presence of all the instructresses.

3. At least twice during each term [*curso*], so that the instructresses may propose whatever their experience declares to them as conducive to the perfection of teaching.

Art. 31. Affairs shall be settled by a plurality of votes and in case of tie the president shall decide.

Art. 32. The secretary shall record the minutes, which, after approval by the corporation, shall be copied in a book, the president authorizing the copy with her rubric, and the secretary with her surname.

In the margin of each minute, the names of those members who were present at the session shall be noted.

Art. 33. It is the secretary's duty to record the reports and communications in fulfilment of the decisions of the board. Nevertheless, the corporation may, when it deems it advisable, charge any other of its members with the recording of any document of this class.

CHAPTER IX

Of disciplinary Councils

Art. 34. The Council shall be composed of at least five members.

Art. 35. The school secretary shall be secretary of the disciplinary Council.

Art. 36. The directress shall convoke the disciplinary Council whenever anything occurs which the Council ought to know.

Art. 37. The decision of the disciplinary Council shall be verbal and summary, and they shall always endeavor to decide definitively on the same day on which the matter is submitted to their hearing.

The order of procedure shall be: Hearing of the deed; deciding whether it is suitable for them to try; the examining of antecedents and witnesses in order to bring out the truth clearly; to hear the accused who shall be cited in the proper manner; and the rendering of the verdict.

If the accused fails to appear of her own wish, the Council shall settle the matter, judging the fault as an aggravating circumstance.

After the minutes have been recorded and signed by the secretary all the members shall affix their rubrics to them.

Art 38. The Council shall not impose other penalties than those enumerated in these regulations, but they may punish the same pupil with several of them.

Art. 39. The verdict shall be published when and as the Council determines; but immediate advice of the penalties imposed shall be given to each pupil, to her father, guardian, or care-taker.

TÍTULO II

OF THE ECONOMIC MANAGEMENT

CHAPTER I

Of the annual budgets

Art. 40. The directress of the school, in conference with the board of instructresses, shall annually compile the annual budgets of receipts and expenditures, both ordinary and extraordinary.

Art. 41. In the ordinary budget of receipts shall be included the amount of the fees for matriculation, degrees, and certificates.

The extraordinary budget shall be composed of the funds which it is calculated will be received in the school in any other way.

Art. 42. In the ordinary budget of expenses, the following shall be included under its proper heading:

1. The salaries which shall be received by the directress, instructresses, employes, and help of the institution.

2. The amounts which are calculated to be necessary for the rent, preservation of the edifice, and its equipment.

3. Expenses of the secretary.

4. Expenses demanded by the teaching and conservation of scientific equipment.

5. One item for unforeseen expenses, which shall not exceed four per cent of the amount of the ordinary expenses of the institution.

Art. 43. In the extraordinary budget shall be figured the expenses which are believed to be necessary for the improvement of the edifice, for the purchase of school equipment or furniture, or for any other object not included in the preceding article.

Art. 44. The directress shall send the budgets to the general governor with a memorandum, if she believes it necessary.

CHAPTER II

Collection, distribution, and payment of accounts

Art. 45. The school shall be guided in matters of collection, distribution of funds, and payment of accounts, by the general rule of accounts.

TÍTULO III

OF TEACHING

CHAPTER I

Of the opening and duration of the term [curso]

Art. 46. The ordinary examinations of studies shall be held in the school from the first to the thirtieth of April, and the extraordinary examinations from the first to the thirtieth of June. The first day of July of each year shall be celebrated in the school by the opening of classes. All the instructresses and assistant teachers shall be present at the ceremony, and the authorities and corporations of the village and those persons who are deemed advisable, in order to give it more solemnity and pomp, shall be invited to it.

Art. 47. The opening ceremonies shall be presided over by the directress, whenever the governor general does not attend.

Art. 48. The ceremony having begun, the secretary of the school shall read a short and simple résumé of the condition of the institution during the preceding year, expressing therein the changes which have occurred in the staff of instructresses, the number of scholars matriculated and examined, the progress made by the teaching, improvements made in the building, increase in scientific equipment, the economic situation, and all the other bits of information which can contribute to give a complete idea of the progress of the institution.

This document shall be printed and afterward inserted in the official newspaper of Manila, publishing therein as an appendix the tables which will serve to prove what was explained in the memorial.

This memorial, together with the inaugural address, which shall be read by the directress, or one of the instructresses, shall be made into a single volume, and copies of it shall be sent to the ministry of the colony, the general government, and scientific and literary corporations.

Art. 49. After the conclusion of the reading, prizes shall be distributed, and the ceremony shall close by the president saying: "His Majesty, the king (whom may God preserve), and, in his name, the queen regent of the kingdom, declares the academic term of such and such a year open in the superior normal school for women teachers in Manila."

Art. 50. Lessons shall begin on the day following the opening of studies, and shall terminate on March 31.

Art. 51. Lessons shall not be suspended during the course, except on Sundays, whole feast days, saints' days, and birthday anniversaries of the king, queen, and prince of Asturia, on the day for the commemoration of the dead, from December 23 until January 2, the three days of the carnival, Ash Wednesday, holy Wednesday, Thursday, Friday, and Saturday, and Easter and Pentecost.

CHAPTER II

Of the order of classes and methods of teaching

Art. 52. Five days before beginning lessons, a representative table shall be affixed in that place in the edifice assigned for announcements expressive of the studies which are taught in the school, the instructresses in charge of them, the textbooks for their study, and the rooms, days, and hours in which the lessons are to be given.

Art. 53. Explanations in all classes shall be in Castilian.

Art. 54. Instructresses shall follow in their teaching the schedules approved by the superior government, in accordance with section 11, of article 11, and shall try to excite emulation among the scholars by contests which shall prove their progress.

Art. 55. The scholars seriously lacking in class in the respect due the instructress shall be expelled from the class by that act and judged by the disciplinary Council.

Art. 56. The instructress shall note daily for the abovesaid purposes, failures of attendance in the scholars, and shall hand in a list of names whenever she thinks it advisable.

She shall also note the manner in which they have answered in the lessons, and to the questions which she has asked them; as well as the acts of restlessness, and the pranks which they have committed.

Art. 57. At the end of each month the instructresses shall hand to the secretary a list of the pupils in their classes, with a note regarding the failure of attendance, lesson, and deportment, which they have incurred, and the qualifications of their memory, intelligence, application, and conduct, so that the persons in charge of them may understand their behavior.

Art. 58. At the end of each month, the instructresses shall also hand in a list of those pupils who have most distinguished themselves in their progress and conduct.

Art. 59. The instructresses shall endeavor to conclude the course of any studies at least twenty days before the conclusion of the term, in order to devote the remaining lessons to a general review which may prepare the scholars for the examination.

CHAPTER III

Of material equipments for instruction

Art. 60. There shall be a sufficient number of rooms in the school, light, well arranged and ventilated, and large enough so that the pupils whom it is calculated will attend may be accommodated.

The seats shall be arranged conveniently and the chair of the instructress shall be elevated so that she may see all her pupils and be distinctly heard.

There shall be a blackboard or oilskin56 near the chair of the instructress for writing and drawing the figures demanded in the teaching.

Rooms for drawing shall be arranged in the manner suitable for these studies.

Art. 61. In addition there shall be:

1. An image of our Lord Jesus Christ, and a picture of his Majesty, the king, in all the classes.

2. The globes, maps, and other objects which are required for the knowledge of geography.

3. The synoptical pictures which are required to facilitate the study of history.

4. A cabinet for physics with the apparatus and instruments indispensable for teaching this study profitably.

5. A classified mineralogical collection.

6. Another zoological collection, in which shall be found the principal species, and if not, then plates which represent them.

7. A botanical garden and its herbarium systematically arranged.

8. A collection of all the solids and instruments deemed necessary for the teaching.

Art. 62. The directress shall see that collections in the cabinets of natural history are formed as completely as possible from the natural products of the archipelago.

Art. 63. Each instructress shall have under her charge the conservation of the material equipment owned by the school for the teaching of her course of study.

TÍTULO IV

OF THE SCHOLARS

CHAPTER I

Of the qualifications which the scholars must possess in order to be admitted to matriculation

Art. 64. In order that the studies of the normal school may produce academical effects, they must be carried on with strict submission to what is prescribed in these regulations.

Art. 65. In order to enter the superior normal school for women teachers, one must pass an examination of the branches of Christian doctrine and sacred history, Castilian grammar, arithmetic, geometry, geography, history of España and Filipinas, hygiene, and needle-work.

Art. 66. The exercises of which the examination for entrance shall consist shall be three in number, in the following form:

Written exercises

1. The writing of a letter or dissertation upon a theme of Christian doctrine, and sacred history, hygiene, or the history of España or of Filipinas.

2. Solution of an arithmetical problem.

3. Execution of a simple geometrical drawing.

Oral exercise

1. Explanatory reading of a complete sentence.

2. Grammatical analysis of a sentence.

3. Answer of a question in geography, and another in each one of the subjects of Christian doctrine, sacred history, hygiene, and history of España or of Filipinas. If any one shall have submitted a theme on any one of these four matters for the dissertation of the written exercise, that subject shall be excluded from the oral exercise.

Practical exercise

Execution of needle-work, under the supervision of the tribunal.

Art. 67. Judges of the entrance examination shall be three instructresses regularly appointed by the directress.

The proofs of this examination shall be the same marks as those for obtaining a course [*ganar curso*].

The pupils shall pay two and one-half pesos for academical fees, which shall be distributed at the close of examination among the instructresses who are judges of the tribunals.

Art. 68. In order to be admitted to matriculation, one must have passed the age of fourteen; petition therefor must be made to the directress of the school; and the petition must be accompanied by the baptismal certificate of the petitioner, by the certificate of good conduct issued by the parish priest of her district, a medical certificate stating that she has proved that she does not suffer from any contagious disease or physical defect which incapacitates her for the duties of teaching, the authorization of her father, tutor, guardian, or husband (if the candidate should be married), and the corresponding personal cedula.

CHAPTER II

Concerning matriculation

Art. 69. On the sixteenth of May annually, the matriculation of the school shall be announced in the official gazette of Manila.

Art. 70. The announcement shall state:

1. The time when the school shall be open for those who have matriculated.

2. The necessary qualifications for admission to the school, and the manner in which these qualifications shall be proved.

3. The fees which must be paid by the pupils.

Art. 71. The matriculation which shall be open from June 1, shall be divided into ordinary or extraordinary, according as it is effected in the months of June or July. In the last five days of this term, the secretary's office shall be open from eight in the morning until four in the afternoon, and on the day which closes the matriculation period, until eight o'clock at night.

Art. 72. Matriculation, whether ordinary or extraordinary, shall be made by means of cedulas of inscription57 made in accordance with the model approved by the general government.

The price of each cedula shall be 1.25 pesos, which shall be paid without distinction by the pupils in the secretary's office of the institution.

Art. 73. Those who desire to enter the school, or come from another institution, shall have a written petition in the form prescribed in the preceding article.

The passing of the entrance examinations and the date thereof in the school shall be entered in the registration of the first study in which the pupil is matriculated.

Art. 74. The pupils, who shall not have matriculated for any reason in the month of June, may do it in the month of July, by paying double fees.

The extension of this last period of time is absolutely prohibited, and the tribunals of examination shall not allow that scholar to be examined whose matriculation is not in accord with this provision.

Art. 75. On July 1 of each year, all the fees paid by those who have matriculated in the term which closes on the day before shall expire, and in virtue of that those pupils who shall not have been examined at that date, as well as those who shall have been suspended, shall require a new matriculation for the following term.

Art. 76. The fees for matriculation shall be paid in two instalments in papeles de pagos al estado,58 half at the time of matriculation, and the other half in the month of February. Those halves of paper shall be united with the personal document of the pupil.

Art. 77. All the registers of matriculation of each term shall be closed on July 31, and, on the following day, the directress shall inform the general government of the result of the inscriptions in all the branches of study.

Art. 78. Any scholar who shall have matriculated in the school may go to any other official school for the purpose of continuing her studies. Those who so desire shall send a petition to the director, and she shall grant it whenever it is not for the purpose of escaping some punishment.

The transfer of those who have matriculated from one institution to another shall only be conceded from the beginning of the term until January 31. If the necessity for such transfer is not proved, the superior government shall be consulted. It shall be accomplished by means of a special inscription for such cases, made out according to a model which shall be sent ex-officio and registered, together with the extract and the study sheet59 of the one interested, to the institution to which the transfer shall have been asked. Said cedula shall be free, and shall confer right to continue the course and be admitted to examination.

Art. 79. Those who are transferred to other institutions shall pay beforehand the academical fees, in accordance with the special inscriptions made for that purpose.

The upper part of the right hand section of these inscriptions shall remain in the documents of the student as a proof of her transference. The lower part [of the right hand section] shall be delivered to her, while the other sections which shall constitute the new matriculation of the pupil, shall be sent ex-officio in a registered package to the directress of the other institution. In the primitive inscription, said transference shall be noted by the secretary rendering useless at the same time and diagonally the examination coupons with a stamp [cajetín], reading "transferred."

Art. 80. The pupils transferred shall present themselves in the new institution within a fitting period.

The inscriptions sent by post shall be united with the others of the same study with the number of order corresponding to them.

Art. 81. The fees for matriculation in the school shall be paid in two instalments: the first when the inscription of the respective studies is proved; and the second in the month of February.

These fees shall amount to 7.50 pesos for all the studies corresponding to each term.

Art. 82. In order to prove the inscription of matriculation the secretary of the school shall follow the following rules:

1. The inscriptions shall be divided into as many groups as there are studies corresponding to each term, enumerating them in correlative order in those groups [*i.e.*, from 1, up].

She shall authorize them with her signature and the seal of the institution, and shall note in addition the name of the study, the number of order in the upper part, leaving for the month of September its repetition in the other sections.

2. A printed paper in accordance with a model shall be supplied to the pupils in the lodge of the portress of the school, with the object of setting forth the group of studies in which they are to matriculate, taking care that after their names they write very distinctly their two surnames, both paternal and maternal.

3. Such paper shall be handed to the secretary of the school, and at the same time the papel de pagos al estado. The one interested shall receive the coupon attached to the same, and the matriculation shall thus be legal, even if the respective inscription shall not be received until the following day.

4. According as the matriculation of each group is made, the list of the pupils shall be made in accordance with the correlative order of its numeration, so that on the second of July, at the commencement of all the classes, the instructors may have said list at their disposal.

This list shall be completed with another list of those pupils who have matriculated in the month of July, and further with those transferred from other institutions, so that the list of the instructor may always be in accord with the book of matriculations in which shall be noted if possible the following:

First, those who are to receive honor; second, those of ordinary matriculation; then, those of extraordinary matriculation; and lastly, those transferred from other centers of teaching; all with one single correlative numeration, so that the last number may always correspond to the total number of inscriptions.

5. After the matriculation has closed, charge shall be taken of the corresponding books, and it shall be ordered that the secretary devote herself during the months of July and August to finishing the details of each inscription, repeating the name of the pupil and that of the group as often as it is noted in the printed form, and noting on the other side the extracts of his study sheet, all with great neatness and distinctness.

The directress shall communicate to the general government the result of the inscriptions on the first of August in the form prescribed.

CHAPTER III

Obligations of the pupils

Art. 83. From the day in which the pupil is entered in the register she shall be subject to the scholastic authority within and without the institution.

Art. 84. Pupils shall be obliged to be punctual in attendance at the class during the whole term. If they shall cease to be punctual for some time without there being any cause therefor which appears legitimate to the instructress, the latter may exclude them from the ordinary examinations, and when they present themselves for the extraordinary examinations in June they cannot aspire to more than a passing mark.

Art. 85. All the pupils shall be obliged to obey and respect the directress and instructresses, both within and without the institution, and to heed the admonitions of the help, charged with the conservation of scholastic order and discipline.

Art. 86. In the register of matriculation of each pupil shall be noted the rewards which she obtains and the punishments which she suffers, by virtue of the decision of the disciplinary Council as well as those imposed by the directress and instructresses, if it be they who resolve to punish her. In both cases the fault, for which the penalty shall have been imposed, shall be mentioned.

Art. 87. The pupils shall be prohibited from addressing their superiors orally or in writing in a body. Those who infringe this rule shall be judged guilty of insubordination.

Art. 88. Pupils shall attend school decently dressed. The directress is authorized to forbid any jewel which takes away from the decorum which ought to rule in an institution of teaching.

CHAPTER IV

Of the examinations

Art. 89. The ordinary examinations of the studies shall be held in the school and at set periods, and the pupils shall pay for this purpose the academical fee of 2.50 pesos for each group.

These fees shall be paid in hard cash in the secretary's office of the school during the month of March, and the pupils shall receive a receipt which shall authorize them without the need of any other academic document, to take the examinations, both ordinary and extraordinary, in the respective group.

Half of the amount of these academic fees shall be assigned to the scientific equipment, and as pecuniary aids to superior and poor pupils; and the other half shall be used for the formation of a common fund, which shall be distributed in equal parts among all the regular instructresses of the school.

Art. 90. The instructresses shall hand to the secretary ten days beforehand a list of the pupils who may be admitted to the ordinary examinations, and another list of those who shall remain for the extraordinary examinations.

Art. 91. On the first of April, the register books shall be distributed among the respective tribunals, the secretaries of the same taking charge of them. After examining them, the examinations shall be begun, commencing with the pupils with registers containing honorary marks, and by those who obtained the mark of excellent for the last term, without any suspension if they shall so petition in a request sent to the directress of the school.

The others shall follow the strict correlative order of the inscriptions, the secretary of the tribunal seeing to it that the pupils sign in the place indicated for that purpose, and after the presentation of their personal cedula,60 and the other requisitions which the tribunal may consider necessary, if there shall be any doubt concerning their personality.

Art. 92. Examinations shall be announced sufficiently beforehand, as well as the locality, day, and hour, in which they shall be held. On each day, moreover, shall be announced the correlative numeration of those persons who shall be examined on the following day.

Those who shall not be present at the ordinary examinations shall remain for the extraordinary examinations.

Art. 93. Each study shall be the object of a special examination and tribunals for term examinations, and competitions for ordinary rewards shall be formed by the instructress of that course and two other instructresses, also officials of the analogous branches designated by the directress, whenever they are not related within the third degree to the pupil.

One of the judges may be replaced by the assistant instructresses.

The term examinations shall consist of questions which shall be asked for at least ten minutes by the judges on three lessons of the schedule of the studies chosen at random.

Art. 94. The ceremonies shall be held in the following manner:

1. As many numbers as the lessons contained in the schedule of the study shall be placed in an urn by the judges.

2. The secretary of the tribunal shall draw three numbers in the presence of the pupil, and the three lessons bearing that number shall be the object of that exercise. The numbers which are drawn from the urn shall be returned to it at the end of the exercise.

3. In the studies of translation and analysis, two lessons shall be chosen by lot, and at the end of the examination on them, the secretary of the tribunal shall open the book which shall have served as textbook for these exercises and shall assign to the pupil the passage which she is to translate and analyze.

4. There shall be a blackboard or a square of oilskin in all the places where examinations are held, so that the pupils may write or make the figures which the judges order them, or which they may believe to be necessary in order to answer fully the questions asked them. Moreover they shall have the apparatus and objects which may be deemed necessary by the tribunal.

Art. 95. At the close of the examinations of each day, the judges, in secret session, and in view of the marks which they ought to have taken during the exercises, shall rank the pupils examined.

These marks shall be: excellent, notable, good, passed, and suspended.

The secretary shall place a list in the lodge of the portress of the school during the days of the examination on which shall appear the marks which the pupils shall have obtained in the examinations.

Art. 96. The marks obtained in the examinations shall be immediately entered in the general register in alphabetical order which shall be started with all those who have matriculated in the school, on the first of September, according to the form approved by the General Division of Public Instruction. In this way, before May 5, they can send to the general government the lists of matriculation as well as of ordinary examination, with their grades, in order that the general summary may be published in the *Gaceta* on the fifteenth day of the same month.

Art. 97. Pupils suspended and those who do not present themselves at the ordinary examinations shall be admitted into the extraordinary examination without other official document than the said voucher stating that they have paid the academical fees in March.

If the first of July arrives without that having been attended to they lose all their fees, and shall have to matriculate again for the following course in accordance with the regulations.

Art. 98. Having noted in the general register the grades of the ordinary examination, they shall proceed, under the supervision of the secretary of the school, to cut the second section of the inscription of the pupils who have passed, in order to join it on their respective documents. The same operation shall be repeated at the end of the examinations in June, except in regard to the pupils who have not passed, to whom the inscriptions refer.

Art. 99. The marks given by the judges shall be decisive and no appeal of any kind shall be received in regard to them.

Art. 100. Those admitted to the extraordinary examinations shall be:

1. The pupils included in the lists of the instructresses as admissible to them.

2. Those admissible to the ordinary examinations who did not appear.

3. Those suspended.

4. Those who desire to obtain a better mark than they obtained in the ordinary examinations.

Art. 101. All the rules relating to the ordinary examinations are applicable to the examinations held in June.

CHAPTER V

Of rewards

Art. 102. Every year rewards, which shall be ordinary and extraordinary, shall be granted in the school.

Ordinary rewards shall be of two kinds: those of the first kind shall consist of matriculation of honor;61 and those of the second in the payment of matriculation and academical fees, books, medals, etc.

Art. 103. Two ordinary rewards shall be granted, one in each course, if the pupils do not exceed fifty in number. If they exceed that number by another fifty or the fraction of fifty pupils, an equal number of honorable mentions may be conceded to them.

Art. 104. The pupils who obtain rewards of the first class shall be entitled to ask the directress for matriculation of honor completely free in the following term and in the same school, whenever such persons do not have unfavorable marks or antecedents in their academical deportment.

Art. 105. The pupils who shall have obtained the mark of excellent in all the examinations of the same term, may become candidates for admission to the competitive exercises for rewards of the first class.

In order to be admitted to the exercises for rewards of the second class, it shall be required that the candidates prove a lack of resources and shall have obtained three marks of excellent in the same term.

Art. 106. Competitive exercises for ordinary rewards shall be held three days after the termination of those for term examinations of the studies, the judges for such exercises being the instructresses who shall have formed the tribunal, during the examination of the branch which was the object of the competition.

Art. 107. In the extraordinary examinations a certificate of honor and grace as teacher of primary elementary teaching, and another as superior shall be conceded.

Art. 108. The competitive exercises for these rewards shall be begun on the twentieth day of June, at twelve o'clock in the morning, before a tribunal composed of five instructresses, under the presidency of the directress.

Art. 109. Those scholars who shall have obtained the mark of excellent in all the exercises may become candidates for the degree of elementary and superior revalida for extraordinary reward.

Art. 110. The cloister of instructresses shall prescribe the subjects in which the exercises for the rewards, both ordinary and extraordinary, shall be the object.

Art. 111. The tribunal shall adjudge the reward to the pupil who shall have handed in the best exercises; and the fact that she who does not receive a favorable mark has competed for a reward shall be noted as a special merit in her study certificate.

Art. 112. The judges shall not speak a word to the one taking the exercise.

Art. 113. The expenses occasioned by the judging of awards shall be paid from the amount arising from the inscriptions and academical fees, three-fifths being assigned for the pay of matriculation and the other two-fifths for the purchase of books and supplies.

CHAPTER VI

Certificates and decisions

Art. 114. The certificates of the academical studies of the pupils may refer to the branches of one single term, or those of two or more, and also to those of the whole course [*carrera*] with or without the corresponding title. The certificates solicited by the pupils, in accordance with the form printed for that purpose, shall be issued by the secretary, on the payment in hard ~~cash~~ d twenty-five centavos, if the certificate shall embrace ~~branch~~es of one group; and two and one-half pesos, if it shall embrace ~~thos~~e or those of all the course [*carrera*], the state seal which the regulations in force prescribe being on account of the secretary.

Art. 115. Certificates made out with the object of a continuance of the studies or the receiving of an academical degree in another institution shall be sent ex-officio and registered, the suitable coupon only being delivered to such person.

Art. 116. Certificates stating that the exercises for revalida, or rather that the respective titles have been issued, shall also be given upon the petition of those interested, for the payment of 1.25 pesos.

Art. 117. Those pupils who shall have obtained three or four honorable mentions, and no conditions [*nota de suspensa*], shall be given all the certificates that they need, without other fees than the amount for the state seal.

Art. 118. Half of the amount of the fees of the documents which are issued by the secretary of the school shall be assigned for printing, state seals, registration of mail, and other like expenses, and the other half shall be divided among the secretary and the employes of the secretary's office, whenever these amounts do not exceed a fourth part of their respective pay.

If they exceed such sum, the remainder shall be employed in improving the archives and other dependencies attached to the secretary's office.

CHAPTER VII

Of faults against academic discipline and means of checking them

Art. 119. Slight faults are:

1. Inattention in regard to the [admonitions of the] help of the institution.

2. Injuries and offenses of slight moment to other pupils.

3. Faults of deportment in the schoolroom.

4. Indecorous words and unquiet acts and pranks.

Grave faults against academic discipline are:

1. Blasphemy, irreligious actions, and immodest actions and words.

2. Passive resistance to superior orders.

3. Insubordination against the directress and instructresses of the school.

4. Grave offenses or insults which wound the other pupils.

5. Any other action which causes grave disturbance in the academical order and discipline.

6. The second occurrence of slight faults, and resistance in suffering the punishment which shall have been imposed for them.

Art. 120. The checking of slight faults belongs to the directress and instructresses, but the hearing of grave faults belongs to the disciplinary Council.

Art. 121. Punishments prescribed for slight faults are:

1. Private censure by the directress of the school.

2. *Idem*, public before her companions.

3. Seclusion in the institution for the space of several days, which may not exceed one week, but attendance at class and permission for the pupil to go home for the night.

4. Increase of failure of attendance up to the number of five.

Art. 122. Grave faults shall be punished by the following penalties:

1. Public admonition, ex-cathedra, by the directress or instructress, according as may be prescribed by the disciplinary Council.

2. Loss of the [studies of the] term.

3. Expulsion from the institution.

4. Disqualification to continue her course.

Art. 123. Punishments 2, 3, and 4, shall be imposed by personal action, which shall be declared by the cloister in full session, the one interested being heard for that purpose; but the confirmation of the governor general shall be indispensable.

Art. 139. The oral exercises for those pupils who are candidates for the elementary teacher's certificate shall consist in answering nine questions on the three branches which shall be chosen by lot from among all the others constituting the general group of the studies of the elementary teacher; and for the candidates to the superior teacher's certificate, in the same exercise, and in like manner for all the branches studied in the four terms.

Art. 140. After the termination of the written and oral exercises the practical exercise in needle-work will begin. This last having ended, the tribunal in the practice school shall be constituted, in the elementary or superior section, according to the class of the pupil in point. Each one of them shall draw a paper from an urn in which there shall be as many as there are branches of study included in the corresponding grade; that is to say, those studies of the elementary for the pupils of that class, and all the studies for the superior, except that of music and singing, which shall not form a part of this exercise.

The subject having been chosen by lot, the one examined shall draw a new ticket from another urn from thirty prepared for that purpose. The number of that ticket shall indicate the point which she is to explain on the development of girls, the elementary spending ten minutes on the explanation and the superior fifteen.

Art. 141. Immediately after the termination of an exercise, the exercise shall be passed upon by secret vote, for which purpose the president shall distribute to each one of the judges three tickets, one of which shall contain an S (sobresaliente [i.e., excellent]), the second one A (aprobada [i.e., passed]), and another one shall be blank (suspensa [i.e., conditioned]).

Art. 142. If each one of the judges deposits a distinct letter in the urn the president shall declare the graduate to have passed; in other cases she shall be qualified according to the vote of the majority.

Art. 143. In order to be admitted to the second exercise, one must have passed in the first; in order to be admitted to the third she must necessarily have passed in the second; and in order to be admitted to the fourth one must have passed the three preceding.

Art. 144. Pupils conditioned in the exercises for confirmation shall not present themselves for new exercises until two months from the date of their condition.

Art. 145. The exercises to which the preceding article refers can be repeated indefinitely, whenever the above-mentioned time intervenes between each two times.

Art. 146. When a pupil repeats the exercises in which she shall have been conditioned, at least one of the judges who shall have participated in the condition shall form part of the tribunal.

Art. 147. For fees of teacher's certificate of superior primary instruction, candidates shall pay in papeles de pagos al estado the sum of forty pesos, besides presenting the fitting stamp which must be affixed to each certificate, and paying in cash two pesos for expenses of issuing the document.

The above-mentioned sum of forty pesos shall be reduced to thirty-five when it is a question of a teacher's certificate of elementary primary instruction, and to seventeen and one-half for the change from elementary teacher's certificate to that of superior.

Half of the amount collected for the purpose of issuing the circulars shall be assigned for printing and other like purposes, and the other half shall be distributed among the secretary and the employes of that office.

Art. 148. The governor general, finding the documents regular, shall issue the certificates with the mark of passed or excellent, which shall bear in plain sight the coupon part of the respective inscriptions which the directress of the school sends him for that purpose, on which he shall note the approval of the exercises and the payment of the fees which the regulations in course prescribe, accompanying it also with a registered copy of the baptismal certificate of the graduate.

Of the practice school

Art. 149. A school of primary teaching, supported by the municipality, shall be joined to the normal school, and, if possible, shall occupy the same building with it, in which the pupils who are candidates for teachers can learn what a school for girls is and practice in it, following the most adequate method and procedure for the teaching of each subject, so that during their course they may obtain the good results which must be promised.

Art. 150. The practice school shall be divided into two sections, which shall be called the elementary and the superior grades. There shall be one teacher in charge of it with a superior certificate, and she shall be called "regent."

Art. 151. The regent shall have one assistant, for whom it shall be sufficient to possess a teacher's certificate of elementary primary instruction, since she shall be in charge of the section peculiar to the certificate which is demanded of her.

Art. 152. The practice school shall not lose its character as a public school for the girls of the village, and shall be supplied in the manner prescribed for others of its class.

Art. 153. The superior normal school for women teachers in Manila shall have at present only day pupils, until the necessities of instruction in the archipelago counsel the admission of resident pupils exactly or in similar form as the normal school for men teachers.

Art. 154. The Augustinian nuns of the Assumption may establish at their account, if they deem it advisable, the admission of resident pupils in the same institution of the school, whenever that is not to the prejudice of the day pupils, or indeed in any other edifice contiguous to or distinct from the school.

Art. 155. All the orders which prevent the fulfilment of the contents of these regulations are abrogated, and the minister of the colonies is authorized to decide the doubts which may arise from the application of the same.

Additional article

The directress and instructresses of the congregation of Augustinian nuns of the Assumption shall have complete liberty for the observance of the statutes of their order.

Madrid, March 31, 1892. Approved by his Majesty.

ROMERO

DECREE OF THE GENERAL GOVERNMENT ELEVATING TO THE GRADE OF SUPERIOR THE NORMAL SCHOOL FOR MEN TEACHERS IN MANILA, AND APPROVING PROVISIONALLY THE NEW REGULATIONS OF THIS SCHOOL

Normal school of teachers:

Your Excellency:

The normal school for men teachers in Manila, established by virtue of the royal organic decree of December 20, 1863, for the purpose of being used as a seminary for men teachers fit to take charge of schools of primary instruction for the natives throughout the Philippine Archipelago, has been fulfilling, since its foundation, the difficult task committed to it by the government of his Majesty, filling the great space which was experienced in these remote provinces from the primitive times of the conquest. With the adoption of a system combining pedagogical instruction and education, at the same time that it has diffused, so far as has been possible, the use of the Castilian language, knowledge of evangelical truths, and the practice of Christian morals, it has propagated the germ of true civilization in all the islands, consolidating, with the most elementary principles of education, the civil life of the villages in their diverse relations in regard to the social organization, and especially with the diverse institutions which unite this archipelago with the mother country.

The immediate truths of that foundation are the greater facility of communication between the natives and the civil, military, ecclesiastical, governmental, judicial, and administrative authorities, and the greater development in the arts and industry, in agriculture and commerce, and in the participation of the natives in the profession of letters and of sciences, and in the exercise of authority and other subordinate charges in the different state offices. Such results have been preceded by an initial period of most laborious formation, for, although the normal school had to be ruled from the beginning by organic regulations adapted to the needs of the region and to the special circumstances of the time and of the individuals for whom it was founded, it had to limit its sphere of action to the most reduced horizons, in accordance with the remarkable state of imperfection and backwardness of the scholars entrusted to it, and of the little time allowable for their fitting instruction and education in the profession of teacher. The perfection of the normal teaching and of its regulation was left, therefore, for the provision of later supplementary orders. For, having seen the moral impossibility of its complete application, according to the ideal demanded of a perfect plan of pedagogical teaching, it had to be molded according to the pressing needs of the villages and to the lack of a staff fit to take charge from the beginning of all the schools of primary instruction in the archipelago.

The absolute lack of suitable men teachers, with actual experience in teaching, was the reason for the studies in the normal school being reduced in the earlier years to supplying hastily the first intellectual and moral needs of the villages. Those having been satisfied, the studies required in article 4 of the regulations for the acquisition of a teacher's certificate of elementary instruction were completed in three years. But although the resident and day pupils had to be fully sixteen years old for admission into the normal school, it resulted that, since the majority of them came from provinces where they generally cease to attend school after the age of twelve, the few ideas which they had learned in those schools were already obliterated from their minds, especially the use and knowledge of Castilian. Consequently, in order that the pupils might study the branches suitable for the teaching profession with understanding of the authors of the textbook, and the explanations of the instructors, it was indispensable to cause said studies to be preceded by a preparatory year, in order that the legal qualifications of ability to pursue their career might be obtained.

At the beginning, the textbooks had to be chosen from among the shortest and most abridged, in consideration of the lack of development of the intellectual faculties of the pupils. That produced in due time the advantage that the new teachers, explaining to the children of their schools the same authors by whom they had been formed, afterwards came themselves better prepared to frequent the classes of the normal school. Furthermore, having left aside the qualification of the young candidates being sixteen years old, in order to enter the preparatory class, the halls of this normal school were from that time filled by the most advanced pupils of the elementary primary schools of the villages, without any notable interruption in the progress of their studies from childhood until the completion of their course.

To this spontaneous and natural modification of the regulations, was due the calling to the teaching profession of the most suitable and advanced pupils whom the normal school now possesses; and if to them be added the best students of the practice school who increased annually the number of the preparatory class, the result is that said selection must greatly redound to the very great advantage of the teaching force. It proceeded then to mitigate the harmful exclusiveness of article 11 of the regulations for the schools and teachers of primary instruction for the natives of this archipelago, permitting the exercise as teachers to the scholars graduating from this normal school of Manila, who had acquired the teacher's certificate before reaching the age of twenty.

Indeed, that the most opportune time for exercising the duties of teacher with advantage and without loss of intellect is immediately after receiving the certificate, is evidenced by the fact that the matters recently learned remain yet fresh in the memory and in the mind of the young teachers; the will is then more active and ready to communicate those matters to the children, and enthusiasm consolidates in this case the vocation of the young teacher and moderates his mind with the habit of work, so that he will persevere in his profession for the rest of his life.

Granting the fondness of the native for instruction, and having seen the increase in this last third of the century of public instruction in Filipinas, thanks to the multitude and variety of official and private teaching centers, it is more and more indispensable every day that the primary teaching of the archipelago be propagated, perfected, and consolidated, giving the greater extension and the preferred place to the pedagogical studies of the normal school for men teachers, by adding to the course of teachers of elementary primary instruction that of superior primary instruction. The intellectual progress of Filipinas, and its hopes for the future, demand a greater development in the instruction and education of the children; and consequently, that the young men, who nobly aspire to become teachers, may obtain the certificate and prerogative of teacher of superior primary instruction. That such are the desires of the government of his Majesty, are evident by the recent creation of a superior normal school for women teachers in Manila, and the constant desire of enlarging the literary studies throughout the Spanish domains.

The necessity of also extending the teaching of this normal school for men teachers in Manila has been so widely recognized, that for some years past the supplementary courses for obtaining the certificate of superior teacher of primary instruction have in fact been studies in said center. It is so much more easy to introduce said improvement, since it can be realized with the same teaching staff, without any greater expense than the actual budget, and even an increase in the years of study can be realized. For, during the first three years, the pupils would study the branches corresponding to the teachers' course of elementary primary instruction, in order to obtain, after passing the examinations of the third year, the certificate by virtue of the examination for degrees only those who shall have obtained in said examination the grades of excellent and passed, besides the fourth year being entitled to obtain the certificate of superior teacher, the studies of the normal school of Manila comparing throughout with those which are pursued in the superior normal schools of the Peninsula.

To the professional exercise of the duties of teacher of superior primary instruction, belong privileges, prerogatives, and emoluments, distinct from those which are enjoyed by teachers of a lower rank. In such case the término competitions of the first and second class would have to belong exclusively to the teachers of superior primary instruction, and in the contests for the ascenso schools they must be preferred to the elementary.

Said competition must take place before a competent tribunal, and must be subjected to the official schedule of the various branches, whose study prepares one for the certificate of superior teacher indispensable for such competitions.

The case foreseen by article 12 of the regulations, namely, of the existence among the supernumerary pupils of a sufficient number of teachers to supply the schools of the archipelago, having been realized, the suppression of the regular [de numero] resident pupils is now proceeding in this normal school.

In accordance, then, with the previous exposition, he who affixes his signature has the honor to recommend to the lofty consideration and approval of your Excellency, so that you may deign to bring, if you judge it suitable, to the notice of his Excellency the minister of the colonies, the subjoined modification of the regulations of the normal school for male teachers of primary instruction for the natives of the Filipinas Islands approved by her Majesty, December 20, 1863. May God preserve your Excellency many years. Manila, November 1, 1893. Your Excellency,

Hermenegildo Jacas

General Division of Civil Administration:
Your Excellency:

So powerful and conclusive are the arguments which the right reverend father director of the normal school for men teachers in Manila adduces, in order to petition your Excellency that said institution enlarge the scope of the studies of its teaching, and have, therefore, in the future, the character of superior, which the director who affixes his signature, honoring himself in making them his own, recommends to your Excellency that taking them under consideration, and in harmony with them, you deign to authorize the subjoined project for a decree. Will your Excellency decide. Manila, November 10, 1893. Your Excellency,

A. AVILÉS

Decree

General government of Filipinas: Civil Administration.

Manila, November 10, 1893.

This general government in the exercise of its powers and in conformity with the recommendation of the General Division of Civil Administration on this date, declares the following:

Article 1. In order to heed the necessities felt more sensibly each day for broadening and perfecting the pedagogical studies for the purpose of forming suitable teachers to whom to entrust the development and progress of primary instruction in the archipelago, the normal school for men teachers of this capital is declared a "superior normal school."

Art. 2. Teachers' certificates which shall be conferred in the future by this institution shall include two grades—elementary and superior.

Art. 3. The studies corresponding to the first grade shall be divided into three courses, and in the form established by the regulations, by which said institution must be ruled, in its article 4.

Art. 4. For the superior degree the same subjects shall be studied with the extension of those which are prescribed in the last section of article 4 of the abovesaid regulations.

Art. 5. The teachers' certificates, obtained in the superior normal school, shall bear equal rights and privileges with those obtained in like institutions in the Peninsula.

Art. 6. The same instructors as those at present in the normal school shall be those charged to teach the subjects belonging to the fourth year.

Art. 7. The regulations drawn up by the director of the superior normal school for men teachers who shall begin to rule with such character, at the beginning of the next term of 1893–94 are provisionally approved.

Let it be communicated, proclaimed, and information thereof given to the ministry of the colonies for its approval.

BLANCO

REGULATIONS OF THE SUPERIOR NORMAL SCHOOL FOR MEN TEACHERS

Of the object of the superior normal school

Article 1. The object of the superior normal school for men teachers in Manila is to serve as a seminary for teachers who may take charge of the schools of primary instruction in the archipelago.

Art. 2. The pupils shall be resident and subject to one and the same rule and discipline. For the present the previous entrance examination shall allow the entrance of day pupils provided that their number does not exceed sixty the first year, and if their antecedents give hope that they can pursue their studies to advantage and that their conduct will be such that it corresponds to the good name of the institution.

Art. 3. [This article is equivalent to Art. 3 of the regulations of December 20, 1863 for the normal school; see *ante*, p. 86.]

Of the studies and their duration

Art. 4. The teaching in the normal school shall include two grades—elementary and superior. The adequate teaching for the acquisition of certificate of teacher of elementary primary instruction shall be distributed over three terms, and one term more shall complete the teaching required for the superior teacher's certificate. The scholars who are candidates for the certificate of teachers of elementary primary teaching must have studied and passed in the following branches:

Christian doctrine explained, in three courses.

Elements of sacred history, comprising two courses.

Castilian language, with exercises of composition and analysis, according to the four parts of the grammar, three courses.

Theory and practice in reading, two courses.

Theory and practice in writing, two courses.

Arithmetic, two courses.

Principles of geometry and surveying, one course.

Principles of geography and history for España and Filipinas, one course.

Principles of agriculture, one course.

Elements of pedagogy, one course.

Rules of etiquette, one course.

Elements of lineal and figure drawing, three courses.

Lessons in vocal and instrumental music, three courses.

Gymnastics, three courses.

The courses in catechism, sacred history, reading, writing, Castilian language, arithmetic, and geometry shall have lessons daily; every other day, geography, history, surveying, and pedagogy; bi-weekly the course in etiquette.

There shall be daily lessons in the academies of music, gymnastics, and drawing.

In order to obtain a teacher's certificate of elementary primary instruction, besides having passed in the branches belonging to the three above-mentioned courses, a revalida examination shall be demanded after having passed the examinations of the last course.

In order to obtain a superior teacher's certificate, one is required: 1—to have obtained the mark of excellent in the revalida examinations for the teacher's certificate of elementary primary instruction; 2—to have taken the increased course in pedagogy, and in addition the legislation in force in regard to primary instruction in Filipinas; 3—principles of religion and ethics, universal history, algebra, industry, commerce, and the ordinary phenomena of nature.

Art. 5. [Equivalent to Art. 5 of the regulations of 1863; see *ante*, p. 87.]

Art. 6. During the last six months of the third course, the pupils shall have practical experience in teaching, by teaching in the classes of the practice school annexed to the normal school established by article 3.

Pupils may not pass from one course to another without proving their fitness in the general examination which shall be held at the end of each year.

An extraordinary examination shall be given to the pupils of the third course, who have not for any reason passed in the ordinary examination at the end of the course.

Art. 7. The teachers of superior primary instruction may select by competition the término schools of the first and second class; and in the contests which are held they shall be preferred in the management, as regular appointees, of the ascenso schools.

Art. 8. The pupils of the normal school, who shall have completed their studies in the elementary course for teachers, having passed their final examinations in proof of their courses, before receiving the teachers' certificates of elementary primary instruction, shall be obliged to stand another examination which shall be called the revalida examination; and in their certificates shall be noted the honorable marks which they shall have merited in said examination.

Teachers who shall have obtained the mark of excellent in the revalida examination, shall be empowered to continue their studies, and to become candidates for the superior teacher's certificate, and can also take regular charge of ascenso schools.

Those who shall not have obtained the mark of excellent in the revalida examination, but that of good or fair, shall also receive teachers' certificates, with the corresponding note, and shall be empowered to take charge of entrada schools. Those who shall have failed in said examinations, if, after the exercise has been repeated, they merit approval, shall receive certificates as teachers of entrada.

Of the pupils of the normal school

Art. 9. Both the resident pupils of the normal school, and the day pupils shall have the following qualifications for admission: 1—they must be natives of the Spanish domains; 2—be fully thirteen years old, this requirement to be proved by baptismal certificate or any other equivalent public document; 3—not suffer any contagious disease, and enjoy sufficient health to discharge the duties peculiar to the charge of teacher; 4—have observed good deportment and prove same by certification of the parish priest of the village of their birth and residence; 5—speak Castilian, know the Christian doctrine, read and write well, know something of Castilian grammar, as far as the regular verbs, inclusive, and the four fundamental operations of arithmetic. All of this shall be exacted in a previous examination held before a tribunal designated by the director.

Art. 10. Only those young men who have the qualifications demanded of the resident pupils, namely, that they live in Manila, or its environs, under the care of their parents, or the charge of a guardian, shall be admitted as day pupils, and in such conditions that one can assume that they have examples of virtue and morality at the domestic hearth. School supplies shall be given to this class of pupils free of charge, if they are poor.

Of the director, teachers, and dependents of the normal school

Art. 11. [The same as Art. 15, of the regulations of December 20, 1863. See *ante*, pp. 91, 92.]

Art. 12. Under the authority of the director there shall be at least six teachers, besides one instructor in drawing, one for vocal music, and one for gymnastics; three assistants, and the number of servants and dependents necessary for the school. One of the teachers shall be at the same time the spiritual instructor of the school, and shall have charge of the direction of the pupils and of presiding over religious ceremonies. Under his peculiar charge shall also be the lessons in sacred history, ethics, and religion. Another of the teachers shall discharge the special duties of prefect of morals, whose principal occupation shall be to accompany the pupils and watch over them in the interior matters of the life of the institution. The other four teachers shall be occupied chiefly in the teaching of other matters.

The classes in vocal music, drawing, and gymnastics, shall be daily and last one hour. A superior término teacher of the first grade shall be appointed for the practice school which is joined to the superior normal school, and he shall guide it under the supervision of the director.

Art. 13. The salary to be received by the director, instructors, assistants, and dependents, as well as the expenses for equipment and the rent of a building, shall be assigned annually in the budgets of the local funds of the islands, in the proper chapter and article.

Of examinations

Art. 14. There shall be a review of all matters studied during that period at the end of each month in each of the classes of the normal school. Every three months there shall be private examinations of all the matters studied during that time, with qualifications and promulgation of the marks obtained by each pupil. A general examination shall be held at the end of the term. This exercise shall be public and shall be held in the presence of the authorities and persons of distinction of the capital, and shall close with the proclamation and distribution of rewards.

Of holidays and vacations

Art. 15. The holidays for the normal school shall be Sundays, Thursdays, feast days, Ash Wednesday, the day commemorated to the faithful dead, and also the saints' days and anniversary birthdays of their Majesties and the prince of Asturias, and the saint's day of the governor general of the archipelago.

The short vacations shall extend from Christmas eve to January 2, and the three carnival days. During said vacations the resident pupils shall remain in the institution.

The long vacations shall last from the close of the examinations at the end of the term in the second fortnight of the month of March until the first day of June. Resident pupils shall pass the period of the long vacations with their families.

Concerning rewards and punishments

Art. 16. The merit of pupils shall be recompensed with honorable marks which shall be entered in the book of the institution, and with annual prizes, whose solemn distribution shall take place at the close of the public examinations.

Art. 17. Punishments shall consist of public censure, deprivation of recess, and separation from the other pupils, and if this is not sufficient, definitive expulsion from the school. Expulsion shall take place irremissibly for the cause of contagious disease, for remarkable laziness, lack of application, and for serious lack of respect toward the teachers, and for bad deportment or depraved morals.

Art. 18. The public reading of the marks of good deportment, application, and progress, shall also serve as reward; and as punishment shall also serve the reading of the contrary marks. This shall be done every three months, assembling for that purpose all the pupils in one place, with their teachers, under the presidency of the director.

Of the interior regulations of the school

Art. 19. [This article is the same as Art. 23 of the regulations of 1863; see *ante*, p. 94.]

Of textbooks

Art. 20. [This article, consisting of two paragraphs, is equivalent to Art. 24 of the regulations of 1863, except that it reads "general government" where the latter reads "superior civil government."]

Concerning special examinations for obtaining assistants' certificates

Art. 21. Examinations shall be held four times each year in the normal school for the obtaining of assistants' certificates. Those who present themselves for the said examinations shall have the qualifications established in art. 9, for those who desire to enter the school. They shall be conversant with some of the matters established in art. 4, in regard to the subjects suitable for the acquisition of teachers' certificates of elementary primary instruction, according to the schedule approved by the superior government. Such examinations shall be public, and shall be held before the directors and teachers of the normal school.

Art. 22. [The same as Art. 26 of the regulations of 1863. See *ante,* p. 95.]

Of the issuing of teachers' and assistants' certificates

Art. 23. The General Division of Civil Administration has the right of issuing certificates as superior elementary and assistant teachers, at the recommendation of the director of the normal school.

Art. 24. [The same as Art. 28 of the regulations of 1863. See *ante,* p. 95.]

Of the competitive examinations to obtain a regular appointment in the término schools of first and second grades.

Art. 25. The vacant término schools of the first and second grades shall be supplied by competitive examinations. Such competitive examinations shall be held whenever the General Division of Civil Administration considers it necessary.

Competitive examinations shall be announced three months beforehand, and all those who shall have obtained a teacher's certificate for superior primary instruction shall be entitled to participate in them.

Art. 26. The examinations shall take place before a tribunal composed of five judges, appointed by the director from among the instructors of the normal school, and shall be ruled by an official schedule drawn up by the same persons, and approved by the superior government. In that schedule shall be contained the matters of the studies peculiar to the teaching profession.

Art. 27. The examination exercises shall be oral and written.

The oral exercises shall consist:

1. In the reply to questions chosen by lot in regard to religion and ethics, pedagogy, Castilian grammar, arithmetic, principles of geography, history of España and the world, principles of algebra and geometry, principles of physics and natural history, and principles of agriculture. Questions in each one of these matters shall be prepared for this purpose in distinct lists, and numbered tickets shall be placed in an urn. The competitor shall draw three tickets, and after reading the questions on religion and ethics for those same numbers, shall reply to at least one of them. Then he shall draw three other tickets for the examination in pedagogy; and so on, for the examination in the other studies. In the drawing of the questions for each subject, there shall always be twenty-five tickets. The questions which are answered shall be replaced by others.

2. In the explanation concerning the capacity of children, in a point relative to any of the subjects above named, the competitor shall read in a textbook of the schools the bit that shall be indicated by one of the examining judges, and shall proceed with the book closed to the explanation of what he has read.

3. In reading from a printed book and a manuscript.

4. In writing on the oilskin the sentence dictated by one of the judges, and then giving the grammatical and logical analysis of the same.

Written exercises shall consist:

1. In writing a page of capital letters according to the system of Iturzaeta on the ruled paper given for that purpose, for which each competitor shall cut the pen which he shall use immediately before the exercise.

2. In writing at the same dictation a composition in Castilian, which shall not be less than one page long, on a subject assigned by the tribunal.

3. In solving in writing the arithmetical problems which shall previously have been agreed on by the judges.

Paper bearing the stamp of the normal school, and the rubric of the president of the tribunal, and a writing desk, shall be furnished to the competitors for all their exercises.

The first exercise shall last an hour and a half, from the time when everything necessary for the same is ready. One hour shall be granted for the second, and for the third the period deemed advisable by the director.

In the marking of the first exercise, attention shall be paid only to the caligraphy, and in the third to the solution of the problems. In the second the writing, spelling, and especially the construction shall be marked.

All the competitors shall perform at one and the same time each one of the written exercises under the eyes of the members of the tribunal, and placed so that they cannot aid one another. The competitors shall not be allowed to consult any book or writing for the second and third exercises. After the time assigned for each one of the exercises, the competitor shall sign his paper and hand it to the president or his substitute.

Art. 28. In case of tie in the exercises between two or more competitors, consideration shall be given to the marks of the certificate, to the years of experience, and to the greater merit contracted in the practice of teaching.

Art. 29. The schools obtained by competition shall be governed permanently by the teachers who obtained them, and such teachers shall be entitled to the emoluments prescribed in the budgets corresponding to their rank.

Art. 30. The competitors who shall not, however, have passed those examinations, shall be preferred to those of their own class who, although they have the same marks in their certificates, shall not have obtained approbation in such exercises.

Manila, November 10, 1893. Approved.

Blanco

SCHOOL LEGISLATION, 1863–1894

Plan of primary instruction in Filipinas. See *ante*, pp. 76–86.

Normal Schools

December 20, 1863. Regulations for the normal school for men teachers. See ante, pp. 86–95.

July 22, 1864. Royal order, declaring a ticket for the passage of the Jesuit fathers assigned to the normal school of Manila.

November 24, 1864. Decree of the superior civil government, in which are dictated some precautionary measures for the installation of the normal school. The number of regular resident pupils is fixed with expression of those who belong to each province of the archipelago in proportion to the respective census of the village, and that of supernumerary resident pupils. Admissions of petitions of candidates for this class of appointments and matriculation for day pupils is declared open.

November 29, 1864. Circular of the superior civil government, directed to the chiefs of the provinces and of the districts, dictating rules for the provision of the places of regular resident pupils in the normal school for men teachers in Manila.

January 19, 1865. Royal order, approving the allowances for Jesuit fathers and brothers of the normal school, and for equipment of the same.

May 30, 1865. Royal order no. 175, of the ministry of the colonies, approving all the measures adopted by the superior civil government for the inauguration of the normal school for men teachers, and expressing the pleasure with which her Majesty saw the zeal manifested in the installation of said institution.

July 17, 1865. Decree of the superior civil government, ordering that the corporals and sergeants of the army who so desire be admitted into the normal school for men teachers.

March 13, 1866. Decree of the superior civil government, dictating rules for the establishment of a school of primary instruction for boys in the normal school for men teachers.

June 25, 1866. Royal order, no. 293, of the ministry of the colonies, naming the sum of ten pesos per month as the board for resident pupils of the normal school for men teachers, and reducing the regular places to forty.

December 24, 1866. Decree of the superior civil government, ruling that the vacancies of regular resident pupils of the normal school for men teachers be filled by the pupils who attend the school of primary instruction, established within the normal school, and by others who may solicit them.

March 22, 1869. Decree of the superior civil government, arranging that the term in the normal school for men teachers begin in June and end in March, the examinations being held in the latter month.

December 2, 1870. Order of the supreme government, modifying article 4 of the regulations of the normal school for men teachers, of December 20, 1863; and arranging that the fees for matriculation in the normal school be reduced to six escudos per study.

November 23, 1871. Project of regulations for a normal school for women teachers in Filipinas.

January 11, 1872. Royal order, ruling that the girls' school of Nueva-Cáceres be erected into a normal school and seminary for women teachers.

June 14, 1872. Decree of the superior civil government, reducing the places for regular resident pupils of the normal school for men teachers in Manila to thirty.

May 26, 1873. Order of the executive authority, authorizing the one hundred villages of the diocese of Nueva-Cáceres to each send a young woman to the girls' school in said city, so that such young women may afterward direct the schools in their respective villages.

May 4, 1874. Decree of the superior civil government, ordering that no petition be sent to it for entrance into the normal school for men teachers without the requisites prescribed in article 9 of the organic regulations for said school, and that the petitions be sent through the medium of the provincial chiefs.

May 21, 1874. Decree of the superior civil government, reducing the number of places for regular resident pupils of the normal school for men teachers in Manila to twenty.

July 28, 1874. Decree of the general government, reducing the number of places for resident pupils of the normal school for men teachers in Manila to fifteen.

August 17, 1874. Decree of the general government, ordering that those pupils of the normal school for men teachers who have twenty voluntary failures of attendance, or thirty involuntary, be stricken from the list.

June 9, 1875. Decree of the general government, constituting in the normal school for women teachers of primary education the school of Santa Isabel of the city and diocese of Nueva-Cáceres.

June 19, 1875. Decree of the general government, approving, with the character of ad interim, the regulations for the normal school for women teachers of primary education in the diocese of Nueva-Cáceres. See this decree, as well as the regulations for the school, *ante*, pp. 142–160.

June 30, 1875. Circular of the government, directed to the governors of the provinces of the diocese of Nueva-Cáceres because of the inauguration of the normal school for women teachers in that city.

April 2, 1878. Decree of the general government, approving the examinations held in September and December, 1877, in the normal school for women teachers in Nueva-Cáceres, and ordering that a teacher's certificate be sent to those pupils examined.

June 22, 1880. Royal order of the ministry of the colonies, creating the chair of the elements employed in the normal school for men teachers in Manila, and ordering that a permanent sum of money be assigned in the budget for this consideration.

September 27, 1880. Royal order, no. 875, of the ministry of the colonies, approving the definitive institution of the normal school for women teachers in Nueva-Cáceres and the regulations of the same, which were approved in the character of ad interim, by superior decree, June 19, 1875.

September 27, 1880. Royal order, no. 880, of the ministry of the colonies, ordering that twenty-five copies of the regulations approved by royal order, number 875, of the same date for the normal school for women teachers in Nueva-Cáceres, be sent to it.

March 11, 1892. Royal decree, creating in Manila a normal school for women teachers in charge of the Augustinian nuns of the Assumption established in the royal school of Santa Isabel in Madrid. See this royal decree, as well as the royal order following, and the regulations, *ante*, pp. 160–210.

May 15, 1893. Announcement of the superior normal school for women teachers, published in the Gaceta, giving information of the opening for matriculation in that institution, the requirements for obtaining it, the fees to be paid for it, and the material for the entrance examination.

November 3, 1893. Decree of the general government, creating the post of professor of the practice school established in the normal school for men teachers in Manila.

November 10, 1893. Decree of the general government, elevating to the grade of superior the normal school for men teachers in Manila, and approving provisionally the new regulations of that school. See this decree, with following regulations, *ante*, pp. 210–228.

December 1, 1893. Decree of the general government, extending to the superior normal school for women teachers the powers which the General Division of Civil Administration has over that for men teachers.

December 15, 1893. Decree of the general government, dictating orders supplementary to the superior decree of November 10, 1893, and to the regulations of the superior normal school for men teachers approved on the same date.

January 30, 1894. Royal order, no. 135, of the ministry of the colonies, authorizing the continuance in the institution of the regular resident pupils of the normal school for men teachers in Manila until the completion of their course.

January 30, 1894. Royal order, no. 136, of the ministry of the colonies, ordering that the rent of the house occupied by the normal school for men teachers in Manila be paid from the budget of the local funds.

February 23, 1894. Decree of the general government, creating a pedagogical academy in the superior normal school for men teachers in Manila.

April 18, 1894. Royal order, no. 280, of the ministry of the colonies, approving the superior decree which elevated to the rank of superior the normal school for men teachers in Manila; the new regulations for the same; the supplementary orders dictated by the superior decree of December 15, 1893; and the appointment of a professor of the practice school established in it.

April 30, 1894. Announcement of the superior normal school for men teachers published in the *Gaceta*, naming date and conditions for the entrance examinations into that institution, as well as for the examinations of assistants, and for the extraordinary examinations for the term of 1893–94.

June 15, 1894. Decree of the general government, modifying article 4 of the superior decree of November 10, 1893, which declared the normal school for men teachers in Manila to be a superior school; and article 2 of the decree of December 15, of the same year.

July 20, 1894. Decree of the general government, approving the organic regulations of the pedagogical academy of the superior formal school for men teachers in Manila; with citation of regulations.

August 17, 1894. Decree of the general government, declaring that the pupils of the normal school who have not passed in their examinations for confirmation which they have to take in order to obtain the teacher's certificate of elementary primary instruction, have sufficient aptitude to receive an assistant teacher's certificate.

Schools of primary instruction

December 20, 1863. Regulations for the schools and teachers of primary instruction for the natives of the Philippine Archipelago. See these regulations, as well as the interior regulations of the same date, and the decree of the superior civil government of February 15, 1864, approving the regulations for the municipal girls' school of Manila, with citation of regulations, *ante*, pp. 96–125.

March 15, 1864. Decree of the superior civil government, appointing the members of the Superior Board of Primary Instruction.

May 17, 1864. Circular of the superior civil government, addressed to the provincial and district chiefs, giving rules for the better establishment of the plan for primary instruction established by royal decree of December 20, 1863, and the regulations of the same date.

June 20, 1864. Royal order, prescribing the model for the staff and equipment of the municipal school for girls in Manila.

October 19, 1864. Decree of the superior civil government, authorizing the Conference of St. Stanislas Kostka62 of the Society of St. Vincent of Paul, to establish a school for primary instruction for boys in the suburbs of San Sebastian of Manila.

December 2, 1864. Decree of the superior civil government, in regard to the special organization and powers of the provincial commission of primary instruction in Manila.

March 1, 1865. Circular of the superior civil government, ordering the provincial and district chiefs to send two reports of the villages of the territory under their charge, in which schools for boys and girls could be established, determining their respective category in accordance with the accompanying models.

January 6, 1866. Royal order, approving the expense of 250 escudos, charged to the local funds for defraying the expenses of the prizes of the girls of the municipal school who show most progress in their examination.

March 1, 1866. Decision of the superior civil government, ordering the director of the normal school for men teachers in Manila to assign an examination for assistant teachers for the first days in June of that year.

March 23, 1866. Decree of the superior civil government, fixing at one escudo per month the quota which must be paid by the children of wealthy families who attend the school of primary instruction established in the normal school for men teachers in Manila.

January 20, 1867. Decree of the superior civil government, prescribing the rank of boys' schools according to the number of inhabitants in each village.

February 15, 1867. Circular of the superior civil government, to the provincial and district chiefs, in regard to the dwelling house for the men teachers, construction and repair of buildings for schools, and purchase of furniture and equipment for the same.

February 16, 1867. Decree of the superior civil government, ordering that the local funds pay the men teachers one peso per year for each boy who attends the writing class, for school supplies and equipment.

June 22, 1867. Decree of the superior civil government, prescribing when it shall proceed to establish in the villages schools for girls; and in regard to the appointment of women teachers to take charge of them.

August 12, 1867. Circular of the superior civil government, to the provincial and district chiefs, determining that they shall send monthly reports of the number of boys attending the schools.

August 30, 1867. Circular of the superior civil government, giving rules for the good discharge of school supervision. See this circular, *ante*, pp. 125–142.

October 30, 1867. Circular of the superior civil government, ordering the provincial chiefs to have the gobernadorcillos proclaim and, moreover, affix to the street corners and in the courts, an edict whose purpose is to stimulate school attendance and the teaching of Castilian; with citation of edict.

November 5, 1867. Royal order, creating a girls' school under the advocacy of Santa Isabel in Nueva-Cáceres, in charge of the sisters of charity, under the supervision of the reverend bishop of the diocese.

November 12, 1867. Decree of the superior civil government, ordering that those who pass in the examinations for substitute women teachers and do not obtain a place for lack of vacancies, be authorized to occupy the first vacancy which occurs.

January 4, 1868. Circular of the superior civil government, recommending the provincial chiefs to send monthly reports of school attendance, and charging them to arouse the zeal of the provincial and the local commissions of primary instruction, so that Castilian may be taught in the schools.

March 14, 1868. Decree of the superior civil government, revising article 26 of the school regulations, so that married women of any age and single women after they have reached the age of twenty years may be appointed teachers.

March 14, 1868. Decree of the superior civil government, ordering that publication of works in the dialects of the country, with the exception of prayer and devotional books and others similar to them, be only permitted when they are printed in two texts, namely, in the dialects and in Castilian, and that such books shall never be assigned for use in the schools.

April 26, 1868. Circular decree of the superior civil government, in regard to the examinations of substitute men teachers; and approval of the regulations of the same, with citation of regulations.

July 18, 1868. Circular of the superior civil government, ordering the publication in the *Gaceta* of a statistical report [*ensayo*] of the schools; and charging the provincial chiefs to send monthly reports showing the number of children present in the same, and stating that Castilian is taught in the same.

August 4, 1868. Statutes for the college-school of Santa Isabel in the city of Nueva-Cáceres.

Título I. Creation, object, and dependency of the college school.

Título II. Of the school of primary instruction for day-school girls; their admission, studies, school hours, and holidays.

Título III. Of the college and of the resident scholars. Object of the college, conditions for admission therein, clothing, board, and food.

Título IV. Interior life of the scholars.

Título V. Studies; distribution of time.

Título VI. Of the frequency of sacraments, attendance, spiritual exercises, holidays, vacations, and absences.

September 2, 1868. Decree of the secretary of the superior civil government, publishing by order of his Excellency in the *Gaceta* a pastoral of his Excellency, the bishop of Nueva-Cáceres, in which the latter urges the parish priests of his diocese to observe very earnestly the duties imposed upon them by the legislation in force for the education of children and the progress of schools.

September 4, 1868. Circular of the superior civil government, to the provincial and district chiefs, charging them that the respective documents accompany recommendations for the issuing of certificates to teachers, and show the pay, between the fixed maximum and minimum in each case, which ought to be granted them.

September 4, 1868. Decree of the superior government, ordering that petitions for money in order to satisfy the rent of the house for men teachers, school equipment, etc., be sent to the sub-intendancy of ways and means.

September 22, 1868. Circular of the superior civil government, to the provincial and district chiefs, recommending to them the exact fulfilment of the circular and regulation for substitute men teachers of April 26 of the same year; that they compel the children of wealthy families to go to school and pay the teacher the prescribed fee; that they contrive to have edifices built for the schools in the villages where there are teachers; and that they inform the latter of their obligation to supply necessary free equipment for writing to the pupils, granting to the substitute as to the normal teachers, one peso annually for said expenses, so that they may be able to exact from them this obligation.

September 30, 1868. Decree of the superior civil government, ordering that substitute teachers be furnished with their corresponding certificates.

October 24, 1868. Decree of the superior civil government, ordering that in case of insolvency, the same methods be employed for the collection of the quotas to be paid by the wealthy pupils to the teachers, that are used for the realization of the public imposts.

October 27, 1868. Decree of the superior civil government, ordering that pupils may attend schools of primary instruction until the age of eighteen, voluntary attendance being from the age of fourteen.

August 5, 1869. Decree of the superior civil government, conferring a commission upon the member of the Superior Board of Primary Instruction, Don José Patricio Clemente, so that he may enter upon an extraordinary visit of supervision of all the public and private institutions of primary education of the province of Manila.

July 16, 1870. Circular of the superior civil government, ordering that when the teachers ask leave to attend to their own affairs or because of a proved illness, they present paid substitutes for themselves.

July 20, 1870. Decree of the superior civil government, ordering that for the lack of assistants with circular, substitute assistants may be appointed for the schools that have more than eighty pupils, by the provincial and district chiefs, at the recommendation of the local supervisors, after conferring with the respective teachers. They shall be given eight escudos per month without right to any other fee.

September 13, 1870. Decree of the superior civil government, ordering that the women teachers shall be paid one peso per year from the local funds for each girl that attends the class in writing, for school equipment.

November 5, 1870. Circular of the superior civil government, recommending the provincial chiefs to request the necessary money for the payment of the teachers from the time that they begin their duties, their salaries, rental for their dwelling house and other emoluments.

December 2, 1870. Order, no. 1179, of the ministry of the colonies, approving the commission conferred by the superior civil government of these islands on Don José Patricio Clemente, for a tour of inspection of the schools of primary teaching in the province of Manila.

December 5, 1870. Order of the supreme government, decreeing the appointment of a board ad interim of public instruction, and decree of "cúmplase"63 of the superior civil government, dated February 23, 1871, in which the above board is appointed.

December 7, 1870. Decree of the superior civil government, authorizing the establishment of a free school of primary instruction for girls, in charge of the sisters of charity in the school of Purísima Concepción [i.e., the most pure conception] installed in the site called La Concordia.

December 17, 1870. Decree of the superior civil government, prescribing that men and women teachers are entitled to receive their salary from the day on which they prove by means of the local supervisors that they have presented themselves and taken charge of the school which they have obtained.

February 23, 1871. Decree of the superior civil government, dissolving the Superior Board of Primary Instruction and ordering that all the antecedent decrees in its possession be surrendered to the ad interim Board of Public Instruction.

March 2, 1871. Decree of the superior civil government, ordering that the ad interim Board of Public Instruction of these islands, apply so far as may be possible, the regulations approved January 26, 1867, for the island of Cuba; with citation of regulation.

March 4, 1871. Decree of the superior civil government, ordering the publication of the plan of studies dictated for the island of Cuba, July 15, 1863, with commands to observe it, so far as might be possible and applicable. Title of the above-cited plan referring to primary education.

April 27, 1871. Royal order of the ministry of the colonies, prescribing the sums which must be paid for the installation of the girls' school of Santa Isabel established in Nueva-Cáceres.

May 7, 1871. Decree of the superior civil government, in regard to the creation of schools and procedures which must be followed by the documents which are drawn up for this purpose; the formation of reports of the existing schools; the establishment of classes for adults and allowances for the teachers for this extraordinary work; the teaching of the Castilian language; supervision of the schools; examinations of the same and rewards for the teachers and pupils who distinguish themselves in them; the pay of the teachers; construction of schools and dwellings for them; material and equipment which the schools must have; compulsory attendance at them; the teaching of Castilian; charge that teaching be free to the poor; exact pay for the teachers.

June 12, 1871. Decree of the superior civil government, ordering that the men and women teacher substitutes be given their corresponding certificates.

July 1, 1871. Decree of the superior civil government, prescribing the textbooks which are to be used in the public schools of primary instruction.

July 19, 1871. Decree of the superior civil government, explaining article 14, of the seventh of May, of this year, relative to the pay of monthly quota by the presence at the school of the wealthy children.

August 26, 1871. Decree of the superior civil government, determining that the rights prescribed in articles 13, 14, and 15, of the seventh of May, of this year, alone be granted, and extended to the teachers graduating from the normal school, and to the substitutes examined with certificates.

September 26, 1871. Decree of the superior civil government, recommending to the provincial commissions of primary instruction, strictness in the examinations of substitute teachers, and that the mark which each one shall merit be placed in the minutes of examination.

October 9, 1871. Decree of the superior civil government, ordering that no petition be admitted asking for permission to print and annotate the text in these islands of works of different nature, whether literary or devoted to public instruction, unless such is directed by the proprietors or authors themselves or by those who are fully authorized by such.

October 12, 1871. Royal order of the ministry of the colonies, asking the superior civil government of these islands for the names of the teachers who distinguished themselves by their zeal for the good of teaching, their intelligence and power to work, in order to inform the Ministry of Public Works [*Fomento*], so that, if it deems it advisable, it may reward them as those of the Peninsula, by sending them collections of books for the formation of popular libraries.

January 13, 1872.64 Circular of the superior civil government, arousing the zeal of provincial and local authorities, and the parochial clergy so that they may urge forward the propagation and progress of primary teaching and the construction of ways of communication.

February 14, 1872. Decree of the superior civil government, ordering that the president of the provincial commission of primary instruction in Manila be present at all the meetings held by the commission, with power to delegate for other urgent occupation his authority to the most important member of the ayuntamiento; that two members of the ayuntamiento be present as members [of the board]; that the secretary of the civil government of the province be a member ex-officio of said commission; that announcements be published for the convocation to a meeting; and that such meeting may be held by the president, three members, and the secretary.

September 30, 1872. Decree of the superior civil government, granting to the provincial and district chiefs, right of participation in the taking of possession and leaving by the teachers of primary instruction.

February 21, 1873. Decree of the superior civil government, in regard to the salaries of teachers, men and women, and their assistants.

March 12, 1873. Circular of the superior civil government, recommending that the Castilian language be taught in the schools of primary instruction.

May 27, 1873. Circular of the superior civil government, ordering that the provincial commissions of primary instruction propose the most advisable measures so that teaching may be obligatory for all and gratuitous for the poor.

May 30, 1873. Circular of the superior civil government, ordering the provincial chiefs to send a report made in accordance with the subjoined model, in which shall be given the number of villages and schools in each province, the men and women teachers who taught in them, and the number of children who attended and those who studied Castilian.

June 10, 1873. Circular of the superior civil government, charging the provincial chiefs with the exact observance of the superior decree of February 21 of the same year, in regard to the salaries of teachers and assistants.

July 26, 1873. Decree of the superior civil government, ordering the governors of the archipelago to send a detailed note of the names, qualifications, and circumstances, of the regularly-appointed teachers, who shall distinguish themselves most in each province, in order that he may recommend them to the government of his Majesty, so that if he considers it well he may reward them with popular libraries according to the royal order of October 12, 1871.

October 10, 1873. Decree of the superior civil government, charging the provincial supervisors of primary instruction to acquire a *Quadro sinóptico de las islas Filipinas* [i.e., Synoptical chart of the Filipinas Islands] by Don Leon Salcedo, for teaching in the schools.

September 9, 1874. Decree of the general government, prescribing that appointments, issuing of certificates, licenses, promotions, and other things belonging to those functionaries, as well as in general all the affairs of government and progress, belong to the General Division of Civil Administration.

September 24, 1874. Decree of the general government, ordering that the vice-presidency of the ad interim Board of Public Instruction be held by the director general of civil administration.

March 31, 1875. Decree of the general government, ordering the provincial chiefs to construct schools and dwelling-houses for the teachers.

October 29, 1875. Royal order, no. 648, of the ministry of the colonies, copying the royal decree of the same date, in which among other extremes, referring to secondary education and to superior education, the powers entrusted to the ad interim Board of Public Instruction be declared ended.

January 15, 1876. Decree of the general government, declaring at an end the powers entrusted to the ad interim Board of Public Instruction.

January 15, 1876. Decree of the general government, ordering among other extremes bearing on secondary and superior education, that the matters referring to public and private instruction be managed and despatched by the general government in its functions of civil administration, and that the Superior Board of Primary Instruction be called Superior Board of Public Instruction of Filipinas, with the organization which is prescribed.

May 17, 1876. Royal order, no. 388, of the ministry of the colonies, ordering that the zeal of persons conversant with the various dialects of the archipelago be stimulated, so that a grammar may be compiled in each dialect for the teaching of the Castilian language in the schools of primary letters, for the purpose of obtaining the diffusion of said language; and that, with like object, the reforms which it is advisable to introduce in legislation in regard to primary instruction, be proposed.

June 7, 1876. Royal order, no. 324, of the ministry of the colonies, ordering among other extremes referring to secondary and superior education, that the Superior Board of Primary Instruction be reestablished in the manner prescribed in article 15 of the royal decree of December 20, 1863.

July 22, 1876. Circular of the general government, giving rules for the observance of royal order, no. 388, of May 17, of the same year.

August 16, 1876. Decree of the general government, reëstablishing the Superior Board of Primary Instruction, and designating the persons who were to compose it.

June 5, 1877. Royal order of the ministry of the colonies, approving the preceding decree.

September 10, 1878. Circular of the General Division of Civil Administration to the provincial chiefs, ordering them to furnish localities for the schools, either by renting or constructing buildings; that the teachers be paid their salaries and fees promptly; that a proof report, in accordance with the subjoined form, be sent of the situation of each province, to the department of primary instruction; and that the petitions of the teachers, asking for some favor or demanding their salary, be sent to said center with the fitting information.

November 6, 1878. Royal order, decreeing that instructors of primary education in the colonies be paid half their salary during the time that they are on leave in the Peninsula for sickness, and the other half to those who act as substitutes for them.

May 20, 1879. Royal order of the ministry of the colonies, in which is shown the pleasure with which his Majesty heard that a boys' school had been started in Nueva-Cáceres, at the expense of the reverend bishop of the diocese.

July 14, 1880. Royal order, no. 625, of the ministry of the colonies, in regard to places for the taking of possession by the teachers, transfers, cessation of duties, and licenses that the same may enjoy.

July 14, 1880. Royal order, no. 668, of the ministry of the colonies, ordering that the provincial chiefs proceed to the construction of edifices for schools, with dwelling-houses for the teachers, by making use of the personal services [of the natives]; charging the gobernadorcillos of the villages with the keeping and conservation of the equipment; paying the expenses with the amount of a fourth part of the fee paid to the teachers by well-to-do children; ordering that the teachers be paid monthly a sum equal to the fourth part of their salary for school equipment; imposing on them the obligation to keep an inventory book of the apparatus and equipment of their respective schools, as well as other books of matriculation and daily attendance; ordering that the General Division of Civil Administration make annually at auction the purchase of the necessary school supplies; and dictating other important measures for the purchase, distribution, and conservation of school equipment and supplies.

September 1, 1880. Circular of the General Division of Civil Administration, animating the provincial chiefs to contrive to have Castilian taught in the schools by all the means in their power.

October 5, 1881. Circular of the secretary of the royal Audiencia of Manila, communicating the decision of the entire tribunal of September 23, of the same year, by which it is ordered that the judges of first instance may avail themselves for written recognizances of the [services of] men teachers with certificates who have graduated from the normal school.

December 27, 1881. Decree of the General Division of Civil Administration, ordering that the boys' schools of Manila and its suburbs have a competitive contest.

March 10, 1882. Circular of the secretary of the royal Audiencia, transcribing a letter of the supreme tribunal, in which it was communicated that the government assembly of the same had approved the decision of the entire tribunal of the abovesaid Audiencia, of September 23, 1881, in reference to the fact that written recognizances be made by men teachers graduating from the normal school established in the villages.

March 24, 1882. Circular of the General Division of Civil Administration, prescribing the salaries to be received by substitute teachers without certificates.

September 12, 1883. Decree of the general government, in regard to compulsory teaching of the Castilian language in the schools; punishments of the teachers who do not keep it; annual inspection of the governors of the schools, giving account of the result in each one of them; examinations in the same, and the rewards and recompenses for the scholars and teachers who distinguish themselves in them; provision of the ascenso schools and término schools of second class for aid and correction to the parents of children from seven to twelve years old who do not attend the schools. Declaration that those employes who cannot talk, read, and write Castilian, cannot receive their prescribed pay. The provincial chiefs are ordered to send a proof report of the primary instruction in their respective territories and a secret memorandum in regard to the same matter. An assembly shall be called for a gathering, in which the authors of the best grammars written in the dialects of the country for the teaching of Castilian shall be rewarded; it is recommended to the General Division of Civil Administration that it study and recommend the increase which it is advisable to give to the pay of the teachers, and the creation of a special body of paid provincial supervisors.

September 25, 1883. Circular of the General Division of Civil Administration, sending to the provincial chiefs the form to which the proof report of primary instruction in their respective territories, which they were to make by virtue of the order in the first transitory prescription of the preceding decree, must conform.

September 25, 1883. Decree of the General Division of Civil Administration, convoking an assembly for rewarding the [authors of the] best Castilian grammars written in the principal dialects of the country for the schools, and fixing the conditions of said assembly.

October 6, 1885. Decree of the general government, granting to the original Hispano-Tagálog grammar, of the right reverend father Fray Toribio Minguella,65 the privileges established in rule 6 of the preceding decree; holding a new assembly for the reward of Castilian grammars written in the Visayan, Cebuyan, Ilocan, Vicol, Pangasinan, or Pampango; and marking the conditions of this new assembly.

February 17, 1886. Circular of the General Division of Civil Administration, recommending to the provincial supervisors of primary instruction to immediately copy for the local reverend or learned supervisors the orders received from said center in regard to teachers.

June 30, 1887. Decree of the general government, encouraging the provincial chiefs and the reverend parish priests, to contrive by all means to have the Castilian language taught in the schools, imposing on them the obligation of personally making the tour of annual inspection, at least to the schools, and another tour by the secretaries of the [local] governments, giving account afterwards of the progress in said teaching and recommending at the same time recompenses or punishment which the teachers deserve on account of their interest or neglect.

July 11, 1887. Circular of the General Division of Civil Administration, charging the provincial chiefs with the exact observance of the orders dictated in regard to primary instruction for the purpose of having Castilian spoken in all the villages; they shall employ rigor in the examinations of substitute teachers, and be careful that the assistant substitutes who are appointed be persons suitable for teaching.

January 13, 1888. Decree of the general government, declaring a competition in the boys' término school of the first class among teachers with certificates from the normal school, who shall have had one year's practice in teaching and giving rules for the holding of said competitions; with programs for the oral examination in said competitions.

July 31, 1888. Circular of the general government, addressed to the provincial chiefs ordering that they make an extraordinary inspection of the school, after which they shall remit to the said general government the various data which are expressed, so that an exact idea of the condition of those schools may be formed.

January 16, 1889. Decree of the general government, ordering that the allowances which they receive in hard cash for school equipment be not paid to the men and women teachers; and creating a board for the purchase of said equipment, and prescribing rules for the provision of the above-mentioned supplies to the schools.

January 16, 1889. Decree of the general government, ordering that the sums which are given in coin for the rewards of the pupils, cease to be given to the teachers, and that the administrative board of school supplies created by the preceding decree, purchase in the public market for said object, primers of agriculture, and then grammars, geographies and other useful books.

January 29, 1889. Royal order, no. 75, of the ministry of the colonies, enjoining the most punctual observance of the orders dictated for obtaining the diffusion of the Castilian language among the natives of these islands, and ordering that the ministry be informed of the results of the visits, which the provincial chiefs are obliged to make to all the schools of the territory under their command, in order to be able to judge rightly the progress which is obtained, and to grant the due recompense to the teachers.

February 4, 1889. Decree of the general government, making regulations for the schools of primary instruction in the archipelago. Division of the various schools into sections and subjects which are to be taught in each one of them; copy books; textbooks; compulsory attendance at the schools; class hours; classes in religion; books of matriculation; and daily register of attendance.

February 4, 1889. Decree of the general government, approving the schedule to which the examination of regularly-appointed women teachers must conform.

February 5, 1889. Decree of the general government, prescribing rules for the construction and conservation of supplies for the schools, making use for this of the services of the personal tax, and the gratuitous cutting of timber in the public mountains, and recommending the reverend parish priests to watch over the schools and see that this decree is fulfilled.

February 9, 1889. Circular of the General Division of Civil Administration, prescribing the stamp tax which must be paid for the certificates of men and women teachers, and assistants, and for the credentials of the same.

March 5, 1889. Decree of the general government, prohibiting boys and girls in the schools from going out to receive the authorities; ordering that whenever any authority who may inspect the schools comes to the village, all the scholars of the same schools assemble therein with their respective teachers; and that the provincial governors impose a fine of ten pesos on the gobernadorcillos and teachers who infringe this decree.

March 30, 1889. Decree of the General Division of Civil Administration, communicating the decision of the superior government, in which it is ordered that the teachers be paid their salaries, house-rent, etc., in the same villages of their residence, by the gobernadorcillos, with the sums collected by imposts of the local treasury, and prescribing rules for effecting said payment.

December 14, 1889. Circular of the general government, ordering the observance of what is prescribed by articles 31 to 34 of the regulations of schools in 1863; that the teachers keep a register of matriculation and another of daily school attendance in accordance with the subjoined forms, and an inventory book giving values of the equipment and supplies in their schools; another of the books given to the children as prizes, and a blank book, in which to copy the orders dictated in regard to primary instruction; that the admission of children to the schools be preceded by a written order of the religious or learned parish priest; that the teaching be divided into the section determined by the superior decree of February 4, of this year; that the class hours be from seven to ten in the morning and from half past two to five in the afternoon; that the provincial supervisors send monthly proof reports of the schools; that the teachers may sell the textbooks which are sent them at the price fixed by the board; that they may make petitions for the supplies that they need every three months; that instruction be compulsory for children from six to twelve years old, while those from four to six and from twelve to eighteen may attend voluntarily; and that private schools be subject to the orders in force for titular schools.

June 30, 1890. Decree of the General Division of Civil Administration, recommending the observance of the circular of the general government, of December 14, 1889, and publishing it again in the *Gaceta*.

July 3, 1890. Circular of the General Division of Civil Administration, ordering that the copies written by the children in the schools be dated and signed by the same and conserved by the teachers.

January 16, 1891. Royal order, no. 58, of the ministry of the colonies, relating to the provincial and municipal budgets of these islands for said year, in which is ordered, among other extremes, the constitution of an administrative board of school supplies.

May 1, 1891. Decree of the general government, designating the persons, who being electors, were to form part of the administrative board of school material.

March 2, 1892. Royal order, no. 116, of the ministry of the colonies, approving the monthly allowance granted to the secretary and clerks of the administrative board of school supplies.

July 29, 1892. Decree of the general government, increasing the salaries of men and women teachers and assistants which were to be assigned in the projects of the budgets of 1893; and ordering the form of the provision of those places and the creation of territorial examining commissions of teachers in Vigan, Nueva-Cáceres, Cebú, and Jaro.

August 3, 1892. Decree of the general government, giving information that the ministry of the colonies had authorized by telegraph the increase of the salary of the teachers proposed by said government.

August 8, 1892. Decree of the general government, giving information that the ministry of the colonies had given telegraphic authorization to increase the sum for school supplies to 100,000 pesos.

August 11, 1892. Decree of the general government, granting annual allowances to men and women teachers with good marks, and more than fifteen years of service.

October 19, 1892. Decree of the general government, ordering the constitution of territorial examining commissions of teachers in Vigan, Nueva-Cáceres, Cebú, and Jaro, prescribing the persons who are to form them; as well as the creation of examining commissions, also of substitute and assistant teachers in the normal schools in Manila and Nueva-Cáceres; said commissions giving rules for examinations of substitute and assistant teachers; and ordering that the provincial commissions of primary instruction cease their duties of examining them.

December 8, 1892. Royal order of the ministry of the colonies, approving the creation of a girls' school in Yap (Carolinas).

February 27, 1893. Decree of the general government, prescribing the distribution and classification of the schools of primary instruction of the archipelago, and giving rules for their provision; with a table of distribution and classification of the schools.

February 27, 1893. Decree of the general government, approving the schedules for the examinations of men and women teachers, substitutes, and assistants of primary instruction; with schedules cited.

March 29, 1893. Decree of the general government, declaring the book entitled El pez de madera [i.e., The Wooden Fish],66 as a textbook in reading for the public schools of the archipelago.

May 1, 1893. Decree of the General Division of Civil Administration, granting free examinations for obtaining certificates as elementary women teachers in the superior normal school for women teachers in Manila, who shall be submitted to the schedules of that institution, and only during the first two years following its installation, namely, in the courses for the years 1893–94 and 1894–95.

July 28, 1893. Decree of the General Division of Civil Administration, allowing competition between various boys' schools of the rank of término of the first and second class and término schools, and contest for boys' and girls' ascenso and entrada schools.

August 21, 1893. Decree of the General Division of Civil Administration, allowing competition in the boys' school of Bacalor (Pampanga).

August 23, 1893. Decree of the General Division of Civil Administration, continuing for a fortnight the period for the admission of petitions in the contest for teachers, decreed July 28 of the said year for the provision of ascenso and entrada schools.

August 31, 1893. Decree of the General Division of Civil Administration, continuing the time for the admission of petitions of men and women teachers who wish to take part in the competitions announced by the decree of July 28, and August 21, of the same year.

September 5, 1893. Schedules for the competitions at the girls' término schools.

September 29, 1893. Decree of the general government, in regard to the pay of salaries to teachers' assistants.

November 1, 1893. Decree of the general government, declaring a pamphlet entitled Sistema métrico decimal de pesas y medidas [i.e., Decimal Metrical System of Weights and Measures]67 a textbook for the public schools of the archipelago.

November 24, 1893. Decree of the general government, allowing those who are more than sixteen years of age and less than twenty and have a teacher's certificate to manage schools in the character of ad interim.

May 14, 1894. Decree of the general government, declaring the book entitled Cartilla higiénica [i.e., Hygienic Primer]68 a textbook of compulsory reading for the public schools of the archipelago.

July 20, 1894. Decree of the general government ordering two previous payments to be made for traveling expenses to men and women teachers and assistants who may be appointed to the charge of schools located in provinces distant from those in which they reside, and who petition it.

[Grifol y Aliaga's book concludes with two appendices. The first appendix contains several official documents concerning legislation in education, the titles of which are as follows:]

May 17, 1864. Circular of the superior civil government, to the provincial and district chiefs, giving rules for the better establishment of the plan of primary instruction established by royal decree of December 20, 1863, and regulations of the same date.

November 29, 1864. Circular of the superior civil government, directed to the provincial and district chiefs, dictating rules for the provision of the places of regular resident pupils of the normal school for men teachers in Manila.

May 20, 1865. Royal order, number 175, of the ministry of the colonies, approving all the measures adopted by the superior civil government for the inauguration of the normal school for men teachers, and expressing the pleasure with which her Majesty saw the zeal shown in the installation of said institution.

[The second appendix consists of an enumeration of the textbooks for the superior normal school for men teachers in Manila; for the normal school for women teachers in Manila; and for the schools of primary instruction.]

1 A royal order of November 19, 1815, provided for charity schools in the convents of friars and nuns, for primary education, to give instruction in the Christian doctrine, in good morals, and in the first letters to the children of the poor, from the age of ten to twelve. (Barrantes, Instrucción primaria, p. 77.)

2 Vicente Barrantes, from whom these extracts are taken, was for some years secretary to the governor-general at Manila. See Report of Commissioner of Education, 1902, ii, p. 2219.

3 Fred W. Atkinson, formerly general superintendent of public instruction in the Philippines, says: "The early work of the Jesuits in training the Filipinos was commendable, and along right lines in furnishing a common school education. It would have been productive of permanently good results if this order had not been supplanted by the local padres, under whose direction the common branches suffered through lack of attention." See Report of Commissioner of Education, 1900–1901, ii, p. 1317.

4 July 27, 1863, several copies of the plan of public instruction approved for the island of Cuba on the fifteenth of the same month were sent by royal

order to the governor of the Philippines, with the object of having the proper measure drawn up, and the advisable plan proposed to the ministry, in regard to the application of said plan to those islands. By decree of October 6, Echagüe created a board of reform of the plan of studies, in order to meet the requirements of the preceding royal order. See Montero y Vidal, iii, p. 403.

5 See a summary of Barrantes's book in Report of Commissioner of Education, 1902, ii, pp. 2219–2224.

6 "Before this date public schools were hardly known in the Philippines, and instruction was confined solely to the children of parents able to pay for it." See Census of Philippines, iii, p. 576.

7 In the decree of the superior government, of May 7, 1871, occurs the following interesting description of conditions of the schools in the Philippines: "There are at present an infinite number of villages without schools; there are entire provinces without edifices where schools can be located; there are also many schools, or rather all the schools of the archipelago, with the exception of a few in the capital, which do not possess the material equipment for education and teaching; the children have to sit on the ground, and remain there for hours and hours, packed together as if they were not what they are; books are not given to them; they have no writing desks; they are not given pens, ink, or books. Those schools do not merit the name of such; they are not schools, sad it is to say so: they are pernicious collections of children, where since they do not gain anything morally or intellectually, they lose much, and most of all in their good physical development; in fine those schools are an expense, and show no result." The same decree states the need of economic and administrative reforms in the Philippines, and the need of "roads, canals, ports, postal communications, both inside and outside the archipelago, telegraphs, professional institutions of superior instruction, an active life without fetters for industry, trade, and agriculture;" but all this must be for the greatest use of the greatest number, and all monopoly must be avoided. "To obtain it human means offer no other mean more energetic, more prompt, and powerful, than the creation and organization of the village school, and its supervision, and its location and erection in the most healthful and convenient place, clean, neat, and modestly furnished, so that it may attract the glances of all," and may thus be of the greatest good. See Grifol y Aliaga, pp. 218, 219.

8 The parish priests of the Philippines were called "reverend" or "devout" according as they were regulars or native seculars. See Barrantes's Instrucción primaria, p. 10.

9 See the titles of these orders from 1863 to 1894, post.

10 The Spanish government evinced a great interest "in giving the Filipinos a primary education commensurate with the standing of a civilized nation; but the intentions of the government were frustrated by ... the religious orders." The "great error of the Spanish nation" consisted "in placing in the hands of a few institutions [the religious orders] the future of her colonies in the extreme east, institutions which did not exist in their native country, and which sought only the private interests of the corporation or order to which they belonged. This entire plan of public instruction lived in the minds of the Spanish legislators, but was never put into practice." Tomás G. del Rosario, in Census of Philippines, iii, p. 582.

11 By 1894 there were 2,143 public schools in the Philippines, and 173 sets of provisions regulating them, or tending to the intellectual development of the people. These laws were only superficial. See Tomás G. del Rosario, Census of Philippines, iii, p. 593.

12 The central treasury of ways and means (Grifol y Aliaga, p. 3, note 2) having been suppressed, the expenses of this institution are at present [1894] defrayed as a charge on chapter 1, art. 1. of the budget of the local funds of the central treasury. In the budget of 1893–94, the appropriation of 10,450 pesos was set aside in the following manner:

		pesos
1	director,	800
6	professors, each 600 pesos,	4,800
1	drawing teacher,	600
1	vocal music teacher,	480
1	gymnastic teacher,	400
3	assistants, each 400 pesos,	1,200
15	resident pupils, each 120 pesos, for only three months,	450
	Wages of the attendants and servants of the school,	600
	For office expenses, conservation, and innovation of furniture, and other effects,	1,120
	Total,	10,450

13 The last classification made of the schools of this archipelago was that approved by superior decree, February 27, 1893, which was published in the Manila Gaceta, May 10 following. (Grifol y Aliaga, p. 4, note 5.)

14 "What contributed greatly, also, to the general backwardness of primary instruction was the small salary paid teachers, as it was impossible for them to live on what was paid them.... The small salary paralyzed any good will and ambition to work." T. G. del Rosario in Census of Philippines, iii, p. 595. See also, ante, p. 80, note 20.

15 Commonly called directorcillos (Grifol y Aliaga, p. 5, note 2).

16 The principalia was formed of those natives who have occupied petty government posts in the islands. See VOL. XVII, p. 331.

17 It is to be understood that the office of superior civil governor is equivalent to the present office of governor general (Grifol y Aliaga, p. 6, note 3).

18 This superior commission, appointed by superior decree of March 15, 1864, was suppressed by another decree of the superior civil government, February 23, 1871, in accordance with order no. 1183, of the ministry of the colonies, of December 5, 1870, by which was created the ad interim Superior Board of Public Instruction (Grifol y Aliaga, p. 6, note 4).

19 Now judge of first instance (Grifol y Aliaga, p. 6, note 5).

20 Now manager or subdelegate of the public treasury.

21 See Wm. B. Freer's Philippine Experiences of an American Teacher, chapter viii, pp. 97–109, for an account of methods used in normal instruction after American occupation.

22 Those pupils styled throughout this translation "regular" or in Spanish de numero, are those appointed directly by the government, the "de numero" (of the number) indicating that a certain number were thus appointed. The supernumerary (literally, "above the number") resident pupils are all others.

23 The clothing recommended by a sub-commission of the superior commission of primary instruction, November 24, 1864, (Grifol y Aliaga, p. 20), for regular and supernumerary resident pupils of the Manila normal school, was as follows:

		Estimated price	
		pesos fuertes	centavos
2	pairs of white pantaloons,	3	0
2	pairs of colored pantaloons,	3	0
2	white jackets,	2	0
1	coat of black alpaca,	2	50

2	black ribbons for the neck,	0	25
1	black cap, with the initials E. N. in silver, according to model,	2	0
2	pairs of shoes,	2	0
1	pair of chinelas [i.e., heelless slipper],	0	50
10	white shirts,	10	0
2	colored shirts,	1	50
12	pocket handkerchiefs,	1	0
12	pairs of socks,	1	0
4	pairs of underdrawers,	1	25
1	mat,	0	50
1	pillow,	0	75
4	pillow-cases,	0	75
4	sheets,	6	0
2	bed covers,	2	0
	Clothesbrush, comb, scissors, etc.,	1	0
	Total	40	0

24 i.e., All-Souls' day.

25 The three days preceding Lent.

26 The United States government continued this school, and gave it the support ($8,880, Mexican) formerly furnished by the Spanish government. See Report of Philippine Commission, 1900, i, p. 36.

27 May 21, 1840, Governor Lardizábal communicated to the Audiencia a royal order of October 4, 1839, in regard to the necessary conditions to be observed for the introduction and circulation of books in the islands, the previous designation of those deserving censure, given by his Majesty's fiscal, a censor being later appointed by the government, and another by the archbishop, the fiscal again reviewing the qualification and the censure; and if "it should result that there was sufficient grounds to prohibit the circulation of any work, because it contains principles, maxims, and doctrines contrary to the rights of the legitimate throne, or to the religion of the State, the book is not only to be taken back, but shipped back immediately." In case

of dispute between the two censors, the fiscal was to decide (royal order, November 19, 1840). See Montero y Vidal, iii, pp. 29, 30.

28 The important circular of the superior civil government of August 30, 1867 (concerning school attendance), treats of the manner of exercise of the supervision of the schools by the parish priests and provincial chiefs. Various other acts of legislation refer to the same matter. (Grifol y Aliaga, p. 118, note 1.)

29 The first two books mentioned are: the Catecismo de la doctrina cristiana, by Gaspar Astete, which has passed through many Spanish editions; and the Catéchisme historique, by Claude Fleury, which has passed through many different editions in many languages. José Francisco de Iturzaeta has published several works on educational subjects.

30 James A. LeRoy (Philippine Life, p. 203) says of the textbooks used in the Philippines: "After 1863, and up to the American conquest, the catechism remained the chief feature of daily work in the primary schools, often relegating all else to an insignificant place—much depending upon the preparation, at best a scanty one, of the teacher. A badly printed little 150 page textbook, prescribed by the government for the schools, was reader, writer, speller, arithmetic, geography, history of Spain and the world (Spain overshadowing), Spanish grammar (quite commonly not taught, because the teacher knew little or nothing of it), and handbook of religious and moral precepts (many pages). This book, moreover, shows how pitifully inadequate was the Filipino child's schooling at the very best; for often not even this textbook was employed, perhaps because the teacher was not prepared to use it."

31 The Philippine school report for 1892, entitled "Report of the children's schools for both sexes, at present in these islands, classified in accordance with the orders of his Excellency, the governor-general, in his decree of July 29, 1892," gives the following data. The schools are classified by grades, i.e., into schools of entrada, ascenso, and finishing schools of the second and first rank; and the order in charge of each village or province is also given. We condense from this report (a manuscript belonging to Rev. T. C. Middleton, O.S.A.), the number of schools in the various provinces, and the order or orders in charge of the same.

Augustinians

Province	No. of Schools
Abra,	28
Antique,	57
Bontoc,	8
Ilocos Norte,	30
Lepanto,	20
Quiangan,	2
Tiagan,	9
Union,	35
Augustinians and Franciscans	
Bulacan,	68
Augustinians and seculars	
Cebú,	120
Capiz,	65
Ilocos Sur,	61
Iloilo,	95
Pampanga,	54
Augustinians, Franciscans, and seculars	
Batangas,	46
Nueva Ecija,	49
Augustinians and Dominicans	
Tarlac,	34
Augustinians and all other orders	
Manila,	84
Franciscans	
Albay,	88
Burias,	4
Camarines Norte,	20
Camarines Sur,	68
Isla del Corregidor,	3
Infanta,	4
Franciscans and Dominicans	

Bataan,	36
Nueva Vizcaya,	16
Franciscans and Recollects	
Misamis,	74
Leite,	89
Principe,	5
Samar,	76
Surigao,	59
Tayabas,	45
Recollects	
Bohol,	94
Cavite,	50
Cottabato,	6
Calamianes,	10
Isla de Negros, occidental,	56
Isla de Negros, oriental,	34
Isabela de Basilan (?)	2
Masbate and Ticao,	23
Mindoro,	44
Paragua,	6
Romblon,	33
Zambales,	48
Recollects and Capuchins	
Carolinas, orientales,	4
Carolinas, occidentales,	3
Recollects and Dominicans	
Morong,	30
Recollects and seculars	
Zamboanga,	15
Dominicans	
Cagayan,	39
Islas Batanes,	14
Isabela de Luzón,	33

Laguna,	56
Pangasinan,	62
Jesuits	
Davao,	11
Dapitan,	12
Capuchins	
Marianas,	4

32 LeRoy, ut supra, pp. 203–204, says: "The advance in primary instruction from 1863 to 1896 was altogether notable, though the figures revealing it are largely superficial, after all, in their significance. The number of school buildings increased in the villages from seven hundred to twenty-one hundred, but the number of pupils did not reach two hundred thousand, in all probability, as against one hundred and thirty-five thousand in 1866."

33 Notwithstanding this admirable prescription, Tomás G. del Rosario, writing in Census of Philippines, iii, p. 595, says concerning the sanitary qualities of the Philippine schools: "The necessary sanitation was not observed in the schools, either to preserve the health of the children or for personal cleanliness, an important purpose of every educational system. Many of the schools were in the filthiest condition. They had no water-closets nor play-grounds, and no instruction was given in physical culture or in social matters."

34 According to article 25 of the penal code in force in these islands, corporal punishments, in addition to that of death, are perpetual chains, perpetual imprisonment, perpetual exile, perpetual banishment, temporal chains, temporal exile, temporal banishment, imprisonment at hard labor, lesser imprisonment, confinement, absolute perpetual and temporal disqualification, and absolute and special perpetual and temporal disqualification for any public charge, right of active or passive suffrage, profession, or trade. (Grifol y Aliaga, p. 123, note 2.)

35 The provisions (Grifol y Aliaga, p. 123, note 3) in force in regard to the salaries of teachers and assistants is that of the superior decree of July 29, 1892, which prescribes the following monthly salaries:

Boys' schools	Pesos
Término schoolteachers of the first grade,	40
Término schoolteachers of the second grade,	30

Ascenso schoolteachers,	22
Entrada schoolteachers,	17
Assistants of the first class,	13
Assistants of the second class,	8
Girls' schools	
Término schoolteachers,	26
Ascenso schoolteachers,	20
Entrada schoolteachers,	15
Assistants of the first class,	12
Assistants of the second class,	8

36 The superior decree of August 11, 1892, conceded annual allowances to men and women teachers who had taught for fifteen years, and had a good record. By the decree of July 20, 1894, traveling expenses were advanced to them. (Grifol y Aliaga, p. 124, note 3.)

37 The post of assistants of the first class belongs only to boys' término schools of the first and second class, and in those of girls to término and ascenso schools. Schools of other grades belong to assistants of the second class. Substitute assistants, namely, those who have no certificate, are entitled only to the monthly pay of four pesos. (Grifol y Aliaga, p. 124, note 4.)

38 Article 4 of the superior decree of May 7, 1871, rules that the teaching in the schools for adults shall last eight months per year, and be given at night, employing two hours every Monday, Thursday, and Saturday of each week. For the increased work, an amount of pay equal to what they received during the day was assigned to the teachers. This decree, as is evident, took away the dominical character given to the adult schools by these regulations of December 20, 1863. Notwithstanding the benefit of the increase of a fourth part of the pay to which teachers are entitled for the adult schools, very few such schools exist. In the budgets in force now, the figures for the payment of salaries for the teaching of adults only reach the sum of 573 pesos distributed among the provinces of Abra, Cebú, and Pampanga, in the proportion of 318, 210, and 45 pesos, respectively. (Grifol y Aliaga, p. 126, note 1.)

39 This Superior Council of Primary Instruction was suppressed by decree of the superior government, February 23, 1871, in accordance with order no. 1183, of the ministry of the colonies, December 5, 1870, by which was created the ad interim Superior Board of Public Instruction, in the manner prescribed by this article and article 15 of the royal decree of August 16, 1876, approved by royal order, June 5 of the following year. (Grifol y Aliaga, p. 126, note 2.)

40 Article 12, of the royal decree of May 19, 1893, relative to the municipal regulation of the villages of Luzón and Visayas, prescribes among the duties of the municipal captain that of "supervisor of the offices, schools, and municipal services." On account of this some have doubted whether the supervision of the schools was taken away from the parish priests to give it to the municipal captains. That doubt has been resolved by paragraph 4 of the provisional regulations of the said royal decree approved by decree of the general government December 9, 1893, for in said paragraph it is stated clearly and distinctly: "Without prejudice to the supervision in instruction which belongs to the parish priest, according to the regulations of 1863, whose powers are not altered in any way, the municipal tribunal shall constantly exercise a watch over primary instruction, etc." In our opinion, the above-mentioned doubt has no call for existence, since the above-mentioned article 12 of the royal decree of May 19, 1893, refers, as one can see by its own words, to the municipal schools, and those which are established in the villages of the archipelago cannot have that character attributed to them, since their expenses are not met by the municipal tribunals, nor does the appointment of the staff belong to them, but both are in charge of the central management. We believe, consequently, that the municipal captains have not even the secondary or supplementary supervision over the present schools of the archipelago, which is given them by paragraph 4 of the provisional regulations of December 9, 1893. (Grifol y Aliaga, pp. 126, 127, note 5.)

41 José de Calasanz, or as he is sometimes called, Joseph de Calasanzio, was born at Peralta, Cataluña, in 1556, and became a well-known ecclesiastic. On the occasion of a visit to Rome in 1592, touched with compassion at the neglected condition of the poor children, he renounced his ecclesiastical honors in Spain and devoted himself to the work of teaching in Rome. There he founded the Congregation of the Piaristes, consisting of regular clerics, about 1,600, whose object was the charitable education of poor children. The congregation was approved in 1617 by Paul V, who permitted members to take the simple vows and adopt their own rules. In 1621 Gregory XV gave them the title of "Regular clerics of the poor, under the protection of the Mother of God, for charitable schools." The work soon spread to the

rest of Italy, and to Germany and Poland. The mother house is at Rome. Its founder, who died in 1648, and was canonized in 1767, refused to accept the honors of bishop or cardinal. See Grande Encyclopédie.

42 Article 9 of the decree of the General Division of Civil Administration, of February 4, 1889, prescribes that on Sunday after mass the boys shall assemble at the school for an hour, so that the religious or parish priest may give them the religious teaching that he deems advisable (Grifol y Aliaga, p. 131, note 1).

43 In 1868, the studies for the normal school for female teachers were given in this school. The report on the education of girls presented by the friars at the exposition at Madrid in 1887 speaks as follows of it: "While strictly speaking there is no other normal school for female teachers than that of Nueva Cáceres, we believe, nevertheless, that this name can be given to the municipal school for girls of this capital, which is the only institution for young women supported from public funds—that is, from the funds of the municipality of Manila. It is true that schoolmistresses can, and actually do, graduate from any girls' school of this capital, and even from any private school, as, according to the law in force to secure this title, the passing of the regular examination is sufficient; but we believe that the only institution of this character in Manila which deserves the title of teachers' school is the municipal school, and we therefore include in the same chapter this school and that of Santa Isabel of Nueva Cáceres." See Census of Philippines, iii, pp. 615, 616.

44 In the Madrid periodical Nuestro Tiempo of November 25, 1905 (pp. 317–331), is an article by Eduardo Sanz y Escartin, of the Royal Academy of Moral and Political Sciences, entitled "La instrucción pública en España" ("Public instruction in Spain"), which gives a good résumé of the condition and needs of education in Spain at present.

45 The Gaceta de Manila is the continuation of the Boletín oficial de Filipinas, [Official Bulletin of Filipinas] which changed its name in accordance with a royal order of May 18, 1860. The first issue of the paper under the new name appeared Tuesday, February 26, 1861, and by a royal order of September 26 following, it was prescribed that all the villages of the archipelago should subscribe for the paper. By a decree issued in February 1861, it was declared that "all the official orders published in the Gaceta de Manila, whatever their origin, are to be regarded as official and authentic text." The Boletín was first issued in 1852, being the continuation of

the Diario de Manila, first published at the end of 1848. See Montero y Vidal, iii, pp. 306, 307; and Politica de España en Filipinas, iii, pp. 94, 95.

46 General Gándara paid special attention to primary education, and very important measures are due to him in the years 1867 and 1868. He was ably seconded by the secretary of the superior government, Vicente Barrantes. See Montero y Vidal, iii, p. 491.

47 Of the girls' school of Nueva-Cáceres, Tomás G. del Rosario says (Census of Philippines, iii, p. 616): "This school was founded by the bishop of that diocese, Fray Francisco Gainza, who inaugurated the studies on April 13, 1868, as a primary school for girls. On June 18, 1871, the studies of the normal school for women were taught there, as they were in that of Manila, by a decree of the government of King Amadeo, of Savoy. On May 26, 1873, the government of the Spanish republic decreed that each of the towns of that ecclesiastical province should hereafter make allowance for a similar number of young girls desirous of obtaining the title of teacher. Up to 1887, 177 girls had obtained certificates as teachers from this educational institution. The sisters of charity are in charge of the institution and of the education of the girls. This educational institution combined the characteristics of a school of primary instruction, a college for the education of boarding pupils, and a school for teachers, or normal school."

48 By decision of his Excellency the governor general, November 18, 1889, this article was revised to the effect that girls could enter the normal school for women teachers in Nueva Cáceres from the age of fourteen, although those with the teachers' certificate could not teach until they reached the age of twenty, according to the regulations. However, those older than sixteen and less than twenty who hold teachers' certificates may have the charge of schools, with the character of ad interim, so long as there are not other teachers with all the legal conditions required; and they are confirmed in these posts when they reach the age of twenty, according to the royal decree of November 24, 1893. (Grifol y Aliaga, p. 45, note 1.)

49 This article (see. Grifol y Aliaga, p. 244) is as follows: "The issuing of teachers' certificates of primary instruction, both normal and substitutes, their appointments to discharge the duties of the public schools, prescribe promotions, licenses, and other things connected with these functionaries, are in charge of the director [general of Civil Administration]."

50 Now the civil governor of Ambos Camarines (Grifol y Aliaga, p. 50, note 2).

51 This article (Grifol y Aliaga, pp. 401, 402) is as follows: "On the receipt of this circular, you shall have a meeting called of the persons who shall compose that provincial commission, in accordance with the above-cited art. 15 [of the royal decree of December 20, 1863]. Therein shall be read the annexed regulations which shall be cited, and those of this circular; and that provincial supervisory commission shall be declared as installed."

52 Of the position of woman in the Philippines and its cause, LeRoy says (Philippine Life, pp. 49, 50), although perhaps a trifle too strongly, as woman in the Philippines seems always to have enjoyed a certain amount of freedom, as compared to her sisters in other oriental countries: "The position of woman in the Philippines is not that typical of the Orient. If we may not say that the Philippines are not at all oriental in this respect, at any rate it is perfectly safe to say that in no other part of the Orient have women relatively so much freedom or do they play so large a part in the control of the family or in social and even industrial affairs. It is a common remark that Filipino women, both of the privileged and of the lower classes, are possessed of more character, and often too of more enterprise, than the men. There seems every reason for ascribing this relative improvement in the position of woman in the Philippines as compared with surrounding countries in the Orient to the influence of the Christian religion and the position which they have assumed under the teaching of the Church and the directorship of the friars."

53 Prueba de curso: the examination which is held at the end of each scholastic year or term, in the months of May and June, or (if it could not be held at that time, or if the student fails to pass) in the month of September of the new term. It must be taken by every pupil in order that he may matriculate the following term.—Francisco Giner de los Rios, of Madrid, of the Free Institution of Teaching.

54 Grado de revalida is the aggregate of exercises and examinations which must be taken by students (in spite of having been examined every year) on the completion of any course (for example that of elementary or superior schoolmaster or mistress), in order to obtain the certificate or diploma of their degree. There are many degrees: doctor, licentiate, bachelor, primary schoolmaster, etc.—Francisco Giner de los Rios.

55 Inscripción: the entering of a student in the school register. This word is also used in general for any record of a name, person, or thing, in a list or register.—Francisco Giner de los Rios.

56 Encerado: a square of oilskin, used as a slate or blackboard. See New Velázquez Dictionary.

57 Cedulas de inscripción are the documents which are given to the students, certifying that they have been registered in the matriculation books.—Francisco Giner de los Rios.

58 Literally, "Paper of payment to the State." This is a kind of stamped paper with its stamp authorized by the State, whose price varies according as the stamp represents the value of an impost which is collected in judicial and many other affairs. In the centers of State teaching, the fees which are to be paid by the students for their matriculation are not paid in money, but by presenting a special paper which is bought in certain shops.—Francisco Ginder de los Rios.

59 Hoja de estudios: the document on which are entered the studies which a student has had, and in which he has been examined, with their official value.—Francisco Giner de los Rios.

60 Cedula personal: an official document declaring the name, occupation, domicile, etc., of the bearer, and serving for identification. See New Velázquez Dictionary.

61 Matrícula de honor: a reward obtained by the best students of each class, by virtue of the term examinations. By this reward they are registered free in the matriculation of the following year.—Francisco Giner de los Rios.

62 St. Stanislas Kostka (or Kotska) was born of a noble Polish family in 1550. While pursuing his studies at Vienna (1563–66), in the Jesuit college, his predilection to the religious life was clearly manifest, but since the provincial would not receive him there without the consent of his parents, he ran away, and tried to gain admission to the Jesuit order in Dilingen, Germany. To avoid the pursuit of his parents he was sent to Rome, where he was received into the order by St. Francis Borja in 1567. Naturally of a delicate constitution, the extreme bodily mortifications which he practiced in his youthful enthusiasm undermined his health, and he died August 14, 1568, at the age of eighteen. See Baring Gould's Lives of the Saints (London, 1898), xiii, pp. 322–325.

63 i.e., the decree of the government, ordering "let it be done."

64 Governor Izquierdo [1871–73] paid considerable attention to primary education, in which he was aided by José Patricio Clemente, secretary of the superior government. See Montero y Vidal, iii, p. 621.

65 The Ensayo de gramática Hispano-Tagala (Manila, 1878) by the Recollect, Fray Toribio Minguella de la Merced. Retana says of this book

(Biblioteca filipina, p. 149): "In my opinion the method of this book is the most suitable for study by Spaniards, who do not haze any knowledge of Latin, studied after the ancient method." Minguella published in 1886, Methodo práctico para que los niños y niñas de las provincias Tagalas aprendan á hablar castellano (Practical method for boys and girls to learn to talk Castilian). This latter book received a reward in public contest.

66 The author of this book is Castor Aguilera y Porta.

67 Its author is Ramón Irureta Goyena.

68 By Benito Francia.

DOMINICAN EDUCATIONAL INSTITUTIONS, 1896-1897

STATISTICS OF THE STUDENTS WHO STUDIED IN THE COLLEGES OF THE DOMINICAN FATHERS IN THE YEAR 1896–1897

College and University of Santo Tomás

The college was founded by the corporation of the Dominicans in 1612, and its foundation approved by King Felipe IV, in December, 1623,1 as appears from the Recopilación de las Indias (ley liii, título xxii, libro i). It was declared a university by brief of his Holiness, Innocent X, in 1645, and King Carlos II received it under his protection and royal patronage in 1680. Finally, King Carlos III, by a decree of March 7, 1785, conferred on it the title of Royal, giving it the titles and honors of the universities of the Spanish monarchy. The collegiates with beca (free) numbered thirty-six in 1896.

Pupils matriculated in 1896 in the different courses

Courses	Degrees conferred	
Course in Theology	15	2
„ in Canons	7	3
„ in Jurisprudence	1,298	17
„ in the Profession of Notary	244	4
„ *in Medicine*	857	8
Course in Pharmacy	169	2
„ in Philosophy and Letters	160	
„ in Sciences	54	
Practitioners of Medicine	205	
„ of Pharmacy	38	
Midwives	12	
Total	3,059	[36]

College of San Juan de Letrán2

This college was founded under the title of San Pedro y San Pablo in the year 1640, for the purpose of giving primary instruction to the poor and orphaned children of Spanish parents. The most reverend master-general, Fray Tomás Turco, confirmed its erection in 1644. The provincial chapter of 1652 accepted it as a house of the province at the request of the governor-general with the approbation of the archbishop of Manila. In the year 1683, it was called the college of San Juan de Letrán, and it has been so called to our day.3

Course for 1896–1897

Rector and father professors		13
Brother masters of primary instruction		4
Resident [internos]	collegiates	220
Half Resident	„	50
Filipino assistants (servants)		8
[Total]		295

Class of day pupils

Matriculated in general studies for the bachelor's degree	5,363
Matriculated for practical studies (specialists)	337
Total	5,700

Titles conferred

Bachelor of Arts	149
Professors of secondary instruction	4
Skilled agriculturalists and appraisers of lands	2
Skilled merchants	17
mechanics	5

College of San Alberto Magno

This college was founded by the Dominican corporation in the year 1891, in the village of Dagupan, in the province of Pangasinan. The building was from the first constructed for the purpose for which it was destined.

Course of 1896–1897

Rector and teachers	8
Brother master of primary instruction	1
Resident pupils	96
Matriculated	842
Total	947

School of Santa Catalina de Sena4

This school is directed by the Dominican sisters and was founded in 1698. In the year 1896 it had:

Nuns who acted as teachers	16
Lay sisters	15
Girls in residence	140
Servants and florists	52
Total	223

School of Nuestra Señora del Rosario, of Lingayén (Pangasinan)

(Founded by the corporation, in 1890)

Nuns who act as teachers	7
Resident pupils	53
Non-resident pupils	13
Servants	10
Total	83

School of Nuestra Señora del Rosario of Vigan (Founded in 1893)

Nuns who act as teachers	7
Pupils in residence	65
Servants	7
[Total]	79

School of Santa Ymelda of Tuguegarao (Cagayán) (Founded in 1892)

Nuns	8
Pupils in residence	77
Non-resident pupils	10
Half pensioners	4
Servants	11
[Total]	110

1 This law is dated Nov. 27, 1623, q.v., VOL. XX, pp. 260, 261.

2 In 1867 the college of San Juan de Letran was declared a college of secondary education. See Montero y Vidal, iii, p. 485.

3 This college was considered as the Institute of the university (note on MS.).

4 The pupils of the schools directed by nuns are girls.

REPORT OF RELIGIOUS SCHOOLS, 1897

Relation of the houses and number of pupils1 whom the sisters of charity had in a school here in Filipinas in the year 1897

1. Here in Manila, they had all the schools which they have at present, namely, the school of La Concordia, that of Santa Ysabel, that of Santa Rosa, and that of Looban.

2. In the school of La Concordia, there were 39 sisters and 300 pupils.

In that of Santa Ysabel 14 sisters and 150 pupils.

In Santa Rosa, 11 sisters and 200 pupils.

In the school of Looban, 11 sisters and 170 collegiates.

3. In addition, they had here in Manila the military hospital, the hospital of St. John of God, the municipal school, and the hospice of San José.

In St. John of God, there were 27 sisters and 400 patients.

In the military hospital, 24 sisters and 300 patients.

In the hospice of San José, 14 sisters and 250 destitute people, counting poor, patients, and orphan children.

In the municipal school, there were 10 sisters and about 300 girls attended it. At present they still have these charitable houses with the exception of the military hospital and the municipal school.

4. Besides these houses here in Manila, they had in the provinces, the schools which they still have.

In Jaro (Iloilo), the school of San José, in which were 12 sisters and 150 scholars.

In Cebu in the same capital, the school of the Immaculate Conception, with 28 sisters and 200 scholars. They have also the hospital and the house of relief.

In Nueva Cáceres (Camarines), the school of Santa Ysabel, in which were 13 sisters and 170 scholars.

In Cavite they also had the hospital of St. John of God, and that of Cañacao. In the former were 16 sisters and 170 patients, and in the latter 16 sisters and 200 patients.

Relation of the number of pupils in the seminary schools here in Filipinas in the year 1897

1. All the seminary schools were in charge of Paulist fathers, except that of Vigan. In the seminary of this city of Manila there were 5 fathers and 3 brothers, while the pupils or seminarists numbered about 40. In addition they had the house which they own at present, in San Marcelino. There were 6 fathers and two brothers whose efforts were devoted to propagating and extending worship, and directing as well the sisters of charity.

2. In the seminary school of Jaro, there were, in the said year, 9 fathers and 2 brothers, and about 600 pupils of whom 200 were regular.

3. In the seminary school of Cebú, there were also 9 fathers and 2 brothers resident, and the number of pupils was about 800, those resident numbering about 300.

4. In that of Nueva Cáceres there was the same number of fathers and brothers as in the seminaries of Jaro and Cebú, while the pupils numbered about 700.

[Endorsed in English: "Congregation of St. Vi[n]cent of Paul."]

1 Throughout the first portion of this document, by "pupils" must be understood "girls."

EDUCATIONAL INSTITUTIONS
OF THE RECOLLECTS

Beaterio de Santa Rita

It is located on the ground plot of San Sebastian, in a district of the same name, outside the walls of Manila, where the Augustinian Recollect fathers have a convent whose foundation dates from the year 1621, and a magnificent iron church dedicated in the year 1891, in which is venerated the miraculous image of our Lady of Carmel.

This beaterio, separated from the convent only by the portico which gives entrance to the church, was founded about the year 1730, and was due principally to our father Fray Andrés de San Fulgencio, who, acceding to the reiterated urgings and petitions of some pious women, who desired to live in retreat from the excitement of the world, built them a house, and gave them the habit of manteletas, or Tertiaries of the Augustinian order.

The preferred occupations in which those pious women who have had the good fortune to take our holy habit in this beaterio, have busied themselves, have been, and are at present, beside their own sanctification, the solid and Christian instruction and education of a certain number of girls; the cleaning and renovating of our church of San Sebastian; and the propagation of worship and devotion to our Lady of Carmel, for whom they act as the perpetual attendants.

They lead a very austere life, and one completely abstracted from the world, scarcely ever leaving the beaterio unless to go to the church, and it is a very remarkable circumstance that in the two hundred years almost, which have elapsed since their foundation, no sister who has taken the habit has abandoned it in order to return to the world.

The inspection and direction of the beaterio belong to the father prior of the convent of San Sebastian, who, with the consent of our father provincial, dictates the suitable provisions for maintaining in that holy house the spirit of piety with which it was founded.

School of San José of Bacolod, Negros

In the intermediary chapter, celebrated in the convent of Manila, October 31, 1895, the installation (in Bacolod, the capital of the island of Negros) of a college of primary and secondary instruction, was determined upon. That determination of the chapter was approved by the most reverend apostolic father, commissary-general of the order, December 18, of the same year 95. January 28, 1896, the very reverend father provincial, Fray Andrés Ferrero, now his Excellency, the bishop of Jaro, petitioned his Excellency the governor-general to have the kindness to authorize him as founder of a school of primary and secondary instruction in the province of Negros under the advocacy of San José, in which they could establish all the courses, the study of which was required in order to obtain the degree of bachelor of arts.

The superior government acceded to the petition by a decree dated February 21, of the same year, on condition of first receiving a favorable report from the very reverend father rector of the royal and pontifical university of Manila. In June of the same year they proceeded to the opening of the school of Bacolod, which was placed under the said university. The disasters that occurred in this archipelago in consequence of the insurrection, have been the cause of this school running for only two years.

Seminary school of Vigan

The corporation of Augustinian Recollects had in its charge the seminary of Vigan between the years 1882 and April, 1895. During that time various courses were added, and, in July, 1892, the complete plan of studies for secondary instruction was established in the said seminary, and it was officially placed under the university of Manila.

School of Santa Rosa

The foundation of this school having been authorized by a royal decree of September 22, 1774, its direction and government (besides that which by right belongs to the diocesan ecclesiastical authority) was committed to the senior auditor, who was afterwards called the president of the royal Audiencia. He was aided by a council of four votes. Thus it continued until December 17, 1891, in which in accordance with a royal order of October 6, of the same year, the general government of these islands appointed as president of the assembly the very reverend father provincial of the Recollects. From that time all the intervention and authority which thitherto had been held by the presidents of the royal Audiencia, were delegated to him.

The individuals composing the Administration Board are appointed by the archbishop of Manila, at the proposal of the father president. The Board informs his reverend Excellency, of the most important decisions which are made so that he may approve them.

THE FRIAR VIEWPOINT

I-EDUCATION

The truth in this matter. If the means are sufficient and efficacious, the ends will be obtained. Uniformity in the method.

There are matters of importance so transcendental in the progressive evolution of peoples, and which determine in so efficacious a manner the greater or less future and civilization of those peoples, that they cannot be less than regarded by men who govern with the most profound attention and persevering study, converting them into the object of their studies, of their zeal, and of their energies. Perhaps nothing occupies the foremost place with more reason and right than education. The desire of happiness is as natural as it is legitimate in man. That desire is so noble and elevated an aspiration, and man feels that desire in the bottom of his soul with so irresistible a force than one may say without any kind of exaggeration, that even unconsciously he is dragged along by it. Hence, every new step that he takes, every ray of light that he perceives, every unknown point that he discovers in that road, induces one to believe that it is one factor more for arrival at a safe port, one greater facility which he acquires for the attainment of that end. And since that end in man cannot be more than the highest end, hence it is that he feels in an invincible manner the necessity of its possession, which is that which constitutes the highest perfection of that privileged creature [man]. Now, then, in order to attain possession of that end, it is necessary to know it, and in order that it may have a practical result, one must know the means which conduce to it, and perfect them so that the result may be complete. Most marvelously is this trust filled by the teaching which has as its direct object the education and perfection of the faculties of man, which are the only means conducive to the knowledge and possession of God—the supreme end, hence, the highest happiness of man. Education is the object and noble finality of teaching, the unfolding and perfection of the faculties of man, both in the physical order, and in the intellectual, esthetic, and moral; to develop the physical energies, producing the most perfect health and robustness of the body, to extend the horizons of the intelligence, the greater number of points of knowledge conducing to the discovery of truth proportioning it; increasing and ennobling man's sentiments for beauty, and directing the will along the road of the good and the just, and removing it from their opposites, the evil and unjust. It is the primordial object and noblest end of every man who governs to endeavor to broaden, extend, and perfect instruction among the peoples under the control of his government and direction.

It is the most sacred duty of every gubernatorial authority to excogitate and choose the most suitable, safe, and correct methods of teaching for the attainment of so sacred an end. It cannot be even doubted that the authors of our traditional legislation for the Indias had other motives than the accuracy and rectitude in the creation of the laws concerning instruction, or other primordial end in it than the knowledge and adoration of God, the supreme end of man on earth; and as a means, the knowledge of the divine mysteries, of the revealed truths, in a word, of the Catholic religion, among the human beings of the New World. Rapid without doubt was the progress which the Catholic faith made in the immense territories of that unknown world, notwithstanding the interminable series of difficulties which our fervent missionaries, covetous to gain souls for God, were to meet in the evangelization of so many races and so numerous peoples divided by so diverse languages, which were so many other obstacles superable by their strong desire and never-satisfied zeal. In order to conquer those difficulties, and that that zeal might be more productive for the cause of religion, and more advantageous for the believers, fifty-eight years after the immortal Colón had discovered this world full of marvels, the first law was dictated in regard to the creation of schools for the teaching of Castilian, signed by Carlos V while governing at Valladolid, June 7, and reproduced July 17, 1550. Such is law xviii, título i, book vi, which reads as follows.

"Having made particular examination in regard to whether, even in the most perfect language of the Indians, the ministers of our holy Catholic faith can explain themselves well and fittingly, we have recognized that that is impossible without committing great discords and imperfections; and although chairs are founded where the priests who shall instruct the Indians may be taught, this is not a fitting remedy because of the great diversity of languages; and having resolved that it will be advantageous to introduce the Castilian language: we command teachers to be given to the Indians, in order to teach those who wish of their own accord to study it, in the way which will be of least trouble and without expense to them. It has appeared that this can be well done by the sacristans, as in the villages of these kingdoms they teach reading, writing, and the Christian doctrine."

But one can immediately understand that teachers who taught without any charge, who might be sacristans, and Indians who wished to study voluntarily, were not fitting factors to attain the most praiseworthy end which the legislator proposed to himself; and in fact it could not have given the desired result since eighty-four years afterwards, law v, título xiii, book i, was issued by Felipe IV, without indicating the means, in Madrid, March 2, 1634, and repeated two years afterward, on November 4, which reads as follows: "We ask and request the archbishops and the bishops to provide and order the curas and missionaries of the Indians in their dioceses, by the use of the mildest means, to arrange and direct that all the Indians be taught the Spanish language, and in that language the Christian doctrine, so that they may become more capable of understanding the mysteries of our holy Catholic faith and so that other advantages may be gained for their salvation, and follow in their government and method of life." The fulfilment of both laws [was] recorded by the royal decree of March 20, 1686,1 and those laws were at the same time extended to Filipinas, since the desire of the legislator was the same in both parts, namely, "to consult upon what is the most efficacious means for destroying the idolatries incurred at present by the majority of the Indians as was true at the beginning of their conversion, etc.," as is said in the above-mentioned royal decree. From that decree one infers a wholesome instruction for Filipinas; but it is no wonder that the Filipinos have not learned Castilian, and that they abandon their primitive superstitions with difficulty, when the Americans of greater capacity than they, with greater means, with a powerful and constant stream of Christian civilization, carried by numerous missionaries, and a greater European emigration, after two centuries did not know the Castilian speech, and the majority were sunk in their idolatries, a thing which does not occur with the masses of the Filipinos, although they are not a little superstitious, a quality exhibited in more or less degree by numerous peoples of Europa after so many centuries of illumination.

For the same end and filled with the same spirit was issued the royal decree of April 16, 1770, which, like the preceding one, was also extended to Filipinas, as were also other later ones, all of which were animated by the most Christian zeal, so that the Indians might learn better the mysteries and doctrinal points of the Catholic religion, for the easier and surer salvation of their souls. Without danger of taking from these laws any valuable data, in accordance with the necessity which counsels it, let us reduce ourselves for the moment to a review of the orders given directly for Filipinas which are found in the celebrated ordinances, first in those given by Corcuera in the year 1642, revised by Cruzat in 1696, and added to by their successors. Among them is one, the 52d, of Governor-general Solis, marquis of Obando, dated October 19, 1752. Among other things that ordinance says: "Through my desires of aiding with the greatest exactness the spiritual and temporal welfare of those vassals, supplying them with all the means of acquiring and consolidating it, I have resolved to order, as by the present I do order and command, said governors, corregidors, alcaldes-mayor, and other justices of these islands, that exactly and punctually, and without interpretation or opinion, they give and cause to be given the most opportune measures, so that in the villages of their districts they demand, establish, and found, from this day forward, schools where the children of the natives and other inhabitants of their districts may be educated and taught (in primary letters in the Castilian or Spanish language), seeing to it earnestly and carefully that they study, learn, and receive education in that language and not in that of the country or any other. They shall work for its greater increase, extension, and intelligence, without consenting or allowing ... this determination to be violated, or schools of any other language to be erected or started, under penalty of five hundred [pesos?] applied in the manner decreed by this superior government.... For that purpose, and so that it may have the fullest effect, I revoke, annul, and declare of no use and value ordinance 29, which declares that Spaniards shall not be allowed to live in or remain in the villages of the Indians; for in the future they must be admitted to such residence. The alcaldes-mayor and justices shall see to it that such people live in a Christian manner and according to the commands of God; and they shall arrest, punish, and exile those who fail in this matter. This is to be understood of the schools which are to be supported and maintained at the cost of the villages themselves and of the funds which the communal treasuries shall have assigned for those of the languages of the country (for as abovesaid the latter must cease and shall cease in proportion as the schools for teaching in the Castilian language shall be built and established); and for the attainment of the duties and posts of governors and other honorable military posts it shall be a necessary qualification that those on whom they are conferred be the most capable, experienced, and clever in being able to read, talk, and write, in the above-mentioned Spanish language, and such posts must be given to such persons and not to others," etc.

In accordance with all that which is faithfully quoted in regard to this particular, is ordinance 25 of the zealous Raón in 1768, which reads as follows: "As it is very important that there be good schoolteachers for the teaching of the Indians, and as it is advisable for them to learn the Spanish language in order to know the Christian doctrine better, and since the salary of one peso and one cabán of rice, which it is the custom to give them from the communal funds each month, is very little, it is ordered that the alcaldes, with the intervention of the curas, or missionary ministers, make a computation of the salary which can be given in each village (in proportion to its tributes) to the schoolteacher, giving an account thereof to the superior government for its approval.... For, with the increase of salaries, better teachers can be had and the end of law xviii, título i, book vi, as will be related hereafter, can be better attained." This is fulfilled at greater length in ordinance or article 93, reading as follows: "In accordance with section 52 of the ancient ordinances, and 17 of those drawn up by governor Don Pedro Manuel de Arandía, it is strictly and rigorously ordered the alcaldes-mayor, and asked and petitioned from the father ministers, that each one, in so far as concerns him, shall apply his zeal to the end that in all the villages there should be one schoolmaster well instructed in the Spanish language, and that he teach the Indians to read and write in it, the Christian doctrine, and other prayers, as is ordered by the king, our sovereign, in his royal decree of June 5, 1754, because of the most serious disadvantages which result by doing the contrary to the religion and the state. For the attainment of so important teaching, the salary of each teacher shall be paid punctually from the communal funds, namely, one peso and one cabán of rice per month. Permission is given to the above-mentioned alcaldes-mayor so that, in the large villages and in proportion to the capacity of said teachers, they may increase their salary by giving information thereof to the superior government for its approval, as is stated in section 25. The above-mentioned teachers shall be informed that, if they do not teach the Indians, and instruct them in the Spanish language, they will be condemned to make restitution of the pay which they shall have received, and shall be deprived of holding any post in these islands and punished at the will of said alcaldes. The latter, especially in their visit to the villages of their provinces, shall investigate with particular care the observance of the abovesaid, and shall inform the superior government.... It is to be noted that for any slight omission of the alcaldes in regard to this most important point, they shall incur the indignation of the superior tribunals, and shall be rigorously punished and fined in proportion to their lack of zeal and fulfilment of this section; for experience has taught that for particular ends and unjust laxity or neglect they have proceeded hitherto with little zeal and with total want of observance of law xviii, título i, book vi, which is corroborated and confirmed by many royal decrees and by the abovesaid sections of the ordinances preceding that law."

Since we are decided to make an exact and complete adjustment of accounts treating of this matter, we transcribe here, in order to attain that, whatever has to do most especially with both ancient and modern legislation, in order to remove at once the mask under which the detractors of the religious orders have been masquerading, blaming them openly for the backward state of the Filipino villages, for their deficiency in education and especially for the ignorance of Castilian, without other proof than the completely gratuitous assertion that those religious orders have constantly opposed the development of education and, in a resolute manner, the study of Castilian.2

In order to prove this supposed opposition, they adduce as an argument (which is negative, and, consequently, of no value) the fact that although the teaching (and with it the Castilian speech) was ordered from the beginning of the conquest with evident insistence and under heavy penalties, the established laws have not given the abundant results which were to be desired. Now, because those results have not been obtained, are the missionaries to blame? The supposition made in order to hurl this crimination upon the religious orders is not serious nor can it be cited by persons who esteem themselves as sensible and reasonable beings.

Before that criminal supposition and that groundless crimination it is fitting to ask: "Were those laws, given with the most just desire and the most holy finality, as is that of christianizing those idolatrous souls and guaranteeing them in the faith of Jesus Christ, suitable for the production of the desired ends? Were the means, which were proposed in those laws, conducive to the end which was being prosecuted? Nay, more, granting the sufficiency of those laws and the propriety of those means for the American districts, since those laws were given for them, was it within the bonds of reason to adapt them with equal propriety and sufficiency to Filipinas?" If it is impossible to grant the first, it is evidently impossible to assent to the second as certain.

It has been shown that law xviii was given in the year 1550, or fifty-eight years after the discovery of the New World. One hundred and forty-two years later that order was repeated by means of law v, of 1634, the fulfilment of which was recorded in 1686, or one hundred and ninety-four years after our arrival on the American coasts. Those laws had been, if not barren, of little fruit, whenever the cause for repeating that law was to banish the idolatries in which the majority of the Indians are now sunk, as they were at the beginning of the conversions. How can that development in instruction be acquired "with Indians who would like to learn, when taught by teachers without pay, and which, so that the teachers might not cost anything, could be well done by the sacristans," who would immediately be Indians like the pupils, doubtless stupid in learning and incapable of teaching the Catholic doctrine in Castilian? Now then, if those laws were inefficient in the American districts, a country more compact, could they be more efficient in Filipinas, which is composed of many islands; could those means exercise more influence on the intellects of those islanders who are of less capacity than the Americans, and the latter were directly invaded by a constant and powerful stream of civilization, catechised and administered by a numerous pleiad of missionaries when the islands of Urdaneta and Legazpi did not receive more than the residues or crumbs, which, both of the former and the latter, came by way of Acapulco—in America with an invader who carried almost all before him, and who tended by his number to cause the pure primitive race to disappear, exactly the contrary to what occurs in the Filipino country, where the native race, in an imposing mass, is above all absorption, this idea being sufficient only so that not even with very many means more powerful than those hitherto placed in practice can they attain the effects which the laws demand?

Consequently, the laws were not adaptable to that country for which they were not made, and not even was that country known when law xviii was given. Neither have the means or factors which have been put in play since, been in relation, even remote relation, with the ends whose attainment is desired.

On one hand, the great scarcity of missionaries scattered among so numerous islands (each one occupying a most extensive territory, with scarcely any communication [with one another], with a work both arduous and multiple, in all the orders, especially in the learning of so diverse and most difficult languages, and the adaptation of these languages in regard to their characters, phonetics, pronunciation, etc., to our characters, spelling, etc., a knowledge attained afterward by prolonged and constant phonological and philological studies), abandoned to their own resources and energies, since it is known that for many dozens of leguas there was no other Spaniard than the missionary, occupied preferably in the administration of sacraments and evangelization and the conservation of so numerous fields of Christendom; on the other hand the means which the laws granted them, entirely null and void, as has been shown, as is also the result obtained by the last royal decree of 1686, by which it is newly ordered "that schools be established and teachers appointed for the Indians, in order to teach the Castilian language to those who would voluntarily wish to learn it, in the way that may be of less trouble to them and without expense;" and with this clause of voluntary instruction, without trouble and without expense, since the natives were scattered in so many and so distant villages or reductions, and had no teachers, not since they knew the Castilian language, but that they could not even know it except by a rudimentary method in their own language: was there any possibility even that that beautiful language whose knowledge would have freed the missionary from so many sorrows, from so painful labor, from so continual anxieties as the detractors of those orders cannot even imagine, could be taught? Notwithstanding, it will be proved by unassailable documents that those missionaries with some useless laws, most of them deficient, have obtained what no one else could have obtained.

Those religious orders, then, have not been the enemies, but the great friends, of instruction. They Have not been opposed, nor only slight lovers of its development, but decided well-wishers, and even enthusiasts in its greater development; and in order to achieve that, the missionaries and parish priests have done that which very few, perhaps no one, could have done: namely, to create schools wherever they preached the gospel; to support them by all means, and even pay them from their scant savings; to bring to a head all classes of philological work; to compile methods, grammars, innumerable dictionaries, books of doctrine, of doctrinal discourses, and many others which besides illuminating the understanding, strengthened the souls in the faith, in accordance with the spirit of those laws.

Furthermore, do the detractors of the religious believe that, if the alcaldes, corregidors, and justices, threatened with very severe penalties by those laws, were convinced of the fact that the missionaries were opposed to the teaching in that part which was viable or feasible, they would not have used their authority to punish, correct, or prevent, that opposition? The ordinances above copied are a copy of the laws given for America, as already mentioned, and suffer in great measure from their peculiarity and lack of application, especially in what regards the teaching of Castilian.

It was in every point impossible that, with the elements possessed by the alcaldes-mayor, corregidors, and governors, they could have observed ordinance 52 of the marquis of Obando. That ordinance contains orders that are positively impracticable and even contradictory. On one side it is ordered "that schools be erected where the children of the natives may be educated (in primary letters in the Castilian language) seeing to it that in this language and not in that of the country, or in any other, they study, be taught, and educated, and that schools of another language be not erected or started under penalty of 500 [pesos?] applied at the will of this superior government." This is ordered absolutely and without any limitation in immense districts where there is not a single school of Castilian, nor methods, nor grammars, nor dictionaries, nor any other method of teaching that language, nor teachers to teach it, nor scarcely any Indians who have been able to learn it, as they have not had any great familiarity with Spaniards who were prohibited by ordinance 29 from residing in the villages of the Indians. This happened in the year 1752. That prohibition was suppressed by the above-mentioned ordinance 52. By the same ordinance was prescribed the quota which the communal funds were to pay to the teachers, which makes one see immediately the contradiction of the finality of the preceding order with that stating "because as abovesaid, these languages must cease and shall cease in proportion as schools for the Castilian language shall be erected and established;" the only ones who were ordered to pay.

It results, therefore, quite evidently, both from the context of the latter ordinance and from ordinance 17 of Arandía, and 25 and 93 of Raón, that in the Filipino provinces and districts there were no means of establishing instruction in Castilian; and that the only schools which were ordered to be paid from the communal funds were those which should be established with that instruction. Consequently, neither the alcaldes and other justices threatened with very severe penalties, and "the anger of the superior tribunals" nor the teachers "condemned to make restitution of the pay which they had received," and punished according to the order of the alcaldes, could make in their promises and villages those laws, given in the Peninsula and in the official residence of the first authority of the islands, viable or practicable. How many laws are there which are very good and of elevated ends, but barren and unpractical, as they lack practical meaning! However, in the midst of so many contradictions and difficulties, in the midst of a work so toilsome and without rest, in spite of the penury and scarcity which God alone can, and knows how to, appreciate, in constant struggle with the elements and the Moros, having to create it and conserve it all, it can be no less than contemplated with pride by every good Spaniard that those heroic and humble sons of España attended from the beginning of the conquest to teaching with a zeal worthy of all praise.

A precious testimony of this is that mentioned by the erudite father Augustín María, O.S.A. in his Historia del Insigne convento de San Pablo de Manila [i.e., History of the glorious convent of San Pablo in Manila], which is preserved unedited in the archives of said convent, when he says: "In the same year (1571) was founded this convent and church of San Pablo, which is the chief one of this province, the capitular house for novitiates, and of studies in grammar, arts, theology, and canons for Indians and creoles, until the Jesuits came and opened public schools." Passing by those teaching centers created in Manila by the religious orders scarcely yet born in those islands, omitting the introduction of printing, a powerful means for progress, by those orders, some decades after their establishment in the islands, and limiting ourselves only to the creation of schools and the progress of primary instruction, we do not fear to affirm that before our legislators occupied themselves in giving laws for teaching in Filipinas, laws had been proclaimed in the assemblies of the religious orders. Before the famous ordinances of Obando and of Raón had been published, the printing houses of the said orders had already printed works entitled: Práctica del Ministerio que siguen los religiosos del orden de N. P. S. Agustín en Philippinas [i.e., Practice of the ministry followed by the religious of the order of our father St. Augustine in Philippinas]; and the Práctica de párrocos dominicana [i.e., Practice of the Dominican parish priest]. Before treating of one or the other it is a duty of historical justice to discard the two above-cited laws given for the New World, the first in 1550, fifteen years before the conquest of Filipinas, and the second in 1634, and both recorded in the royal decree of 1686,3 given likewise for América and all extended to the archipelago of Legazpi. Now then, much before those last dates, the Augustinian order in its tenth provincial chapter, held May 9, 1596, in which the reverend father, Fray Lorenzo de León, was elected provincial, among the acts and resolutions which it established, which are capitular laws, compulsory on all the religious of the province, was the following: "It is enjoined upon all the ministers of Indians, that just as the schoolboys are taught to read and write, they be taught also to speak our Spanish language, because of the great culture and profit which follow therefrom." That document was providentially conserved in the secretary's office of the convent of San Pablo in Manila, notwithstanding the devastation which that convent suffered and the loss of precious documents during the English invasion.

They did not cease to hope for the abundant fruits which resulted from such wise rules as the above, and the schools were created and continued to increase in a remarkable manner. In order that there might be uniformity in the method of teaching, in the Augustinian provincial chapter, held in Manila in August 1712, the practice of the ministry prescribed in the [provincial] chapter of April 19, 1698, was ordered to be observed in definite terms. That was directed even in the chapter held May 17, 1716, in which it was ordered by minute 21 that the provincial elect, reverend father Fray Tomás Ortiz "should make a Práctica del Ministerio" [i.e., Practice of the Ministry] and after it was made to send it through the provinces, "so that all the religious might observe it;" he did that, signing the circular which accompanied said Práctica, at Tondo, August 10, of the abovesaid year. From this Práctica, we copy the following paragraph in regard to the schools: ``Number 79. Not only by a decree of his Majesty, but also by his own obligation, the minister must use all diligence and care in promoting and conserving the schools for children in the villages. And when he encounters difficulty in this, it will be advisable, and many times necessary, for him to make use of the alcaldes-mayor, so that they may obtain by their influence what the ministers could not obtain in this matter by their own efforts. And if the parents refuse to send their children, the ministers shall also be able to inform the alcaldes-mayor [i.e., sub-alcaldes] of it in order that the latter may force them to do it. And above all, the minister ought to be very happy in contriving to conserve the schools, and in suffering with patience the great resistance which is found among the natives to the schools. It will be well to care for them with some expenses for their conservation, for they are very useful and necessary." Beyond this valuable paragraph are prescribed the days for school and the hours and exercises in which the children are to be employed.

This same Práctica del Ministerio remarkably increased by its author, the reverend father Fray Tomás Ortiz, was printed in "Manila, in the convent of Nuestra Señora de los Angeles [i.e., Our Lady of the Angels], in the year 1731," and we copy from it, for the eternal and most valuable testimony in proof of our assertion, the principal paragraph, which reads as follows:

"158. The father ministers, in fulfilment of their duty, are obliged to procure, by all means and methods possible, and, if necessary, by means of royal justices, that all the villages, both capitals and visitas, shall have schools, and that all the boys attend them daily. If the natives of the visitas refuse or are unable to support schools, the boys of those visitas shall be obliged to go to the schools of the capitals, for in addition to the schools being so necessary as are attested by ecclesiastical and secular laws, the absence of schools occasions many spiritual and temporal losses, as is taught by experience. Among others, one is the vast ignorance suffered in much of what is necessary for confession in order that they may become Christians and live like rational people.

"In order to be able to conquer the difficulties which some generally find in maintaining schools, it is necessary for the father ministers to procure and solicit two things: one is that ministers be assigned with salaries suitable for their support; the other is that the children have primers or books for reading and paper for writing. When these two things cannot be obtained by other means than at the cost of the father ministers, they must not therefore excuse themselves from giving what is necessary for the said two things. For, besides the fact that they will be doing a great alms thereby, they will also obtain great relief in the teaching of the boys, and will avoid many spiritual and temporal losses of the villages, to which by their office they are obliged. And if the end cannot be obtained without the means, so also the schools cannot be obtained without any expense, or the teaching of youth without the schools, or the spiritual welfare of souls without the teaching, etc. For the same reasons respectively, endeavor shall be made to maintain schools for little girls, which shall be held in the houses of the teachers where they shall learn to read and pray, for which great prudence is necessary."

Another very notable paragraph, in which are prescribed the days for school, attendance, method, subjects, etc., follows this paragraph which is worthy of the highest praise. That paragraph imposes the obligation on the children of great practical sense, that after "mass is finished (which they were to hear every day) they shall kiss the father's hand. By this diligence the latter can ascertain those who do not attend, and force them to attend, etc."

In order that one may see the rare unanimity existing among the religious corporations in a matter as transcendental as is that of education, it is very fitting to transcribe here some paragraphs of the instructions which the reverend father, Fray Manuel del Río, provincial at that time of the Dominicans, gave to his religious under date of August 31, 1739, which were printed in Manila in the same year, and which we have entitled *Práctica del párroco dominicana* [*i.e.*, *Practice of the Dominican parish priest*] as the valuable copy which we possess has no title page. It reads as follows:

"The king, our sovereign, orders that there be schools in all the villages of the Indians in order to teach them reading, writing, and the doctrine. In those schools the ministers must work zealously and earnestly, as it is a thing which is of so great importance for the education and spiritual gain of their souls. Schools shall also be established in the visitas, especially if they are large or distant from the capital, and in those visitas which are furnished with no schoolteacher because they are small or near the capital, the lads shall be obliged to attend the school at the capital. All the lads, whether chief or timaoas, must attend the school, and they, and their parents or relatives must be obliged to do so, so that they may not be exempted from that attendance by any excuse or pretext, except the singers, who will be taught to read and write in the school of the cantors. For the more exact fulfilment of this, a list shall be made of those who ought to attend the school, and a copy of it shall be given to the said teacher. This shall be read frequently in the school, noting those who fail in order to punish them.

"In order to maintain said schools and the attendance of the lads therein without the excuses which some generally offer of not having primers, pens, or paper for writing, it is necessary for the minister to solicit the one who has those things for sale in the village, for those who can buy them. Those who find it impossible to do so shall be furnished by the minister with those articles by way of alms, and in that, besides the merit acquired by this virtue, he will gather the fruit of the welfare and the gain of their souls.

"Girls' schools shall also be formed by causing them to go to the house of their teacher, so that they may learn to read and sew, and also learn the doctrine. But they shall not be obliged to attend church daily, as are the boys, but only on Saturday or any other day assigned for the reciting of the rosary and the examination in the doctrine."

It is to be noted that both provincials, as well as their successors, imposed on their subjects the obligation to faithfully observe what is prescribed in the *Práctica* and respective instructions, which the ministers of the Lord fulfilled with especial solicitude and constancy, since only in this way could they gather the most copious fruits which we all admire.

The unity of thought and action which the religious corporations had in a matter so primordial as is teaching is also to be noted. Evidently it is to be inferred from those beautiful periods that the religious were trying to pay the teachers, having recourse even to the alcaldes when that was necessary; and when that could not be obtained they themselves paid the teacher the fruit of his labors as well as supplying also the children with everything necessary for their instruction, such as primers, books, papers, pens, etc. For that, no quota was put in the budget, since, as is seen, that most essential datum is not mentioned in the laws, ordinances, and royal decrees above given. It is also to be noted that, in the rules above cited, there is no mention of other than boys' schools, but none for girls, while all were alike considered, both of those of the capital or villages and those of the barrios, with an equal vigilance by our missionaries, who from the first, established compulsory attendance as absolutely indispensable, in contradiction to the old laws, in which was noted the tendency to liberty or non-compulsion, as is inferred from the royal decree of November 5, 1782,4 given for Charcas (Méjico) and extended to Filipinas confirmed by the law of June 11, 1815, which cites it in its two extremes.

In this way those humble religious worked out the laws as much as possible, although it cost them much, by rectifying what was not viable and by supplying the deficiencies of those laws, especially in the matters pertaining to the salaries of the teachers, and payment for school supplies, which, on account of the scarcity of funds from the treasury, the legislature was compelled to establish as is established in this last royal decree above cited: "That, for the salary of teachers, the products of foundations, where there shall be any, be applied in the first place, and for the others, the products of the property of the community, in accordance with the terms of the laws." But since the foundations, in case there were any, existed only in the capitals, which were at the same time the episcopal residence, and the communal funds were in general exhausted, it was the same thing as determining that the parish priests would continue to pay the expenses from their poor living, or find some means which would give that so desired and difficult result. This penury of the treasury which was felt equally in España and in Filipinas obliged his Majesty to extend to these islands the royal decree of October 20, 1817, which reads as follows:

"The existing state of exhaustion of my royal treasury does not permit that so great a sum be set aside for the endowment of these schools as would be necessary for so important an object; but the convents of all the religious orders scattered throughout my kingdoms may in great measure supply this impossibility...." There was no need to put this royal decree in force in the Filipinas, since, in the majority of the convents or parish houses, schools for boys had already been established in their lower part, and those for girls in the houses of the women teachers, and other houses made for that purpose. It is but right to note how much the missionary always labored for the education of the woman whose better gifts he recognized always. He created numerous schools for her instruction, and paid for them from his living, quite contrary to the total inattention which the administration paid to the schools and teachers for girls, until the regulations of December 20, 1863 were formulated, the eighth article of which orders that "there shall be a boys' school and another school for girls in every village, whatever its number of souls."

Article 2 of these regulations,5 quite distinct from the path of the ancient legislation, recognized, in accordance with the conduct and laws of the religious orders, the necessity of establishing compulsion in primary teaching; and firm in this principle, it ordered that "the primary instruction should be compulsory for all the natives, to the degree that the inattendance of the child might be penalized by virtue of art. 2, with the fine of from one-half to two reals." Neither is the legislation exclusive with relation to the study of Castilian, as is seen by the context of its art. 3; it ordains education gratis to the poor by art. 4; and the well-to-do shall pay the teacher a moderate monthly fee, which shall be prescribed by the governor of each province, after conferring with the parish priest and gobernadorcillo. Paper, copybooks, ink, and pens shall be given free to all the children by the teacher, who, at the proper time, shall receive for this service one duro per month, for every child who writes, in accordance with the ruling made by a decree of the superior government, February 16, 1867. Very suitable measures were to be taken, all in accord with the action of the parish priest, in order not to give any occasion for fraud. That was a very well taken resolution, for it stimulated the zeal of the teacher, who received on this account a sum not to be despised, which, together with the quota of the well-to-do children and the monthly pay which he received, according to art. 22, consisting of 12, 15, and 20 pesos, according as the school of which he was in charge was entrada, ascenso, or término, he received a pay quite sufficient for his needs, enjoying in addition, by art. 23, a free dwelling-house for himself and family, and in due season the pension prescribed by art. 24.

Article 32 determines the powers of the parish priest as local supervisor, which, although they were conceded with a certain timidity, were perhaps believed to be excessive or unnecessary, and it seems its abolition was clearly agreed upon by art. 12 in declaring the municipal captain "supervisor of the schools." This blow must be judged as a very strong one in the lofty governmental spheres of the islands, for the genuine representation of the parish priests in the villages is one of the functions most natural to their charge, both as teachers of the Catholic doctrine and ethics, and in the role of traditional supporters of the schools, although in art. 102 was established the following as an explanation to art. 12 of the decree: "Without prejudice to the supervision which belongs in the instruction to the parish priests according to the regulations of December 1863, whose powers are not at all altered, the tribunal shall watch carefully over primary instruction; shall demand the teaching of Castilian in the schools; shall oblige the inhabitants to send their children to them; and shall stimulate instruction by means of adequate examinations and rewards. Said tribunal shall place in operation the most practical means for the diffusion of the Spanish language among the inhabitants, deciding upon those means in meetings with the parish priests and the delegates of the principalía."

At first view one observes the good desire which the author of said article shelters when he says that the powers conceded to the parish priest as supervisor of schools by art. 20 of the regulations of the same shall not be changed in any point, without perceiving that directly afterward it created another authority in opposition to that of the parish priest, if not with all the powers of the latter, because those which he possesses as teacher in ethics and the doctrine do not admit of transmission, yet clearly of all the others, and in them with prior rank.

It is evident that, by the context of this article, the power of "watching carefully over primary instruction" is conceded to the captain, which is identical with the first part of art. 32 of the school regulations conceded to the parish priest which reads as follows: "To visit the schools as often as possible." This is the first part of that article, and the second part "and to see that the regulations are observed," whose art. 3 orders that "the teachers shall have special care that the pupils have practical exercise in speaking the Castilian language," is of identical meaning and effect with the power conceded to the captain, which declares, "he shall demand that Castilian be taught in the schools." This power is followed by those of "he shall compel the inhabitants to send their children to the schools, and shall stimulate instruction by means of adequate examinations and rewards;" both powers similar to those which are conceded to the parish priests by the third part of said art. 32, which declares, "To promote the attendance of children at the schools." To supplement this with the compulsory virtue, he is authorized by art. 2, explained and ratified in No. 3 of the decree of the superior government of August 30, 1867, to be able to admonish and compel parents, who are slow in sending their children to the schools, by means of fines from one-half to two reals, and that which is conceded to him, in accordance with annual examinations, by art. 13, and art. 7 of the decree of the superior government, of May 7, 1871, which declares: "The reverend and learned parish priests, accompanied by the gobernadorcillos and by the principalías of the villages, shall visit the schools monthly, shall hold examinations every three months, etc." By this one can see that the parish priest conserves the first place, even in this, over the gobernadorcillo and principalía, by whom he is accompanied, in order to give more luster to the ceremony. That happens in no act or meeting of the present municipality, in which the parish priest has no other functions than those of intervention and counsel, included in that which is signified in the last paragraph of the above-mentioned art. 102, which says when referring to the municipal captain: "He shall put in force the most practical means for the diffusion of the Spanish language among the inhabitants, agreeing upon those means in meetings with the parish priests and delegates of the principalía;" and although it is established that the creation of the Sunday schools of which art. 29 of the regulations speaks, which are also of the intervention of the parish priest, as are the boys' schools, falls completely to his share, as the means, if not sole, yet the one most efficacious and of practical application, it would result as in all the other powers which have been enumerated as conceded to the parish priest by the school regulations and to the captain by decree and municipal regulations—it would result, we say—at each step in an encounter and rivalry in which the parish priests would come out second best, for the simple reason, repeated to satiety in innumerable articles of the decree and municipal regulations, that the action of the parish priest is nothing more than supervision and counsel,6 with the added abasement that "his presence shall not be included in the number of those who shall concur in the validity of the deliberations," as is prescribed by art. 49 of the decree and 64 of the regulations. Sad then, is, and at once, graceless, the function of the parish priest compared to the action of the captain and of the board which is executive.

It seems unnecessary to say that the action and powers of the parish priest in his duties as local supervisor of schools result in the theoretical legal sphere of action, completely null and void, and that action carried to the practical field of action exposes it to continual rivalries, numerous frictions, and even deep quarrels between two authorities, who in that, as in everything which belongs to the multiple affairs of the village, ought to be in perfect accord, as is demanded jointly by the lofty interests of religion and of the fatherland, of the spiritual welfare and of the material order and peace of the villages.

And as that duality, besides being shameful and lowering for the parish priests, is inviolable, and since by another part art. 12 of the decree and

102 of the regulations, both above cited, in the form in which they have been compiled, do not fill any need or space, as all that which is ordained therein is a repetition of what has been already decreed, there is no reason for their existence, to the evident common harm, and to the small shame of the parish priest, who deserves eternal gratitude for his labors, for his solicitude, and for the zeal which he has ever displayed, and in the midst of the greatest sacrifices, for the instruction.

Nearly three centuries, since 1565, when the first Augustinians, the companions of Legazpi and Salcedo reached the Filipinas shores, until 1863, the year in which regulations were first made for primary instruction, outlined only hitherto in numerous laws and royal decrees which it was impossible to fulfil, as is proved, for almost three centuries, we say, of bold zeal bordering on the inconceivable, of constant anxiety and watching, of unusual effort, which borders on the heroic, and with remarkable expenses never paid back, ignored by most people, and recognized and praised by very few: are these not sufficient, not only so that the liberty to exercise the noblest charge which Church and fatherland have confided to them for centuries in the teaching of the schools, which is intimately associated with the teaching in the pulpit, be conceded to the parish priests, but that also by justice illumined by gratitude, the necessary law, moral force, aid, and support, for the exercise, with perfect repose and without any impediment, and more, without any asperity and struggle, of that sacred duty so full of trouble and bitterness for him, so full of results most beneficial for religion and fatherland, be conceded to him? If, then, one desire to concede to the parish priest the position which is in justice due him in education, if there is to be granted to the missionary that which the most rudimentary gratitude urges, it is of imperious necessity that that mortifying and abasing duality be radically destroyed, for it renders useless all the energies of the parish priest supervisor, and stifles his noble and disinterested aid offered without tax for the service of the holy ideals of God and fatherland. Perhaps the parish priest is deprived of this salutary intervention because such intervention is believed unnecessary, superfluous or prejudicial to the lofty interests of the fatherland or of the well-being of the native? Today necessarily more than ever, through the deep-colored dripping of the blood of the insurrection,7 one can see with the clearness of noonday that the intervention of the parish priest ought to be established in all the orders, in order that it might again take the lofty position which was overthrown thirty years ago. Is it, perhaps, because the intervention of the parish priests will be a barrier, or obstacle, even to the sustained mark of true progress in education in general, or of Castilian in particular? But this is perfectly utopian, and even an argument now of bad taste. The religious orders enemies of true progress! Perhaps they are not the ones who in their teaching have created everything today existing in Filipinas? Are not the religious corporations those who have always formed their ranks in the vanguard of science, and today especially both in the Peninsula, and in the Magellian Archipelago, do not numerous colleges nourish with special predilection on the part of the public? As an incontestible proof of this truth, let one concede without difficulty what shall afterwards be proposed as a supplement of that existing today.

The argument of Castilian is a mythical argument of more than long standing, since it has been proved quite clearly during the preceding centuries that there has been an absolute lack of material for teaching it. The patronizing enthusiasts of the Castilian, who think it to be a panacea, so that the Indian may learn everything and obtain the social height of the peoples of another race and of other capacities, and who are persuaded, or appear to be so, that "what is of importance above all else is that the Indian learn Castilian in order to understand and to identify himself with the Castila," are laboring under a false belief. We sincerely believe that the native, if he once come to understand the Castila in the genuine meaning of the word, will never come to identify himself with them. Thus it was explained by a distinguished man of talent, both illustrious and liberal, Don Patricio de la Escosura,8 the least monastic man in España and the one most favorable to the friars in Filipinas of his epoch, as he himself declared in most ample phrase; a man of government and administration, who throwing aside as was proper the vulgar opinion that the friars were opposed to the teaching of Castilian, assigned in his famous Memoria on Filipinas "of the parish priests, I say, little must be expected in this matter;" in order to affirm as follows: "And by this I do not pretend, and much less, deny to them their apostolic zeal, their desire for the common good, and the importance of the services which they have lent to religion and the mother country, and are lending and may lend in the future;" and adding some years later in his prologue to the small work Recuerdos [i.e., Remembrances] which could better be entitled Infundios [i.e., Fables] of Señor Cañamaque: "Let the friars in the archipelago be suppressed, and that country will soon be an entirely savage region of the globe, where there will scarcely remain a vestige or perhaps a remembrance of Spanish domination. That is a truth, for all those who know and judge impartially concerning the archipelago, of axiomatic authority." And that truth established, he immediately asked: "Why then is not that force utilized, in whose existence and supreme efficacy all agree? Why are not the friars charged as much as possible with the responsibility of the immense authority which they in fact exercise by associating them officially and in reasonable terms with the governmental and administrative action in Filipinas?" Why? For a very simple reason. Because governments, like ministers of the crown and royal commissaries in Filipinas, like Señor Escosura, suffer prejudices and embrace opinions so original and vulgar as that of the opposition of the religious corporations to the teaching of Castilian, a universal panacea as abovesaid, to knowing everything, and which will enable the native to conquer every sort of obstacle; for this most clear talent, and we say it truly, caused to be based on the ignorance of Castilian "so much ignorance and so absurd superstitions at the end of three centuries, and in spite of the efforts of the Spanish legislator to civilize the Indians. So long as the Indian," he adds, "speaks his primitive language, it is approximately impossible to withdraw him completely from his prejudices, from his superstition, erroneous ideas, and the puerilities belonging to the savage condition. So long as he understands the Castilian with difficulty, ... how can he have clear notions of his duties, and of his rights—he who cannot understand the laws more than by the medium of some interpreter?..."

What candor and how little understanding of the native, or what excess of political or party idea!

That illustrious statistician believed that the knowledge of Castilian and the unity of the language could not be in any time a favorable base for the insurrection, which was one of the contrary arguments which he was opposing, for, he was asserting in general that "neither the population through its number, nor the native race through its nature and special conditions, are here capable of independence at any time. This country is not a continent, but an archipelago. Its diverse provinces are for the greater part, distinct islands; ... and so long as there is a Spanish military marine in these waters, supposing that any serious insurrection should arise (which seems to me highly improbable) there is nothing easier than to circumscribe it to the locality in which it should be born, and consequently to stifle it in its cradle." A few lines afterwards he says: "The Indians here, I repeat, can never become independent. They feel that also for the present, although perhaps they do not understand it; and furthermore by instinct they prefer at all times Spaniards to foreigners, on whom they look moreover with unfavorable caution." What an illusion, and what an enormous disillusion! How great would be the deception of Señor Escosura if he would come to life in his grave! Without troubling us with the argument of the Castilian, or taking into account the circumstances that he lays down in regard to the multiplicity of islands which are extremely unfavorable for their defense, according to his way of thinking, what would he say now if he lifted his head and observed that the knowledge of Castilian has been considerably extended—perhaps four times as much as when he went as royal commissary to Filipinas, in order to write that Memoria; that, if not the lawyers, the men of most letters and knowledge of Castilian, the intelligent, and those of the most cultured native society, in which figures a numerous pleiad composed of advocates, physicians, pharmacists, painters, engravers, normal and elementary teachers, municipal captains, past-captains, cuadrilleros,9 and hundreds more of those who understand one another and are in the way of identifying themselves with the Castila, as Señor Escosura would say, are the leaders, are those who captain and direct the enormous native multitudes who are related to them in thought and action, and stimulate and spread that bloody rebellion which is spreading through all the islands like an immense spot of oil, in spite of the fact that they are so numerous and are defended by a respectable squadron; of that insurrection, which scarcely born and without arms, presents itself powerful, and armed in the greater part of Luzón and certain other provinces, and latent or masked in all the remaining provinces; of that insurrection which without any preamble of liberties, and of little more than two years of limited exercise of municipal autonomy, is beginning to proclaim and demand independence, and passing to active life is establishing a government and is exercising perfect dominion for more than one-half year in an entire province a few leguas from Manila, at the very foot of a strong fort and under the fire of its arsenal, in spite of the numerous squadron which touches its coasts. What would the author of that Memoria, abounding in liberties and so ample in his criticism, say? He would say much of that which he then censured in his opponents. He would ingenuously and solemnly assert in the face of the bloody panorama of so enormous hetacombs that he had been deceived, and he would even add that it is at least rash to sow the winds, which become, as a logical sequel, fatal whirlwinds to finish us; that the implanting of a certain class of reforms and liberties is a rash work; and would adduce the reason which he gave in the above-cited prologue when treating in regard to the difficulty of implanting with result in those islands "certain literary and scientific professions;" namely, "that given the physical and intellectual qualifications of their race, it would be rash to expect that they would ever compare with Europeans. The Indian learns much more readily than we do; but he forgets with the same readiness, and retrogrades to his primitive condition." It seems impossible how a man of so clear judgment and so exact concepts in regard to persons could stumble so transcendently as is found throughout in his Memoria. How powerful is the strength of consistency. The political ideal, like the sectarian, annuls the deepest and most righteous convictions.

But let us turn backwards a piece to pick up an end not allowed to fall to chance. We said that, as a proof that the religious orders have neither now nor ever been opposed to the teaching, one would concede without difficulty what we are going to set forth as a supplement of what exists today.

It is known by all, and is demonstrated quite clearly, that the traditional laws for teaching, if admirably penetrated by the spirit, profoundly Catholic, of their epoch, were very deficient, and in no small measure impracticable in Filipinas, because they lack almost all the means indispensable for the happy attainment which legislators and missionaries ardently desired; equally notorious is it, and also demonstrated, that the absolute lack of legal rules and regulations to facilitate their obligation accentuated more strongly the deficiency of those laws. We say legal, because the few regulations that there were, and which were practiced, were those of which mention has already been made in the Práctica del Ministerio of 1712, circulated as was compulsory, by their provincial among the Augustinian parish priests, revised in the provincial chapter of 1716, and amplified and printed in 1731; and the Instrucciones morales y religiosas [i.e., Moral and religious Instructions],10 printed in 1739 for the use of the Dominican fathers—a lamentable lack which disappeared with the publication of the regulations of December 20, 1863.

This law which was successively perfected by numerous decrees of the superior government of the islands, especially by generals Izquierdo, Gándara, and Weyler, who were filled with the praiseworthy desire for the teaching; this law together with the opening of the Suez Canal, which has produced a notable increase in the European population,11 and by this and by the facility of numerous communications and most valuable commercial transactions, has been an abundant fount of education and progress, which must be perfected and heightened so that what ought to be an abundant and beneficial irrigation for so valuable possessions may not be converted into a devastating torrent.

But even after this which we might call a giant's step in the history of the Filipinas, their progress and their relations with Europa, within the islands even, very much still needs to be done. It is a fact that the coasting trade steam vessels have acquired an increase more considerable than could have been imagined twenty years ago, while the sail-coasting trade has not been diminished for this reason, but increased. But just as the maritime communications have acquired great facility, communications by land have deteriorated not a little, and the neighborhood roads of all the islands have been falling into complete neglect since the day when the days of forced labor began to be reduced, and this tax became redeemable [in money].

If the greater number of roads in good condition with their corresponding log bridges over the creeks and the simple plank over the narrow valleys are absolutely indispensable for commercial transactions, for the advisable development of primary instruction, the capital is the constant attendance of the children at the school. In order that this may be attained, it is quite necessary to construct those roads, for in their majority they have no existence, and where they have fallen into neglect they must be made passable alike for the dry season and for the rainy season, prohibiting and rigorously fining the owners of the adjacent fields who cut the roads in order to make fields or runnels of water for the same. This being done, it is equally necessary that the small barrios and isolated groups of dwellings be grouped together, thus forming large barrios; or those already existing be united in such manner that they form districts of seventy to eighty citizens as a minimum.

Not a little labor and repeated orders will it cost to form these groups, since it is known that the native feels as no one else the homesickness for the forest, an effect perhaps of his humid temperament, perhaps the reminiscence of his primitive condition; and when this is done, to establish municipal schools for both sexes in all the barrios which consist of more than one hundred citizens, or uniting two for this purpose, which are distant more than three kilometers from the central schools or from the village, which is the distance demanded by the law for the compulsory attendance of the children. These Schools, with the necessary conditions of ventilation, capacity, and security, ought to be erected by the respective municipalities, in accordance with the simple lithograph plans which must be furnished gratis by the body of civil engineers which shall be conserved, as was formerly done, in the archives of said tribunals, in order that they might be used when the time came. The men and women teachers who shall be normal [graduates] shall have the option of petitioning these posts, and if they should not be supplied with them, the former teacher may petition them under the condition of capacity, which they shall prove by a preceding examination held before the provincial board of primary instruction, in case that they shall not already have stood a prior examination. Both of them shall be suitably paid according to circumstances, and that quota shall be completed with another small particular quota from each well-to-do child.

It is of great convenience for the ends of fitness, and especially of morality, that men or women teachers shall not be appointed either in the villages or in the barrios of the villages, without a previous report of the parish priests of their native towns, to the effect that they do not fall short of the age of twelve years, and naming the villages where they shall have been resident; and that the parish priests have the power of suspending them, according to the tenor of the second authorization of art. 32 of the school regulations and the superior decree of August 30, 1867, informing the provincial supervisor for the definitive sentence, if this last measure of rigor shall have been used; naming or recommending, according to the cases of casual or definitive suspension, the substitute with his respective pay.

An unequivocal proof that the religious corporations not only are not trying to escape the instruction, but that they are promoting it with all their strength, is that they believe and sustain both in Manila and in the provinces, numerous schools and refuges for both sexes. And so that so praiseworthy desires, as the said corporations are found to possess in this matter, may have a happy outcome, and so that the provinces may reckon an abundant seminary of the youth of both sexes, which in due time shall be converted into an intelligent and capable staff of teachers, which shall have as its base morality and unconditional love for España, who shall cause those two sacred loves—love of virtue and love of fatherland—to spring up in the hearts of their pupils, not only should the above-mentioned corporations be empowered but also furnished all the means of establishing normal schools for men and women teachers in the principal provinces of the archipelago, under the direction and care of those corporations, in order by this means to assure the Catholic and social education, which carry with themselves a deep and abiding love for España.

No one, in better conditions than the religious orders, who by means of the parish priests are at the front of the villages, can proceed with more accuracy and knowledge of the cause in the selection of the youth who shall people those schools, for no one, better than the parish priests, has a more perfect knowledge of the moral and intellectual conditions of those youth and of their inclinations and ancestral inheritance from their forbears, the absolutely necessary factors for obtaining the beneficent result which it is desired to obtain, namely, the most complete moral, intellectual, and truly conceived patriotic regeneration, profoundly disturbed by a not small number of causes, which rapidly developing within the envenomed surrounding of masonry, and powerfully pushed forward by that impious sect, have produced grievous days for España and Filipinas, in which the precious blood of their sons has been abundantly shed, causing thereby enormous expenses to the Peninsula, and a half century of retrogression for the islands, together with the infamous blot of the highest ingratitude of its rebellious sons. Now more than ever is this means of regeneration demanded.

And we faithfully believe that that means of regeneration ought to be placed in practice as soon as possible, the government removing on its part every kind of obstacle, especially of documents and information. That is the point on which these initiatives are wrecked, or are indefinitely detained, as happened to the zealous and untiring Señor Gainza in regard to his school of Santa Isabel—the normal school for women teachers in Nueva Cáceres—who after having struggled for a long time in the offices of the superior government, of administration, instruction, and engineers, was compelled to resolve his cherished project by presenting it personally to Queen Doña Isabel, who fully and kindly acceded to his supplication, and even thus with the valuable license of her Majesty communicated in due form, that eminent prelate still met all sorts of difficulties, from the provincial chief, which only disappeared with his departure from the same. In order that these labors might have a homogeneous result and those normal schools respond efficaciously to the concept of the fatherland, it is not advisable that the instruction in them be given by others than Spanish corporations, and consequently, by Spanish religious, who are the ones who can really impress that love, prohibiting, as a consequence of this standard, the teaching of the schools already established, be they private or not, from being given in any other language than the Spanish, or in ordinary conversation, that any other language than the Castilian be used, without this at all preventing other languages from being taught.

For the better order, progress, and homogeneity, it is indispensable that one bear in mind the capacity of the natives, in order to assign the list of studies which they are to take. That must be proportioned in all institutions to their nature, and those studies, as is evident, must be suppressed, which either give an unadvisable or useless result, because of being outside the intellectual sphere of the native. Still more evident is the necessity of the instruction for the natives obeying a uniform plan of method and social education, in order to avoid ill feeling among the teaching communities, and peculiarities and comparisons, which by themselves are always odious, and which cause not a little mischief among the natives, who, if they are not distinguished by their character and reasoning, yet are by nature very observant, and lay great stress on all external details, so that without troubling themselves in seeking the cause, they form their opinion or standard; and from that time on they will not be inclined toward those things which the masons and separatists are pursuing with the greatest of rancor by finding in those same things more obstacles for the attainment of their evil purposes.

The list of studies, as well as the method of teaching and of education will be the first and immediate end of the studies, opinion, and formula which the Superior Board of Public Instruction shall bear to its conclusion with singular interest. This board shall form the consequent schedules and above-mentioned methods, which it shall subject to the approbation of the general government of the archipelago.

The abovesaid superior board may be composed of the following gentlemen: the archbishop of Manila; the intendant of the public treasury; the president of the Audiencia; civil governor of Manila; secretary of the superior government; one councilor of administration; the provincials of the Augustinians, Franciscans, Dominicans, and Recollects; the rectors of the university, of the normal school, and of the seminary. To it shall be submitted the revision of the present schedules, both for the normal schools and in so far as the schedules of the studies of primary and secondary and higher education need to be revised; and at the same time the method of teaching and of education for both sexes, the execution of which, as I have just said, will be accomplished under the character of its importance and immediate necessity.

The attention of every studious and observing man, who has lived in residence in the Filipino provinces, is not a little struck by the excessive number of young men, who having taken more or less courses in Manila, but without concluding the course begun, or even taking the degree of bachelor, after their parents have spent considerable sums on them, return to their villages with very little or no virtue, but with many vices. At first sight one notes in these young men an irritating radical attitude and a freedom mixed with unendurable arrogance and vanity. Their fellow countrymen, whom they disdain because they possess, although in a superficial manner, the Castilian speech full of phrases and sounds, which would make the most reserved Viscayan laugh, and of high-sounding words which they use without understanding their real significance, immediately look up to them as so many Senecas. They are persuaded that they are perfect gentlemen, for by dint of seeing them practiced they have learned a few social formulas; they wear a cravat, and boots, and pantaloons of the latest style. For the rest, they are completely devoid of fundamental knowledge, and of the fundamentals of knowledge in the studies which they have taken, and have acquired only a slight tint of the part, let us say the bark of those studies, which they conclude by forgetting in proportion as time passes and their passions increase. These young men who forget what they have learned with so great facility, do not, as a general rule, devote themselves to any work, for they do not like work and cannot perform any; for the habits that they have contracted are very different—habits of pastime, idleness, and the waste of their paternal capital. In such condition are those who, as a rule, furnish the contingent of the staff of those who are employed without pay, of aspirants, and amanuenses with little pay of the offices and municipalities, while the most intelligent and skilful devote themselves to making writs for parties in litigation, a very handy matter, and one never finished among the natives, not even by force of many deceptions and the loss of great interests.

And that our opinion is not formed from the smoke of straw, and lightly, is proved by the numerous lists of matriculations which accompany the conscientious and well written memorials by trustworthy Dominican fathers, especially those which were published in the years 1883 and 1887, because of the expositions of Amsterdam and Filipinas, in Madrid. We cannot resist the temptation to transcribe here a valuable paragraph, which wonderfully meets our purpose. It is taken from the writing signed by the excellent Dominican, Father Buitrago, for the last-mentioned exposition. It is as follows: "The first thing which offers itself to the consideration of the reader, is the multitude of the inscriptions of matriculation, and the small proportionate number of approvals. On this point, the first thing that offers is to investigate the causes of that disproportion, which is a great surprise to those who are ignorant of the special conditions under which secondary teaching in this country is found. Many of the young men who matriculate for it, have scarcely any or no desire to obtain a passing mark in their courses, their only object being to learn the Castilian language, and to know, in order that they may afterward occupy a more important position in their villages, some of the customs of the Spaniards. Those who come to Manila with the decided intention of terminating a literary career are relatively very few. In this matter their families exact but little also. And then there is added the method of living in this place, crowded together in their greatest part in private houses under the nominal vigilance of their landlords or landladies, as they call the owners of the houses in which they are lodged. Consequently, not few in this capital are reared in idleness and learn the vices of Europeans without taking on their good qualities. The rector of the university can do nothing on this point, for the rules allow students to matriculate two or three times or even more often, in the same course, in spite of their not passing in it."

Before such an inundation of wise men, whose scholastic modesty suffers with a serene mind and with immovable resignation [resignación de estuco] three and more failures in one study, there is no other means, since the lash cannot be legally used, or the oak rod of the oldtime dominie, than to put in practice a salutary strictness in the examinations of the secondary education, and to revise the regulations more strictly, in order thereby to free the provinces of that inundation of learning which parches the fields for lack of arms to work them, uses up the savings of the wealthy families, fills the villages with vampires who suck the sweat of the poor or careless with impunity, increases the lawsuits and ill feeling in the villages, makes of the municipalities and offices a workshop of intrigue, and gives a numerous contingent to the lodges and to separatism.

And as the above-mentioned author of the said *Memoria* adds: "It is apparent to us at times that (the rector) actively negotiated to subject the lodging houses for students to one set of regulations, in order to watch over their moral and literary conduct better; but such efforts have had no result;" it is thoroughly necessary to create a law, in which the rector shall be authorized to extend his zeal, vigilance, and action to such houses, and also to subject all the day students of Manila, without distinction of establishments, to the university police of the rector and his agents, reëstablishing in this regard the ancient university right. For that purpose, full powers ought to be given to the rector, so that, now by himself in faults of less degree, and now by the university Council in the greater, he may impose academical fines, and even ask the aid of public force in case of necessity, beginning by demanding from each young man who wishes to matriculate, the certificate or report of good conduct given by the parish priest of the village whence he comes. This requirement is of exceptional advisability, not only for the general ends of the instruction, but also for the more perfect selection of the persons who, on devoting themselves to the noble employment of teaching, shall form the understanding and the heart of future generations.

Only in this manner can we succeed in getting the Filipino youth to acquire the conditions and habits of morality and study, until they reach the end of their capacity. Only in this manner can we succeed in giving to the fatherland, grateful children, to Filipinas, honored citizens, to society, useful members, to families, children who honor the white hairs of their parents, and to the public posts a suitable staff, without pretensions, and faithful in the performance of their duties; and that they shall be consequently, fervent Catholics, who shall never forget what the parish priest taught them when they were children, in his simple doctrinal lessons, and who shall be heard afterwards to repeat to their teachers, to bless the divine cross which illumined their intellects and saved their souls, and to bless España, which amid the folds of its yellow banner or crowning its standards, brought the cross triumphant to those shores, and with it Christian civilization and true progress.

II

"Until the end of the year 1863 in which was dictated the memorable royal decree, which established a plan of primary instruction in Filipinas, and which arranged for the creation of schools of primary instruction in all the villages of the islands, ánd the creation of a normal school in Manila, whence should graduate well-educated and religious teachers who should take the foremost places in those institutions, it might be said that there had been no legislation in regard to primary instruction in these islands. For, although it is certain that precepts directed to the attainment of education by the natives, and very particularly the teaching of the beautiful Spanish language, are not lacking (some of those precepts being contained in the Leyes de Indias, and in the edicts of good government), it is a fact that those precepts are isolated arrangements without conclusions, the product of the good desire which has always animated the Spanish monarchs and their worthy representatives in the archipelago for the advancement and prosperity of these islands, but without resting upon a firm foundation for lack of the elements for its existence.

"Before the above-mentioned epoch the reverend and learned parish priests of the villages came to fill in great measure and voluntarily the noble ends of propagating primary instruction throughout these distant regions by the aid of their own pupils, the most advanced of whom dedicated themselves to the teaching of their fellow citizens, although they received but very little remuneration for their work and care, and there was no consideration of teachers or titles which accredited them as such."12

In fact the religious corporations in Filipinas were those who busied themselves with the interest which the matter deserved in primary instruction, which was abandoned almost entirely by the authorities until the year 1863, notwithstanding the repeated recommendations, orders, and laws of our monarchs and of the Councils of Indias. The religious were the first teachers of primary letters in Filipinas, as they were afterwards in secondary instruction, in the superior teaching with faculties, and in the principal arts and trades which the Indians learned. By the advice of the religious, the villages constructed the first schools. The religious directed the works; they gave the instruction, until they had pupils who could be substituted for them and leave them free for the spiritual administration of the faithful; and they, the religious, paid the wages of those improvised teachers, without official title or character as such, but sufficiently instructed to teach the tiny people their first letters, and to succeed in obtaining that seventy-five per cent of the inhabitants [of the Filipino village] might learn how to read and write correctly. Señor Hilarión,13 archbishop of Manila, was able to say to the most excellent Ayuntamiento of that city when provincial of the calced Augustinians: "There are multitudes of villages, such as Argao, Dalaguete, and Bolhoon, in Cebú, and many in the province of Iloilo, in which it is difficult to find a single boy or girl who does not know how to read or write, an advantage which many cities of our España have not yet succeeded in obtaining."

The pay that the religious could give to the teachers educated by them was moderate, but in faith none of the detractors of the monastic corporations of Filipinas had given as much, or even the half, for so beneficial a work.

The religious not only provided large, roomy, and ventilated places for the primary instruction of the two sects, and acted as teachers until the most advanced pupils could use something of what was supplied them in teaching, but also provided the schools with the suitable and necessary furnishings in which the industry and genius of the parish-priest regular came to aid their pecuniary appeals and the absolute lack of the materials for teaching. There was no ink, paper, or pens. The first was not necessary for the new papyrus, which was no other than the magnificent leaf of the banana, and the pen was a small bit of bamboo cut in the manner of a pen. From each leaf of the banana they could get twenty or thirty pages of a larger size than those of Iturzaeta. On the other side of the leaf, covered with fine down and smooth as that of velvet, the Indians wrote their letters with the bamboo cut in the form of a pen or of the ancient stylus. What was thus written was not very permanent, nor was there any need that it should be, for the copy pages were not kept as a justification of the expenses of writing allowed by the teachers according to rule later, because of the distrustful or cautious official administration. Since the material was plentiful and free the children were allowed to write as many pages as they wished. More, in fact, they would be seen seated and writing at all hours of the day, not only in their houses, but also in the square, in the street, on the roads, for in all parts they had ready at hand bananas and bamboos, and a stone or any other kind of an object was used as a desk. And, since the aptitude of the native Filipino is so remarkable for imitation, and his patience so great, they did not stop their writing until they imitated ours with the greatest perfection. The religious also wrote the books and primers for their reading, formerly in manuscript, then printed in their own dialect, so that they might profit from the maxims and doctrine, and history and religion, in proportion as they became proficient in reading.

Notwithstanding, after 1863, when the government took charge of education, and the normal school directed by the Jesuit fathers provided the villages with normal teachers under official title and pay, the religious ceased to continue to foment education in their villages, yet not only as local supervisors, with which character they were invested by the memorable decree of that date—the foundation of all the circulars, decrees, and instructions which afterward fell upon that historical document in a vast jumble—but also since the boys and girls of the barrios distant from the villages twenty kilometers and sometimes more, were not able on account of the distance to be present at the official school, did the parish-priest religious, attentive and vigilant, hasten in their anxiety to supply with their pecuniary resources the official deficiencies in every barrio or visita. They had schools built of light materials but solid and well built, in which teachers, both male and female, appointed and paid by the parish priests, gave primary instruction in reading, writing, and arithmetic; and sewing and embroidery to the girls. Finally, the parish priests also supplied them with paper, pens, ink, books, thread, needles, and all the other materials needed in teaching. The said schools were visited by the parish priests, if not periodically, yet whenever the duties of their ministries would permit. All the boys and girls of the nearby barrios attended those schools. Every Sunday after mass, masters and mistresses, with their respective scholars presented to their parish priests their copy books, sums, sewing, and embroidery, which they had made during the week. In order to comprehend the significance of all that has been set forth to this point, one must bear in mind that the population in Filipinas is found much scattered in groups of houses called barrios or visitas, more or less densely populated, and separated by a greater or less distance from one another. So true is this that of the fourteen thousand inhabitants of the village of Ogton, verbi gratia, scarcely four thousand lived within the radius of the village. This scattering of the inhabitants throughout the jurisdiction of the villages, if it were meet and convenient at the beginning of the conquest, in order that the barrios or the visitas might become the nucleus of future villages, yet had no reason for existence, during the last half of the past century in the very densely populated provinces like that of Iloilo and others. The inhabitants of the barrios distant from the village, from authority, and from the parish priests, could not be watched and attended to by the paternal solicitude of the latter, so much, or so well as those of the village, who lived under his immediate eye. Many of the priests themselves were suspected by the authorities as breeders of evil doers and criminals, for in the distant barrios people of evil life gathered, combined their thefts, and concealed the thefts. They were the pests of the civil guard and of the local authorities, and the constant preoccupation of the parish priests who saw that they were not fulfilling their religious duties as good Christians, and who, in order to administer the sacraments to them, had to go on horseback, by chair [horimon] or by hammock, whether it rained in torrents, or the equatorial sun melted their brains. Many times, and in distinct seasons and occasions, the superior authority of the islands ordered that the barrios be incorporated into the villages. Not being able to succeed in that, they ordered the small barrios to be fused into the greater, and roads to be opened which would put them in communication with the mother village. Not even this could they obtain because of the inborn passivity of the Indians. The one most harmed by that order of things was the parish priest who had the duty of watching over those scattered sheep, and giving them the food of the spirit to the danger of his health, and the exhaustion of his purse, by paying the wages of the teachers and for the materials used in teaching for the schools of the barrios.14

When the schools were already running with regularity, and the fruits which were produced under the accurate direction and immediate inspection of the parish priests were plentiful, the superior government of the islands took possession of the department of education, and in the above-mentioned decree of 1863, gave official character to the schools instituted by the parish priests. It conceded titles as teachers ad interim to those who were then in charge of the schools appointed by the religious. It assigned them a moderate pay, but one much greater than that received from the parish priests, whose resources were certainly very meager, and with which they had to attend to other duties which their ministry imposed on them. But the government left in most complete abandonment the settlement of the barrios composed generally of two-thirds of the total number of souls. We have already related how and in what manner the parish priests supplied the governmental omission. Teachers ad interim were gradually substituted by the normal teachers as they graduated from the normal school. Indeed in the last years of the past century there were but few schools not ruled over by teachers of the normal school. Did education gain much by the semi-academical title of the new teachers? Did the language of the fatherland become more general? At first, we must reply with all truth that while the normal teachers remained under the immediate supervision of the parish priests, authorized by the official rules to suspend them and fashion them suitably, education made excellent progress. But when they were emancipated from the supervision of the parish-priest religious by the decree of sad memory countersigned by Señor Maura in 1893, creating the municipalities to which passed the supervision and management of the schools and the teachers, education went into a decline.15 The presence of the children became purely nominal in the triplicate report which the masters and mistresses sent monthly to the government of the province. That report had to be visoed by the parish priests, but the governors received and approved them without that requisite, disdaining and despising the signature of the parish priests. In that the latter understood that the visto bueno [i.e., approval] was a farce, which, taken seriously, lessened the reputation of and gained ill will for them, without any profit to the teachers and municipal captains. Consequently, it was all the same for the results whether they signed the said reports, or did not sign them. But if was painful to contemplate the empty benches in the school, from which those regular and interminable rows of four hundred or five hundred boys, and two other rows of as many or more girls, reduced afterwards to two or three dozen at the most, no longer went to the church after the afternoon class. That happened and we have seen it. It was one, and not of the least serious, misfortunes that came upon the country because of the unfortunate decree in regard to the Filipino municipalities.

On the creation of the normal school the government proposed as its principal object the rapid and quick diffusion of Castilian as the bond of union between the mother country and the colony. The end was good and praiseworthy, but a mistake was made in the means by which it was to be obtained, for those means were neither sufficient nor efficacious. Departing even from the false supposition that all the normal teachers constantly directed their efforts to teaching Castilian to the children, nothing serious and positive could be obtained. In the schools the children read and wrote in Castilian, learned the grammar by heart, and some teachers gave the explanation in Castilian also. The teacher asked questions in Castilian, and the scholars replied in certain dialogues, which they learned by heart.16 But what was the result? The children did not understand one iota of the master's explanation. They answered in the dialogue like parrots, and the few phrases which they learned in the harmonious language of Cervantes, they forgot before they reached home, if not in the very school itself, because they did not again hear them either when playing with their comrades or in their homes, or in the school itself. For the constant and daily presence in the school left much to be desired, especially during the last decade of Spanish rule. Before the creation of the municipalities to which Señor Maura gave the local supervision of the schools, the parish priests visited them frequently. Every afternoon when the boys and girls were dismissed from school they went to the church in two lines, and the parish priest observed and even counted the number of those who were present, and when many of them were absent, they asked the teachers for their report of the absent children, called on their parents, and with flattery, admonitions, or threats, succeeded in getting the latter to see that their children were punctual in attendance. Furthermore, they clothed at their expense the poor boys and girls who excused their non-attendance at school because they had no pantaloons, or were without a skirt with which to cover the body. Later, with the municipalities, neither the municipal captains nor anyone else took care of the daily attendance of teachers and scholars in the school. If primary instruction in Filipinas had gone on in this way for considerable time it would have pitifully retrograded.

We have already seen the intervention which the parish priests had in primary education before the decree of 63, after that date, and also after the never sufficiently-deplored decree in regard to the municipalities, proposed for the royal signature by the then minister of the colonies, Don Antonio Maura, in 1893. But, notwithstanding that, there are many Spaniards who blame the parish-priest religious for the ignorance of the Indians of Castilian. Why this charge, both gratuitous and unjust? Some have argued that the parish priests should personally teach Castilian to the native children. In order to understand the absurdity of so great a pretension, one need only bear in mind that the parish-priest regulars in Filipinas had in their charge the spiritual administration of the villages, the number of souls in the smallest of which was not less than six thousand, and for the greater part reached ten thousand, fourteen thousand, and even twenty thousand, and more. For that work only a few parish priests had a coadjutor, and those among the Tagálogs, two or three Indian coadjutors, who aided them in the administration of the sacrament to the well and sick. It was also the duty of the parish priest to reply to consultations, give advices, direct communications, exercise the duties of alcaldes, justices of the peace, decisions, etc.; for in all that they had to take action, as neither the municipal alcalde nor the justice of peace of the village understood Castilian, and least of all, understood the orders, reports, acts, and measures. And it is asked us, if, after attending to so varied occupations, some peculiar to their ministry, others imposed by charity and by necessity, the parish priests would have time, willingness, or pleasure, in officiating as masters of Castilian without pay; however, there is still more. The parish priests were the local presidents of the boards of health and of locusts, public works, industrial and urban contribution, citizen and tributary poll, etc., etc., and we are asked, I repeat, if with all these trifles and mummeries the parish priest would have time even to rest, at the very least.

Others carried their pretension even to meddling with sacred matters of the temple and interfering with the parochial dwelling, demanding from the parish priests that the theological moral preaching, and the explanation of the Christian doctrine be in Castilian, as if it were the duty of the parish priest to please four deluded people, and not to instruct his parishioners who, not understanding Castilian, would have obtained from the catechism and from the sermon that which the negro did from the story. The same is true of the demand that the religious should address their servants in our beautiful language. Seeing that the Indian servants did the reverse of what their Spanish masters ordered them, and seeing the desperation of the latter for the said reason, why should the religious have to be subjected to like impatience when they could avoid it by addressing their servants in their own language? So general was the opinion that the religious were opposed to the Indians learning Castilian that Governor-general Despujols, in his visits to the Ilonga capital, apostrophized the parish-priest religious harshly, who had gone in commission to salute him. "You," he said to them, "are the ones who oppose the diffusion of Castilian in the country." Such were the words of that Catalonian, who claimed that a colony separated from the mother country by thousands of miles, and almost abandoned for that reason until the opening of the isthmus of Suez, should know and speak the Castilian, which is not known or spoken as yet in Cataluña, or in other provinces of España. It was very convenient for the Spaniards who went to Filipinas on business or as employes, and even necessary for them to understand the Indians, and they demanded that the latter learn Castilian. It was also very convenient and comfortable for the religious, since the learning of a dialect of the country cost them at least a year's study and practice. But was it not easier and more just that forty or fifty thousand Spaniards learn the language of the country since they needed it to live and do business in it, than to make six or seven millions of Indians, very few of whom needed to know it, learn Spanish?

Father Zúñiga17 already declared in his time: "It has been ordered that books be not printed in the Tagálog language, that the Indians learn the doctrine in the Castilian language, and that the fathers preach to them in that language. The religious, in order to observe that command preached to them in Spanish and in Tagálog, but to ask them to confess some Indians who only knew the doctrine in a language which they did not understand and that the parish priests should be satisfied by preaching to their parishioners in a language of which the latter were ignorant, was almost the same as asking them for that which Diocletian asked from the Christians, and they would rather die willingly before fulfilling it.... In order that one may see the inconsistency of those who rule, it is sufficient to know their method of procedure in regard to plays. These Indians, as I have said, are very fond of plays, and the most influential people are those who become actors. Since such people do not generally know the Castilian language, they petition that they be allowed to play in their own language, and there is not the slightest hesitation in allowing plays in the Tagálog language in all the villages of this province, even in that of Binondo, which is only separated from the city [of Manila].

"And it is asked that the parish priests preach in Spanish!"18

In 1590, we find in the records of our province the following most note-worthy minute of the provincial chapter: "Likewise, it shall be charged upon all the ministers of the Indians that, just as the lads of the school are taught to read and to write, they also shall learn to talk our Spanish tongue because of the great culture and profit which follow therefrom (Archives of St. Augustine in Manila)." This was the rule made by the Augustinian fathers in 1590, and still there are some who accuse the religious of having been opposed to the diffusion of Castilian in Filipinas.

The decree in which the religious were charged to teach Castilian in the kingdoms of Indias is as follows: "By Don Felipe IV, in Madrid, March 2, 1634; and November 4, 1636, law v. That the curas arrange to teach the Indians the Castilian language and the Christian doctrine in the same language.

"We ask and charge the archbishops and bishops to provide and order in their dioceses the curas and instructors of the Indians, by using the gentlest means, to arrange and direct all the Indians to be taught the Spanish language, and that they be taught the Christian doctrine in that language, so that they may become more apt in the mysteries of our Catholic faith, and profit for their salvation, and attain other advantages in their government and mode of living." —Book i, título xiii.

"We could cite other dispositions19 but these are sufficient to cause the noble propositions of our governors-general and the first apostles of Christianity in that country to be appreciated. Apart from the fact that in former times the friar could not alone carry the weight of the extraordinary labor, which is inferred from the teaching of a language which can be contained in the head of but very few Indians, the aspiration that our language supplant the many which are spoken in Filipinas can be only completely illusory."

We cannot resist the desire to reproduce here some paragraphs of the Carta abierta [i.e., open letter] which was directed through the columns of La Época by Señor Retana to Don Manuel Becerra, who was then minister of the Colonies.20

"I do not see, Señor Don Manuel, that a single Spaniard exists who would not be delighted to know that peoples who live many leguas from ours use the Spanish language as their own language. Why should we not be proud when we are persuaded that in both Americas live about forty millions of individuals who speak our beautiful language? Consequently, I esteem as most meritorious that vehement desire of yours to effect that there in Filipinas the Malays abandon their monotonous and poor dialects, and choose as their language that which we talk in Castilla. Very meritorious is it in fact among us to sustain so fine a theory; and I say, among us, for if you were English and set forth your laudable propositions in the House of Lords, or the House of Commons, of diffusing the language of the mother-country among the natives of unequal colonies, you may be assured, Señor Becerra, that on all sides of the circle there would come marks and even cries of disapproval. For it is a matter sufficiently well known in Great Britain and in Holland; and in a certain manner in France also, it is not maintained, not even in theory, that it is advisable for the conquered races to know the language of the ruling race. The great Macaulay, a liberal democrat, freethinker, a sincere and enthusiastic man, published his desire that Christianity be propagated in India, but he never spoke of a propagation of the English language in the Hindoostan Empire.

"Think, Señor Don Manuel, and grant me that if it were possible to please all the Spaniards to have our language propagated in all quarters of the world, there may be *some persons* who, thinking like the *English*, may conceive that that propagation would be unadvisable, from the viewpoint of politics.

"But by deprecating such tiquis miquis21 since I hold, so far as I am concerned, that today our fellow countrymen who think in the English fashion in this manner are exceptional, let us come to the real root of the matter. It is an easy thing for you, Don Manuel, to see that it is practicable in a brief space of time to place the Castilian in the head of seven millions of Filipino Indians. Permit me to make a citation which is of pearls. Not many months ago the director of the royal college of the Escorial, or, to be more explicit, Fray Francisco Valdés, a man of superior talent who has lived in Filipinas for eighteen or twenty years, said: 'Our language cannot be substituted advantageously for the Tagálog, so long as the social education of that people does not experience profound and radical transformations.' And the same author adds: 'And since the total transformation of the customs and manner of living of a race is not the work of one year, much less of one century, hence, our firm conviction that great as may be our strength and much as the fondness of the Indian for Castilian may be exaggerated, the latter will never be the common idiom of Filipinas.'

"Do you think of tearing out the entrails of seven millions of individuals by giving them other new ones in this manner all at once? For the peculiar idiom is born in the peculiar country, and develops with the individual, and there is no human strength, which in many years can tear it out. At one step from us lie Cataluña and Vascongadas, where no success is had in making the speech of Cervantes common to individuals for whom the resonant drapery of our rich language is very loose, and whom it suffocates. Much less could it be so [in Filipinas]!

"Those who make the greatest propaganda are not, indeed, the masters. As many masters as there are in Cavite, there are in Bulacan, for example, or more, and in Cavite the people talk fairly good Castilian, while in Bulacan they scarcely talk any. Why? Because in Cavite there are many Spaniards who live there, while in Bulacan there are perhaps not fifty. For the rest another citation and the conclusion. The famous student of Filipinas, now the bishop of Jaca, Fray Francisco Valdés, says: 'There are many Indians who come to know quite well the material of the Spanish word; but the internal signification and the logical character of our beautiful language is for them an undecipherable secret. Our meanings [giros] and phrases are opposed to their peculiar fashion of conceiving and correlating ideas. From this discrepancy in the association of ideas, they produce literary products as nonsensical as the one below. This example is chosen from among innumerable others of the same kind, as it is the work of a master who passed among those of his class and was really one of the best instructed. The matter is an invitation elegantly printed and gotten up on the occasion of the mass called vara which the gobernadorcillos usually cause to be celebrated with great pomp on that day when they receive from the governor the vara or staff of command. It is as follows: On the nineteenth day, in the morning, and of the present full moon, the mass of my vara will be held in this church under my charge, for God has gratuitously granted me this honorable charge. I invite you, therefore, to my house, so that from that moment the vacancy of my heart having been freed, it may become full by your presence, until my last hour sounds on the clock of the Eternal.'" Come now Don Manuel, what do you say to this?22

"We might extend our remarks to much greater length23 in this important matter in order to prove that the 'Ordeno y mando'24 of those who govern always falls to pieces before insuperable difficulties, and therefore to accuse the religious of being the reason why Castilian is not popular in Filipinas when we have the most eloquent data that in the villages ruled by secular priests of the country, there is less Castilian spoken than in the parishes ruled over by the friars, is an immense simplicity into which only the malevolent can fall or those who do not know those races by experience.—Consult Barrantes's La Instrucción primaria en Filipinas; and Father Valdés's El Archipiélago Filipino."25

If the Spanish government desired that the Castilian language be rapidly diffused in Filipinas, the normal school or the teachers who graduated from it were not the most efficient and suitable means, but the establishment in the Filipino villages of five hundred thousand Spanish families. The servants of those families, and familiarity and converse with the native families would have done in a short time, what never would have succeeded by means of the normal teachers, and which the other educational schools in which the native dialects would not be allowed to be spoken, would have taken centuries in obtaining. It was observed that in the ports and in the capitals where the Spanish element was numerous, almost all the Indians spoke Castilian. Consequently, this same thing would have happened in the villages in which fifty or one hundred Spanish families would have been settled. Neither was it the mission of the parish-priest religious to teach

Castilian to the Indians, nor did they have time to dedicate themselves to it. Neither would they have succeeded in that in a long time, not even with all their prestige and competency. Nor did they need as parish priests that the Indian should know Castilian, although as Spaniards they desired it, and very greatly. For, very strongly did it come to them that language, religion, and customs, are strong chains which united mother countries to colonies.

No one could be in a position to know the needs of the country, to feel its forces and appreciate its progress as could the parish-priest religious. Individual members of respectable communities consecrated to the spiritual and material happiness of the Indians, passed, but the spirit which guided their footsteps toward so noble an end, without separating itself any distance from the preconceived plan, always existed. When the opportunity to give greater amplitude to education, and to open up new and vaster horizons to the studious youth of the country, came, the parish priests were the ones who recognized that need and satisfied it. By a royal decree of June 8, 1585, King Don Felipe II arranged for the foundation of the college of San José, which was destined for the education and teaching of the children of Spaniards resident in Filipinas. Lessons in Latin, rhetoric, and philosophy, were given in that college by distinguished Jesuit fathers. The restrictions placed as to the number and quality of the pupils did not satisfy the need for more centers of learning, which the Filipino youth urgently demanded within a little time. His Excellency, the archbishop of Manila, Señor Benavides, a Dominican, projected the foundation of the college of Santo Tomás, aided by his Excellency, Don Fray Diego de Soria of the same order, bishop of Nueva Segovia.26 With the one thousand pesos fuertes donated by Señor Benavides and the four thousand by Señor Soria, and the acquisition of the libraries of both, the works were commenced in the year 1610. In 1617, the college was in condition of being admitted as a house by the province of the Dominican fathers in the islands. In 1620, having been provided with professors, it opened its halls to the Filipino youth without distinction of race. King Don Felipe IV took the college under his special protection by a royal decree of November 27, 1623. Some years later, its royal protector obtained from his Holiness, Pope Innocent X, the fitting bull given November 20, 1644, by which the said college was erected into a university, and the latter decorated with the honorable titles of Royal and Pontifical. By a royal decree of May 17, 1680, it was admitted solemnly under the royal protection, and his Majesty, the king, was declared its patron. By another royal decree of December 7, 1781, the statutes approved by the government of the colony, October 20, 1786, were formed. It continued and is at present in charge of its founders, the learned and virtuous Dominican fathers. That royal college and pontifical university has a rector religious, and all the professors except those of medicine and pharmacy are also Dominicans.

The studious youth who saw in the new center of teaching the glorious future which invited them by the golden laurels of learning, came in crowds to fill the cloisters of the new university, which, narrow and reduced for containing within their halls so many young men desirous of learning and instruction, begged the aid of another institution which should share with the university in the task of the teacher. The time urged, the necessity was pressing, there was no time to think of the construction of a new edifice for circumstances did not permit it. Then there was fitted up as a college the school of primary instruction instituted by the illustrious Spaniard, Don Gerónimo Guerrero, of glorious memory, whose name should pass to posterity so that he may be blessed eternally by Spaniards and Filipinos, since he dedicated his wealth, his labors, and his care to their instruction and education, not only instructing them in the primary letters, but also supporting them and clothing them with his own resources and with the alms which other charitable persons who were desirous of contributing in so deserving a work gave him. The efforts of that remarkable Spaniard deserved the protection of the government of the mother country and the support of the Council of Indias. The king remunerated them by granting him an encomienda in Ilocos as an aid in that blessed establishment, and God rewarded it by conceding him the religious vocation which induced him to take the habit in the order of the Dominican fathers. He ceded to the latter his schoolhouse, his encomienda, and all his goods, with the sole condition that the said fathers were to take charge of the gratuitous education and teaching of the poor Spanish and native boys. The condition having been accepted by the Dominican fathers the schoolhouse of the worthy Spaniard and now virtuous religious was erected into a college under the advocacy of San Juan de Letrán, July 18, 1640, by license from the governor-general and from the archbishop. Since that college was a school, it had also as its object the elemental instruction and education of abandoned and poor children, in order to make of them good citizens and excellent military men for the defense of the plaza of Manila, and the colony. Erected into a college, the students continued therein the study of philosophy, theology, and canons, in order that those who showed aptitude and merited that dignity, might be ordained as priests. Later, all the young men who cared to devote themselves to the study of secondary education were admitted as pensioned inmates. At the end of that course, and after they had taken their degree, they went to the university of Santo Tomás to take up the higher branches. The above-mentioned college was always very useful and commendable. A blessed asylum in its origin, it has always been until today the institution of secondary teaching in which the Dominican fathers, subjecting themselves rigorously to the urgent, although ancient plan of studies, have been able to mold themselves to the peculiar capacity of the natives, directing with exquisite prudence, their native qualities to the professional studies which most harmonize with them.

Thus, in proportion as the necessities for education were exacting, the monastic orders, ever attentive to every movement which could be of interest to the colony, continued to create centers of instruction: the Jesuit fathers in the Ateneo and in the normal school in Manila; the Dominicans in the university, Letrán, and Dagupan; the Franciscans, in Camarines; the Augustinian Recollects, in Negros; the calced Augustinians founded in Iloilo colleges of secondary education directed by themselves, which promised to be the dawn of a new era of civilization and culture, if the last Indian rebellion, provoked by the obstinate governors and supported by the Americans had not caused its ruin with a secular work, the wonder of the world, with the colleges, with the Spanish domination, with the country, and with all the existing things gained quietly yet at the cost of great hardships, and of enormous sacrifices in self-denial and virtue.27

The weak sex also were attended to according to their merits by the religious orders. From before the middle of the eighteenth century dates the institution of the school of Santa Rosa, or of Mother Paula, as its foundress was called. She was a religious of the tertiary branch of St. Dominic, who went from Cataluña to Manila to consecrate herself to the welfare of her own class. Having arrived at Manila, she saw that the greatest benefit which her flaming charity could produce was the education and instruction of the young Indian women. In reality, she labored with pious and burning zeal, until she obtained a house, in which she made the foundation of the beaterio school in which the young Indian women received a Christian education. In the holy fear of God, they learned the doctrine and exercised themselves in the labors peculiar to their sex, in order to later dedicate themselves to God and to the moral education of their sex, or to become married, in which estate they gave application and example of the excellent maxims and sane principles which they learned from their glorious foundress. Mother Paula endured many persecutions which she suffered with resignation and patience. She gave her name to the beaterio, which continued as an educational institution and as a retreat for the girls who desired to embrace it temporarily.

Before the beaterio of Santa Rosa, or of Mother Paula, was founded that of Santa Catalina de Sena. The former was the complement of the latter, which in its beginning only took charge of the education of young Spanish women, It is said that its foundation was due to a certain number of women of the tertiary branch of St. Dominic who retired to a house in order to devote themselves to pious exercises, and from which they went out only to hear mass. Others attribute the foundation of that beaterio school in 1696 to the solicitude of Mother Francisca del Espiritu Santo, and to the reverend father, Fray Juan de Santo Domingo. The illustrious author, Fray Joaquin Martinez de Zúñiga, recognizes as foundress of that beaterio in 1694, Doña Antonia Esguerra, but from any of those three opinions which we follow it will always result that the said beaterio school of Santa Catalina de Sena was dedicated from its beginning to the education and teaching given by women religious to the Spanish girls primarily, and admitted afterwards into its classes Indian and mestizo girls. All learned to read, write, reckon, and the work peculiar to their sex.

The prodigious increase of the Filipino population and of the general prosperity of the country, and even more the advanced extension made by culture in all social classes made the above-mentioned beaterio schools insufficient, and, just as other monastic orders came to the aid of the Dominican fathers when the needs of the times demanded it, so also, the sisters of charity came to the aid of the tertiary mothers, and founded the schools of Luban and Concordia in Manila, in Tuguegarao, Pangasinan, Camarines, Iloilo, Cebú, and Ilocos-Sur.

The monastic orders, charged with the superior rule of almost all the literary profession, directors of the scientific movement of the country, could not have forgotten one class of the greatest utility at any time of the scarcity of religious, although it never corresponded as it ought to the desires of its professors, or to that which the high spiritual interests of the Church and of the faithful demanded and hoped from it. The bishops of the country all proceeding from the monastic cloisters founded the conciliar seminaries directed by religious of all the orders, in which the native clergy was educated, instructed, and formed, as an aid to the regular clergy in the beginning, and as parish priests and administrators after the missions and ministries surrendered to the miters by the religious orders.

All the above-mentioned centers of education gave a suitable increase for the end for which they were created. All attained in a short time so high a degree of splendor, that but seldom or never is seen in cultured Europa. They counted their regular pupils by hundreds, and their day pupils by thousands. The confidence of the families in the solid instruction and morality of the religious professors, in the method and facility in the explanation by expert professors who knew the qualities and defects of the scholars, and even the language of the country, and in the moral and religious regimen to which they rigorously submitted both regular and day pupils contributed to so happy a result.

With respect to the condition of education in the last third of the past century, some affirm that it was highly satisfactory, while others have asserted that its backward state and abandonment were pitiful. If we consider that the courses were made, if not by the rule of the statutes approved by the general government of the colony, October 20, 1786, at least by a plan of almost as respectable an antiquity, the secondary and university education had to result as deficient for modern times. If we add the small capacity of the Indians for the sciences, the chronological defects will show up more clearly through the little gain of the scholars in spite of the enlightened efforts of the eleven doctors, and eighteen licentiates of the royal and pontifical university of Santo Tomás.

As if led by the hand we have now come to touch upon one of the Filipino problems discussed so often and with so great heat, and yet without result to the satisfaction of all. We speak of the aptitude and capacity of the Indians for the letters and sciences.

Has the Filipino Indian that aptitude and sufficiency?

Before entering fully upon the question, we ought to advise that we have lived in several Visayan villages for the space of twenty-three years; that we speak the language fluently; that, as a parish priest, we have necessarily had among our duties to treat with Indians of all social classes, from the most enlightened to the rudest; that we have merited their confidence; that we have studied them and observed them at their domestic fireside and in public life; that we know their customs, their passions, their defects, and their good qualities. And if all this, and much more which we could add, is not sufficient to form an exact and definite judgment on the nature of the Indian, we will say that we have consulted the experience of our predecessors, and the parish-priest religious brothers of the habit, friends, and associates who took part in the sacred ministry in villages of other provinces, and we have found our opinions upon this particular in accord with their more valuable opinions. We will say also, in order that our opinion may not be censured as partial, that by the divine grace we wear the habit of our glorious founder, St. Augustine, the wisest and most universal of the holy fathers, the great figure of the fourth century, the wonderful ancient author, the admiration of the moderns, from whom we have inherited our love for study and the sciences, which with prayer and contemplation constitute the foundation and essence of our institute, as it was founded by a saint consecrated all his life to letters and converted to the faith by means of a book: Tolle lege; tolle, lege.28 Lastly, we advise that the Order of St. Augustine, to which I have the good fortune to belong, also built a school in Iloilo, dedicated to secondary education, in which it spent huge sums to make it the equal of the best schools of Europa.

Now then, having set forth these preliminaries, we enter upon the question. More than two centuries ago, the university and the colleges of San José, and San Juan de Letrán, in Manila, opened their halls to the Filipino youth. The Indians annually matriculated by thousands in the various courses which were taught by erudite professors. How many scientific notabilities have resulted from the natives up to the present from the university cloisters? How many Indian theologues, canons, philosophers, moralists [have graduated] from the conciliar seminaries? Not even one by exception, which usually is found in any general rule. At the most we have heard of some good advocate, of some regular theologue, of some mediocre canon, of some advanced pharmacist, or of some clever physician. But those whom we can consider as exceptions to the rule, never reach the top rank of their equals in other countries. This lack is not attributed to the professors, for they were always picked men, and in the university of Manila, the present bishop of Oviedo, Señor Vigil, his Excellency, the lately deceased Cardinal Ceferino, the archbishop of Manila, Father Nozaleda, the illustrious Father Orias, and very many other Dominican fathers who were the honor of their order, of their country, and of all the monastic orders, shone pre-eminently for their learning. We recognize more sufficiency in the European mestizo and the Sangley or Chinese mestizo, than in the pure-blooded Indian; and the mestizos of those races are the ones who distinguish themselves, some notably, as authors, advocates, physicians, canons, and among other literary professions, in which not one single pure-blooded Indian has been found. What does this signify, if not that the deficiency exists in the race, and not in the professors or in the books.29

When we have tried to demonstrate to them some abstract truth, a mystery, a catholic dogma, some philosophical thesis, with the greatest simplicity, clearness, and precision, we have observed that the attention of the Indian, excited and sustained at the beginning, gradually diminished, his eyes wandered, his distraction was manifest. Giving another turn and another form to the exposition, we have succeeded in awakening those sleepy or tired minds, but always for only a few moments. By one example we obtain more than by the most exact dissertations, and by the most clear explanations; for their childish minds, their excessively acute sensibility needs something palpable to bring some light to the darkness of their understandings. We have observed that phenomenon also in the rude as well as the instructed Indians who had learned to reason by logic, and have cultivated the mind by study as far as their mental strengths can go. It must be inferred then that the Filipino Indian is a grown-up child. As a child he cannot go beyond the elemental in the sciences, for his most limited understanding cannot mount in its flight to the heights of the metaphysical.

Examples, similes, and metaphors are the indirect means to make him understand the intangible, the spiritual, and the abstract. There can be no luminous philosophical dissertations, or brilliant theories, or abstruse problems, but examples, many examples to make him perceive the truth and the essence of things, causing him to touch, feel, and perceive, with eyes, ears, touch, and the other bodily senses.

There have not been lacking those who have attributed the incapacity and insufficiency of the Indians to intellectual laziness which corresponds to the laziness peculiar to an equatorial country, where the burning rays of fiery sun enervates the physical and intellectual forces. We neither affirm nor deny this, since it might well happen that the Indians possess, like children, in the beginning in potentiality intellectual faculties in their germ equal and even superior to those of the white race, but we incline to the belief that the Indian of pure blood can never reach in scientific culture to the level of the European. If he ever attains anything in the field of science, it must be because another blood inoculates in his own blood the divine breath of wisdom, and then he will be able to advance somewhat when the cross whitens his olive-colored face, has lowered his prominent cheek-bones, and elevated his flat nose a trifle. Until that time comes, the Indian will always be a grown-up child, as simple, as ignorant, and as credulous as a child, but with all the passions, vices, and defects of the adult.

"In regard to the nature and understanding of the Indians," says Retana, "speaking in general, they are more clever than the American Indians.30 They readily learn any art, and with the same readiness they imitate any work which is placed before them. They make fine clerks and are employed in the accounting offices and other offices in that duty. For, besides the fact that they write well, they are excellent accountants, have capacity for directing a lawsuit, and very sharp in getting the parties to the lawsuit all tangled up. There are good stonemasons, and musicians among them. But in all these things, they only reach a certain degree which they never surpass, either because of laziness, or for the lack of intellect, which we must suppose to be sufficiently limited. For they never invent anything, and all is reduced to their skill of imitation. Those who give themselves to the sciences never surpass a mediocrity in their comprehension.

"He who has had to do with the Indians of Filipinas can do no less than assent to this truth. We find them more clever than ourselves in learning any mechanical work, but more stupid in whatever depends upon the understanding or on the imagination. In so brief a time do they learn the trade of artists, musicians, embroiderers, cobblers, tailors, and whatever is reduced to the mechanical, that they exercise it fairly well in little time. If they are not satisfied with it, they readily give it up and learn another trade.

There are Indians who have gone through all those trades, and they have filled them all well. But not one of them has ever surpassed mediocrity. There has never been an artisan who has invented any improvement in the trade which he learned. They are most ingenious in imitating what they see, but they never invent anything. If those men had the talents of Europeans, why is it possible that one cannot find in three hundred years one who has added anything to what was taught him?

"I can affirm of the Filipinos with whom I have lived for more than sixteen years, that they are handy in every kind of mechanism which is shown to them. They are capable of imitating the most curious works, but they can invent nothing, for they lack imagination and fancy, and are very obtuse in the abstract sciences because they lack understanding.

"Some try to attribute this to the subordination in which the Spaniards hold them. I will ask such people why does not that subordination and submission prevent them from making any mechanical work with a sufficient perfection? The soldiers learn the military exercise quicker than do the Spaniards; the children learn to read readily; most of them write an excellent hand. The girls easily imitate the laces and embroideries of Europa. Why do they not imitate equally well our philosophers, our mathematicians, and our poets? Why do they not make any advance in painting, in music, and in the other sciences which require imagination and understanding?31 More than half of the seculars of the Manila archbishopric are Indians. There are some who have become alcaldes-mayor, officers in the royal army, and advocates in the royal Audiencia. Why have none of them gone beyond a very moderate mediocrity in the sciences to which they have dedicated themselves? Just as among Europeans individuals are found for all kinds of abstract sciences, it must be confessed that in the same manner nations are found who, because of the climate in which they have lived for a long series of generations, have contracted a certain tangency of understanding which disposes them very little to receive metaphysical and spiritual ideas."32

This gives us the key to the fatal results obtained in education in Filipinas. Of the hundreds of students who matriculated annually in the colleges, fifteen per cent did not succeed in obtaining the degree of bachelor, and if those who gained a professional title in the university scarcely reached ten per cent, and of them the greater number were advocates without clients, and physicians without patients, they, united with those who abandoned their books and mutilated their career, were in the villages the greatest calamity that befell the country. They all pompously called themselves pilósopos for filósofos [i.e., philosophers], and they were no more than ignorant and presuming fellows, pettifoggers, intriguers, and lazy, haughty, and vain fellows, who neither could nor would work, or aid their parents in work or trade, but could dress as those in Manila, prink themselves out like women, censuring everything, even the religious acts, in order that they might be esteemed sages. They were, through their vices, a grievous weight to the parish priests; by their laziness and viciousness, an insupportable burden to their families; by their lewdness and intrigues the mine which furnished suits to the lawyers, and for the disaffected and filibuster, as they were almost all of them affiliated with freemasonry, a danger to the government and to the nation.33 All those evil students learned all the evil of the capitals and laden with vices, evil ideas, and morals, they were in the villages a scandal for the majority, a snare for some, and mischievous for all.

"Those deserters from the university," says Escosura, "half instructed with incomplete notions of the sciences which, belonging to the superior education, require to be studied by persons of consideration and social prestige, and above all to be upright, in order that they may not be dangerous to the public safety; those deserters from the university form, I repeat, a class in Filipinas, and are, above all, insatiable leeches who devour the substance of the Indians, so many other founts of lawsuits and quarrels among their fellowcitizens."

Perhaps I shall be asked at this point: "Why since you [religious] see and know all this, why did your religious devote themselves to, and encourage, education?" Because it is very difficult to separate oneself from the influence of the time; for it is impossible to oppose the conquering current of opinion, as the monastic orders of Filipinas did not arrange means to free themselves from the pressure of the government, and to reply to the unjust charge of having retrograded, which those who did not know the country even on the map fulminated against them; and lastly to avoid greater evils. The regular province of the Augustinian fathers was the last to devote itself to superior education among the Indians. When did it do that, and why? When Señor Becerra was minister of the colonies in the years 1887 and 1888, and that minister of sad memory planned an official institute in the capital of Iloilo, the Augustinian fathers saw in the plan of the minister a most grave danger for the country, and they went ahead to ward it off. All we parish-priest regulars of Filipinas saw with pain the advances which freemasonry was making in the country by means of the abandoned advocates and physicians, unfit students, ambitious caciques, wealthy fellows, ruined by their vices or by play—we know the works of the spade against the foundation of Spanish domination which were based on religion, prestige, and superiority of race. We all recognized and experienced the apathy and indifference of the authorities who were not ignorant of the frauds and plans of the lodges; and there were even governors of the provinces who protected them. And if to all that which we knew, recognized, and could not remedy, we had consented that Señor Becerra establish in Iloilo an institute of secondary education with professors who might have been freemasons or atheists, the catastrophe would have been certain and imminent, for such institute would be a seeding place for filibusters and insurgents. In order to avoid that, the Augustinian order planned and constructed at its own expense an edifice which it resolved to dedicate as an institute. That could not be carried out, for the last revolution of '98 came upon them before it was inaugurated.

More beneficial for the country, more in accordance with the monastic traditions, more in harmony with the recommendations of our glorious founder, which were practiced by our virtuous ancestors, would have been the opening of schools of arts and crafts. In reality, although the Spanish government established a few of those schools in Manila, Pampanga, and Iloilo, it was so unseasonable that it was unable to gather the fruits which were promised in their founded hopes. Such is the scarcity of Indian artists and artisans, that of the former there are a few sculptors, engravers, and painters, etc., but of the latter, we can assert that almost all the trades are in the hands of the Chinese, and only carpentry, cabinet-making, architecture, masonry, and some other trades, are exercised by Indians, to whom the parish-priest religious taught them because they needed them for their works and constructions.

It is known that the ancient monks divided their time among prayer, contemplation, study, and manual work. St. Anthony34 and his five thousand monks, as well as all those who afterward imitated the monastic life or that of the desert, employed part of their day in labor with their hands, weaving mats, making shoes, oars, boats, or small skiffs, and other similar labors. Our father, St. Augustine, desired his monks to also devote some hours of the day to manual labor. Accordingly, our predecessors did it. It is true, that the spirit of the respective epochs changed the character of the bodily work, but the monastic corporations of Filipinas, which recognized the incapacity of the Indian for science and deplored the pernicious effects of science poorly digested by the natives, if they could not do away with the action of the governments, the influence of opinion, the pressure of the times, would have had to turn aside, by means of their parish-priest religious, the tendency of the Indians to the literary branches, and to have directed that tendency to those branches of pure imitation, for which it is necessary to recognize, and we do that gladly, that the Filipino Indian has exceptional abilities. At the same time that the university was founded, and the colleges provided, schools and workshops ought to have been established for the natives, which would have obtained the preference in those narrow, dull, and lazy minds, with greater benefits to the country and less harm to all. All the monasteries founded by St. Basil the Great35 had in charge an elementary superior school, and another of arts and crafts joined to it. That ought to be the model of the religious orders in Filipinas, in spite of the governments of the mother country, of the demands of opinion manifestly gone astray on this point, and of the spirit of the epoch which could not have any influence in that country, most especially by their constitution, nature, customs, and government. Had the religious corporations, thoroughly permeated with their Christian and civilizing mission, proceeded in that manner, the contingent of sons with the three pointed design of the square and apron,36 who left the halls of the colleges and became the petty leaders and chief revolutionists who betrayed the mother country and were also the greatest enemies of those who had taught them the little good that they knew, would not have been so numerous.

The cholera, which made ravages in the Filipino Archipelago in 1882, left in the saddest orphanage many children of both sexes and of all the races. They, abandoned, and without resources, wandered through the streets begging public charity. The Spanish women, moved by the disconsolate spectacle, which so many ragged and hungry children offered, formed a society, from which a committee was chosen, which went to the governor-general to beg for food and shelter for those abandoned children. The governor summoned the provincials of the monastic order, as being the natural protectors of the destitute, and creators of the centers of education and learning in the country. He petitioned them for support and aid. The father provincial of the Augustinians, representing his order, took under charge of the province of Santísimo Nombre de Jesús, the support, education, and teaching of the abandoned and orphaned children. The Augustinian fathers assigned for that purpose local sites provisionally in the avenue of San Marcelino, where they gathered the children who were wandering through the city of Manila, and gave them shelter in the temporary barracks. But since the latter had no hygienic conditions, and were not large enough, they transferred the children to the lower parts of the convent of Guadalupe, which were spacious and well ventilated. There they opened workshops of sculpture and ceramics, painting, and modeling, and there they remained until the year 1892, when the schools, workshops, and children were transferred to the building of the new plant constructed for that purpose in the village of Malabon. That place united all the desirable conditions of solidity, decoration, size, and even elegance, which could be desired. There the Augustinian fathers taught the orphans, in addition to their primary letters, painting, designing, sculpture, and modeling, printing, and binding, and indeed the printing plant was bought by the voluntary donation of some religious, through the economies practiced in the missions by dint of privations and of a life of poverty and mortification. We know one of those religious, respectable for his exemplary virtue, who gave for that purpose all his savings, consisting of two thousand pesos. We feel that his humility has prohibited us from placing his name here, so that he may be blessed by all who should hear of a charity and liberality peculiar to the sons of a St. Augustine, who gave even his death-bed to the poor, and suitable also to those of Santo Tomás de Villanueva, father of the poor. That asylum of the orphans, and of the unfortunates abandoned by its founders who had to flee from the ingratitude of the revolutionists, was burned by the shells which the Americans threw to dislodge the Indian rebels who had made forts of it, and being looted afterward by pillaging Chinese who took away even the paving-stones of the lower floor, a cargo of which was surprised by the North American police in the Pasig River, and returned to the Augustinian fathers—the only indemnity which they have received up to date.

The Augustinian fathers also extended their charity to orphan girls. For that purpose they caused sisters of their tertiary branch to go from the Peninsula, who took charge of the education and instruction of the children in the orphanage that was built in Mandaloya at the expense of the said Augustinian fathers. More than three hundred Indian mestizo and Spanish girls received a fine education there, so much so that their work in embroidery, sewing, and the manufacture of artificial flowers, took the prize in the expositions at Madrid and Manila.

So excellent and fine was the education that the orphan girls received in Mandaloya, that it was necessary to accede to the repeated requests of influential families who begged that the Augustinian tertiary mothers receive as pensioners the daughters of many Peninsulars and Spanish mestizos.

1 See this decree in VOL. XLV, pp. 184–186, where it is dated June 20, 1686.

2 Tomás G. del Rosario, cited often in these notes, says (Census of Philippines, iii, pp. 594, 595): "A decree of the general government, issued October 6, 1885, provided for a competition to be followed by prizes for the best grammars written in Visayan, Cebuano, Ilocano, Bícol, Pangasinán, and Pampango, there being one already in Tagálog. Naturally these grammars, which were written in different dialects and taught in the public schools, made it more difficult (and that was the object) for the Spanish language to become general. Matters reached such a stage that teachers were punished

and threatened with deportation, and some were actually deported, for teaching Spanish."

Speaking on the same subject, LeRoy ("Friars in Philippines," in *Political Science Quarterly*, for December, 1903, p. 673) says: "In proclaiming the law of 1893 [the Maura law], Governor-general Blanco instructed the municipal councils to employ 'the most practical means for the diffusion of the Spanish language.' The common assertion that the friars did teach the natives Spanish is contradicted by these provisions and by the numerous decrees from 1585 on; those who frankly admit that they did not spread Spanish, and who hold that it is impracticable to make the natives accept either Spanish or English, have a fair argument to present."

3 See this decree in VOL. XLV, pp. 184–186.

4 This is given by Barrantes, Instrucción primaria, pp. 69–71.

5 For this and following citations of the regulations, see ante.

6 Speaking of the legislation of 1863, LeRoy (Philippine Life, pp. 202, 203) says: "Most significant of all, local school boards of a civil and lay character were ordered established, a feature of the decree which had not by any means been realized when the municipal reform of 1893 was decreed, and which that reform itself did not accomplish. Theoretically, the friars were left in supervision only of religious instruction in the public schools; practically, in four towns out of five, they managed everything about the schools to suit their own will, down almost to the last hours of Spanish rule."

7 The Tagálog insurrection broke out prematurely through betrayal of the plot in August, 1896.

8 Patricio de la Escosura, formerly minister and ambassador in Berlin, member of the Royal Spanish Academy, went to the Philippines about 1863, as royal commissary. His Memoria is important and worth consultation for the history of the islands. It has a prologue by Cañamaque. The first chapter on the teaching of Spanish argues that Spanish be taught the Filipinos. Chapter viii is on the creation of a school of physicians and surgeons. The various chapters of this book, although written as letters to the President of the Council of Ministers, in 1863, were not published until 1882. See Pardo de Tavera's Biblioteca filipina.

9 See VOL. XVII, p. 333. The Cuadrilleros occupied in a certain sense, the position occupied now by the constabulary.

10 The author of this book was Manuel del Rio, who went to the Philippines in 1713, where he labored many years in various villages

of Pangasinán. He was procurator-general of his order, definitor, and provincial; and was bishop-elect of Nueva Segovia at his death. A fuller title of his book is as follows: "Instrucciones morales y religiosas para el govierno, direccion, y acierto en la practica de nuestros ministerios. Que deben observar todos los religiosos de esta nuestra Provincia de el Santo Rossario de Philipinas del Orden de Predicadores." See Peréz and Güemes's Adiciones y continuacion (Manila, 1905), p. 114.

11 The opening of the Suez Canal, as much probably as any other factor promulgated modern ideas in the Philippines, because of the vastly shorter route thus brought about between them and the mother country.

12 The above citation is from Daniel Grifol y Aliaga's prologue to his book La instrucción primaria en Filipinas (note by Zamora, p. 235).

13 Fray Hilarion Diez, O.S.A., who was consecrated archbishop of Manila, October 21, 1827. His death occurred May 7, 1829. See Ferrando's Historia, vi, pp. cliii, cliv.

14 Zamora, speaking in his chapter ix of the intervention of the friar, and discussing in general the accusations against the religious orders, says (pp. 408–452): "The Spaniards in admiration of the sanity of life, of the austerity and purity of the morals of the religious; thankful for their good offices as intermediaries among themselves in their disputes, and among the Indians during rebellions; convinced of the efficacy of their word, and of their intervention in all things; of the necessity of their active and diligent coöperation for the conservation and consolidation of the colony: began to respect, venerate, and recognize in them spontaneously, a certain right to intervene in their affairs, to settle their differences, submit to their judgment their quarrels, and respect their decisions with more submission and conformity than would proceed from the legitimately constituted authority. The governors themselves could not leave the religious out of account in all that they undertook." The Indian learned to distinguish, says Zamora, between the peaceful and helpful friar, who sought only his welfare, and the often brutal and harsh encomendero. "Not otherwise was the origin of the prestige of the religious among Indians and Spaniards;" and the lapse of time furthered it. The governors made use of the friars as ambassadors, counsellors, and in other capacities connected with the government. "The religious were the ones who formed the villages and made a record of their parishioners on the tribute and citizen list." As the friars were the only ones who understood the native dialects and the natives were ignorant of Spanish, the authorities were forced to work through the former, and consequently, the friars had the right of "visé" of the tribute and citizen lists. They became the presiding officers of all local boards, and so had all the power. In the

provinces the dwelling of the parish priest was open to strangers who lodged there as in a hotel. The envy and maliciousness of certain people, however, conspired to take away the power of the parish priest, a reform that was rather agreeable than otherwise to him, as it left him more time for his ministry; but he deplored it as it seemed to threaten the country at no distant future. "The vigilant, noble, and disinterested intervention of the parish priests in all matters was the chief and necessary wheel of the gubernatorial, administrative, and judicial mechanism, in their multiple and complicated attributes and duties. That was exercised with regularity, until, in the last years of Spanish dominion in that country, the impelling force restrained the impulse." The fruit of the "reform" was the contempt of the natives for the Spaniards. "If the religious orders were the cause for the loss of these islands, they were so unconsciously and ignorantly, or consciously and maliciously." Zamora argues that they were not in any way the cause for the loss of the country. "The religious communities knew that the ruin of the country was their own ruin, the end of the Spanish domination, the end even of their existence in Filipinas." "On three bases rested the Spanish domination in Filipinas with its institutions and organisations: religion; the prestige of the parish-priest regulars; and the superiority of race in so great accord with Spanish nobility." To freemasonry was due the destruction of the high ideal of religion, and also the idea of the superiority of race; and to freemasonry is due, then, the loss of the colony. The friars have not committed the abuses with which they have been credited, and were not the cause of the revolution. They were always the upholders of Spanish sovereignty, and protected the natives.

15 The municipal reform of 1893, the "Maura law," in conferring a considerable degree of local autonomy on Philippine towns, made the newly created municipal councils also school boards. It was a further step in taking from the padre the power to "visé" and supervise everything done, small and great, in a town. In promulgating the law, Governor-general Blanco (popular with the Filipinos for his liberal measures) took pains to explain that the priest's school-inspecting powers, so far as religious teaching went, were to be the same as ever. As a matter of fact, this reform of Minister Maura, sent forth amid much accompaniment of proclamas in Spain and the islands, was virtually made a dead-letter under succeeding governors. Its non-enforcement, except in a few towns, was one of the complaints of the insurgents in 1896. See LeRoy "Friars in the Philippines," in Political Science Quarterly for December, 1903, pp. 672, 673.

16 Victor S. Clark (Bulletin of the Bureau of Labor, no. 58, May, 1905; Labor Conditions in the Philippines), says (p. 854): "Practically all the Christian population of Mindanao spoke Spanish in 1883, which indicates

that the statistics probably did not cover the remoter Jesuit mission stations among the Moros. In that year about 21 per cent of the total population reported for the islands could read, but less than 5½ per cent could speak Spanish. In other words, 75 per cent of the persons able to read could do so only in the Malay dialects."

17 Estadismo, chapter xiv (Retana's ed.; note by Zamora).

18 Zúñiga (Estadismo, Retana's ed., i, pp. 299, 300), says of the natives of Tondo province: "The language of these Indians is somewhat corrupted, because a great number of Spanish words have been introduced. That is the only benefit which they have derived from living near Manila, since there are very few who know Spanish. In the suburbs themselves, as well as in Binondo and Santa Cruz, the Tagálog language is spoken. The Spaniards cast the blame on the religious for the Indians not knowing the Spanish language. But let them examine the villages of the seculars, and they will find whether they know more than those of the regular curacies. We cannot succeed in getting them to learn the doctrine, and it is wished that we teach them the Spanish language. There are some Spaniards who believe that we are opposed to them learning it, but this calumny was clearly destroyed in the time of Señor Anda, when it was ordered that no one could become a gobernadorcillo unless he knew Spanish; and it was necessary in almost all the villages to take the servants of the fathers. Now even, if there is any Indian who knows Spanish in the villages, it is because he has served some religious or some Spaniard in Manila. I know very well the method of introducing the Spanish language into Filipinas; but since I know that my plan will not be observed, I shall say only that hitherto, certain absurd means which would not have been used among barbarians, have been taken."

19 Estadismo, appendix A (note by Zamora). This citation is from vol. ii, pp. 59*, *60.

20 The issue of June 5, 1891 (note by Zamora).

21 An expression used in ridicule, like the English folderols. It might be translated "utter nonsense."

22 The Spanish for this invitation is as follows: "El día diecinueve de su mañana y del presente plenilunio tendrá lugar la misa de mi vara en esta Iglesia de mi cargo que Dios gratuitamente me ha concedido esta carga honorosa. Invito á Vd. tanto como á mi casa que desde luego se llenará el vacio acendrado de mi corazón en su asistencia hasta resonar mi última hora en el relox del Eterno." Some of the words are taken in the wrong acceptation.

23 This letter is given by Retana in his edition of Zúñiga's Estadismo, ii, pp. *60–63*.

24 Literally, "I ordain and command" — the form of opening often used in decrees, edicts, etc.

25 This last paragraph is not a part of Retana's letter to Becerra, but it is taken from Retana's words following the letter in his edition of the Estadismo, ii, pp. 63*, *64.

26 The friars virtually controlled secondary and higher instruction in the islands until they were lost to Spain in 1898. The reaction that followed the liberal measures (some of them practical, some foolish) of 1863 to 1870 really strengthened the hold of the friars upon superior education (though one must take into account the competition from the Jesuits in Manila with which the disturbed Dominicans had to deal in increased degree each year). See LeRoy's Philippine Life, p. 205.

27 "The friars maintained control of secondary and higher instruction till the islands were lost to Spain in 1898. A reaction from the liberal policy of 1863 to 1868 was stimulated by the appearance of a radical party in the Philippines, and by an insurrectionary movement at Cavite, in 1872. The friar party declared these to be the natural consequences of 'reform' and when the government changed, as it soon did, the projects of educational reorganization were speedily nullified." James A. LeRoy in Political Science Quarterly, December, 1903, pp. 673, 674.

28 i.e., "Take and read."

29 The comments of Victor S. Clark, in his Labor Conditions in the Philippines (Bulletin no. 58, of Bureau of Labor), in regard to Filipino workmen, are interesting, and show a somewhat different side than that presented by Zamora.

Zamora has left out of account the Filipino patriot, Dr. José Rizal, who was executed by order of the Spanish government, December 30, 1896. Rizal was a pure-blooded Tagálog, and attained highest rank in the Orient as an eye specialist. In addition he was a poet, a sculptor, and a novelist of more than average ability, a wonderful linguist, a widely-read man, and a clear thinker. He studied in the Ateneo Municipal and in Santo Tomás. The two following selections, the first from his novel Noli me tangere, often called the "Filipino bible," and the second from El Filibusterismo (both taken from LeRoy's Philippine Life in town and country, pp. 210–213, and 207, 208) are interesting criticisms of the education of the friars. The first is the reflections of the village philosopher, the second apropos of the teaching of physics in the University of Santo Tomás.

"The country is not the same today as it was twenty years ago.... If you do not see it, it is because you have not seen the former state, have not studied the effect of the immigration of Europeans, of the entrance of new books, and of the going of the young men to study in Europe. It is true that the Royal and Pontifical University of St. Thomas still exists, with its most wise cloister, and certain intelligences still busy themselves in formulating the distinctions and threshing out to the final issue the subtleties of scholasticism. But where will you now find that metaphysical youth of our times, with an archaic education, who tortured his brain and died in full pursuit of sophistries in some remote part of the provinces, without ever having succeeded in understanding the attributes of *being*, or settling the question of *essence* and *existence*, concepts so lofty that they made us forget what was essential in life, our own existence and individuality? Look at the youth of today. Full of enthusiasm at the view of wider horizons, it studies History, Mathematics, Geography, Literature, Physical Science, Languages, all subjects that in our time we heard of with horror as though they were heresies; the greatest freethinker of my time declared all these things inferior to the classifications of Aristotle and the laws of the syllogism. Man has finally comprehended that he is man; he refuses to give himself over to the analysis of his God, to the penetration of the imperceptible, into what he has not seen, and to give laws to the phantasms of his brain; man comprehends that his inheritance is the vast world, dominion over which is within his reach; weary of a task that is useless and presumptuous, he lowers his gaze to earth, and examines his own surroundings.... The experimental sciences have already given their firstfruits; it needs Only time to perfect them. The lawyers of today are being trained in the new teachings of legal philosophy; some begin to shine in the midst of the shadows which surround our courts of justice, and point to a change in the course of affairs.... Look you: the press itself, however backward it might wish to be, is taking a step forward against its will. The Dominicans themselves do not escape this law, but are imitating the Jesuits, their implacable enemies; they give *fiestas* in their cloisters, erect little theatres, write poesies, because, as they are not devoid of intelligence in spite of believing in the fifteenth century, they comprehend that the Jesuits are right and will continue yet to play a part in the future of the young peoples that they have educated.

"But are the Jesuits the companions of Progress? Why, then, are they opposed in Europe?"

"I will answer you like an old scholastic.... One may accompany the course of Progress in three ways, ahead of her, side by side with her, and behind her. The first are those who guide the course of Progress; the second are those who are borne along by her; the last are dragged along, and among them are the Jesuits. Well would they like to direct her course, but, as they see her in the possession of full strength and having other tendencies, they capitulate, preferring to follow rather than be smothered or be left in the middle of the road without light. Well now, we in the Philippines are traveling along at least three centuries behind the car of Progress; we are barely commencing to emerge from the Middle Ages. Hence, the Jesuits, reactionary in Europe, when seen from our point of view represent Progress; the Philippines owe to them their dawning system of instruction, and to them the Natural Sciences, the soul of the nineteenth century, as it has been indebted to the Dominicans for Scholasticism, already dead in spite of Leo XIII—no Pope can revive what common sense has judged and condemned.... The strife is on between the past, which cleaves and clings with curses to the waning feudal castle, and the future, whose song of triumph may be faintly heard off in the distant but splendorous glories of a dawn that is coming, bringing the message of Good-News from other countries."

"The walls were entirely bare; not a drawing, nor an engraving, nor even any kind of a *representation* of an instrument of physics. On occasions there would be lowered from heaven an instrumentlet to be shown from afar to the class, like the Holy of Holies to the prostrate faithful: 'Look at me, but don't touch me.' From time to time, some complacent professor came, a day of the year was assigned for visiting the mysterious 'cabinet,' and admiring from afar the enigmatic apparatus arranged inside the cases. Then no one could complain; that day there were seen much brass, much glass, many tubes, disks, wheels, bells, etc. And the show stopped there, and the Philippines were not turned upside down. For the rest, the students are convinced that these instruments were not bought for them; merry fools would the friars be! The 'cabinet' was made to be shown to foreigners and to high officials from Spain, that, on seeing it, they may nod in approbation, while their guide smiles as if saying: 'You have been thinking you were going to find a lot of backward monks, eh? Well, we are at the height of the century; we have a cabinet!'

"And the foreigners and high officials, obsequiously entertained, afterward wrote in their voyages or reports: 'The Royal and Pontifical University of St. Thomas, of Manila, in charge of the illustrious Dominicans, possesses a magnificent cabinet of physics for the instruction of youth.... There annually take this course some two hundred and fifty students; but, be it on account of the apathy, indolence, scanty capacity of the natives, or through any other cause whatsoever, ethnological or unperceivable, up to date there has not developed a Lavoisier, a Secchi, or a Tyndall, even in miniature, from the Philippine-Malay race!'"

30 See p. 801 of Victor S. Clark's article in Bulletin no. 58, ut supra, for a comparison between the Filipino and the Central and South American Indians.

31 Retana's praises of Rizal, a full-blooded Tagálog, in all these lines, as seen in his Vida y escritos del Dr. José Rizal, a series just concluded (October, 1906), in the Madrid review, Nuestro Tiempo, are the best answer to his own question.

32 See Retana's Estadismo, appendix A (note by Zamora).

33 According to Eduardo Navarro, O.S.A., the first freemason lodge established in the Philippines was the one called Luz Filipina, about 1860, which was established in Cavite under the Gran Oriente Lusitano. It was in immediate correspondence with the Portuguese lodges of Macao and Hongkong. Shortly after another lodge was created in Zamboanga of Peninsulars and creoles resident in Mindanao. Some time after 1868, must have occurred the creation of another lodge composed of foreigners and dependents of the lodge of Hongkong, of the Scottish rite. Into this lodge were admitted some Peninsulars and Filipinos. Shortly after this many other lodges were created under the Grañ Oriente de España. See Navarro's Asuntos filipinos (Madrid, 1897), pp. 221–277. Manuel Sastron (Insurrección en Filipinas, Madrid, 1901, p. 41), who represents the friar standpoint, says: "We believe and affirm in good faith, that, in our opinion, the origin, the primitive cellule of the insurrection of 1896 in Filipinas, is to be found in masonry." The masonic movement was by 1890 widespread in the islands. See also Sawyer's Inhabitants of Philippines, pp. 79–83.

34 St. Anthony the Great, who was an Egyptian, born A.D. 356. His day is January 17. See Baring Gould's Lives of the Saints, i, pp. 249–272.

35 St. Basil the Great was a native of Cappadocian Cæsarea. His death occurred A.D. 379. His day is celebrated on June 14, except by the Greeks who keep January 1 in his memory. See Baring Gould's Lives of the Saints, vi, pp. 192–202.

36 Referring to the Katipunan, or Kataas-taasan Kagalang-gálang Katipunan Nang Mañga Anac Nang Bayan, "Sovereign Worshipful Association of the Sons of the Country." This society, of which it is yet too early to have definite and detailed information, was due in the main to Andrés Bonifacio, a warehouse keeper in the employ of Fressel and Co., of Manila, who became its third president, although primarily founded by Marcelo Hilario del Pilar. This society enrolled in its ranks the common people among the Tagálogs. It is more than likely that the plan of the organization was copied from the masonic lodges, but the analogy stops here. The Katipunan was not masonry. See Sastron's Insurrección, pp. 51–59; Sawyer's Inhabitants, pp. 82, 83; and The Katipunan (Manila, 1902), purporting to be by one Francis St. Clair, although it is claimed by some to have been written by or for the friars.

EDUCATION SINCE AMERICAN OCCUPATION

It is the chief glory of American connection with the Philippines, that no sooner was their easy conquest an assured fact, than attention was directed toward the education of the peoples who thus came under the control of the western democracy. In spite of the more than three centuries of Spanish rule, although many measures had been dictated by the government and by the religious orders, although the college of San José, the Dominican university of Santo Tomás, the college of San Juan de Letran, and various other institutions had flourished for the greater or less part of Spanish domination, and especially, although the active government measures, beginning with the memorable decree of December 20, 1863, had induced a wider result in primary instruction, the educational methods in force in the islands were antiquated, often without result, and narrowing, and to a certain degree tended to shackle rather than to free the mind. The best work was done by the Jesuits who had adopted the most progressive methods used in the islands during Spanish occupancy. The religious orders are not without praise for having established, as early as they did, educational institutions where some Filipinos could, to a certain extent, take on the advantages of the occidental polish and education which Spain had to offer. But it must be remembered that Spain itself has never, since the early days when the great Salamanca University flourished as one of the most advanced outposts of education in the world, been renowned as a center of learning. Hence, it may be said, whatever the cause for its deficiency, that Spain gave to the Philippines the best that it had in the way of education; with the reservation that the remoteness of the colony from the mother country gave opportunity for neglect and carelessness on the part of both official and ecclesiastic, and for the furthering of private or corporation ends, at the expense of and detriment to the colony. Quite apparently, a country cannot give to a colony what it does not itself possess. Had Spain possessed a more modern and effective system of education, doubtless the same would have been true in the Philippines. To determine the reason for the backwardness of education in the islands, therefore, one must examine the causes for its poor condition in Spain, and the two will be found in great measure to be the same. The root of the matter will be found in the close connection between Church and

State—this connection dating back in greatest measure to 1493, when the ecclesiastical patronage of the Spanish monarch became a settled fact, and Church and State were irrevocably bound together—and a misconception as to where the educational function primarily resides—which we take to be a function of government.

We cannot, in the short compass allowed, enter into the discussion of the factors involved, the most important of which is the question of the friar orders and the transference of their power in greater proportion even than in Spain, into the Philippines. Suffice it to say here that those who would blame the friar orders exclusively for the backward state of the Philippines in education as in other things, go astray; and the same is equally true of those who would excuse them altogether. The same remark holds true of the government. Both the religious orders, or even more broadly, the entire ecclesiastical government, and the civil government, are to be reproached for the deplorable condition of Philippine education.

It is the results of the pre-American education that allows the following to be said: "The party which follows the intellectual leadership of Leon Guerrero (director of El Renacimiento) is quietly resisting what they call the 'Anglo-Saxonization' of their people through the schools. These men are really Spanish at heart (the older, mostly so in blood), and they have a Spanish-Latin feeling of hostility to the very name of 'Anglo-Saxon.' They prefer Latin education and educational methods, and Latin molds of civilization. Where they go astray is in their assumption, entirely gratuitous, that they really represent the Filipino people and Filipino ways of thought, desires and aspirations which are to be 'squelched' by this new campaign of instruction in English. Now, superficially, there are little evidences to corroborate this view, as would be inevitable, as the results of three centuries of tutelage according to Spanish models. But the man who looks beneath the surface sees at once that the Filipinos are not 'Latins' and were not 'Latinized,' and that these intellectual Latins, floating at the top of Filipino society are as mistaken as can be in assuming that they are representative of their people. The truth is, the Filipinos, in the mass, are, as regards the purposes of any real education, virgin material to work upon. Not only has their national and social life not been cast over in Latin molds, but Spanish influence was just sufficient, added to their undeveloped state at the time of the conquest, so that there are no 'Filipino molds' of civilization. They are really just ready to be worked upon, and whatever fundamental elements of 'Filipino nationality' there are latent, whatever inherent or acquired social traits properly constituting a 'Filipino soul,' will come to the front with this new opportunity."[1]

It is impossible to give a comprehensive résumé of American efforts toward the education of the Filipinos. The captious critic will emphasize the mistakes which have been made and which will be made in the future, and it is yet perhaps too early to make a pronounced statement as to the results; but this much may be said, and in no spirit of American self-congratulation, namely, that the Filipino is at present enjoying the greatest opportunity that has ever been offered to him to acquire an education. The chief problem of the Philippines has well been said to be that of education.2 Chief among future developments must be industrial education, which will not only train rightly the great dexterity of the Filipino, but also teach him the dignity of work with the hands, whatever his rank or station, and thus help to fit him for, and hasten the time when he shall enjoy greater self-government than he enjoys at present.

Below we give the direct available sources for a study of American education in the Philippines, from which the student may be able to study the question in its many phases. It is to be noted that a study of the present-day education in the islands must always be made hand-in-hand with that of the past. As might be expected, the majority of such sources are government documents.

Public Laws and *Resolutions* passed by the United States Philippine Commission (published by authority of the U. S. Philippine Commission, Manila). The various volumes of these laws contain the following acts concerned with education (number of act and date alone being given).

> 1900—3, Sept. 12; 4, Sept. 12; 11, Oct. 3; 15, Oct. 10; 32, Oct. 24. 1901—69, Jan. 5 (accompanied later in vol. by arguments of Dr. T. H. Pardo de Tavera and others against the rector of the university of Santo Tomás, and the Roman Catholic Church, in regard to the college of San José; and appearing also in *Senate doc.*, no. 190, 56th Congress, 2d session); 74, Jan. 21; 93, Mar. 4; 97, Mar. 9; 110, Mar. 30; 129, May 16; 156, July 1; 163, July 13; 180, July 24; 201, Aug. 13; 222, Sept. 6, 228, Sept. 7; 239, Sept. 25; 248, Oct. 2; 264, Oct. 14; 285, Oct. 29; 291, Nov. 2; 311, Dec. 4. 1902—330, Jan. 9; 339, Jan. 28; 373, Mar. 7; 407, May 24; 415, June 9; 446, Aug. 15; 453, Oct. 8; 490, Oct. 27; 512, Nov. 10; 514, Nov. 11; 524, Nov. 18; 532, Nov. 24; 563, Dec. 22; 565, Dec. 22. 1903—600, Jan. 27; 661, Mar. 5; 672, Mar. 7; 682, Mar. 14; 686, Mar. 17; 734, April 8; 744, April 8; 795, July 23; 807, July 27; 810, July 30; 832, Aug. 12; 837, Aug. 24; 846, Aug. 24; 854, Aug. 26; 858, Aug.

27; 880, Sept. 10; 904, Sept. 25; 917, Oct. 1; 919, Oct. 2; 997, Nov. 17; 1018, Dec. 2. 1904—1048, Feb. 6; 1049, Feb. 11; 1057, Feb. 20; 1085, Mar. 10; 1133, Apr. 28; 1175, June 2; 1188, June 29; 1199, July 19; 1216, Aug. 17; 1225, Aug. 31; 1231, Oct. 14; 1251, Nov. 25; 1275, Dec. 6. 1905—Jan. 12.

Of these the most important is act no. 74 (and its various amendments), establishing a Department of Public Instruction in the Philippines, and appropriating $40,000 for the organization and maintenance of a normal and trade school in Manila, and $15,000 for the organization and maintenance of an agricultural school in the island of Negros, for the year 1901. Many of the acts are appropriations for various purposes. In addition to the above, acts touching archives and laboratories, as well as various other matters, may be considered as having educational value.

Reports of the Philippine Commission (Washington). Of chief value in this publication are the annual reports of the Secretary of Public Instruction, such reports beginning for the year 1902. It is to be noted that these reports contain the following (we cite from the Commission report for 1905, just issued): General report of the secretary of Public Instruction; report of the superintendent of Education; report of the chief of the Bureau of Architecture and Construction of Public Buildings; report of the Public Printer; report of the Bureau of Archives, Patents, Copyrights, etc.; report of the acting librarian of the American circulating Library; report of the editor of the Official Gazette. Special references in the various reports are as follows:

> 1900—i, pp. 17–42; 1901—i, pp. 133–148, ii, pp. 511–575 (appendix FF containing Fred W. Atkinson's report); 1902— first annual report of the Secretary of Public Instruction, year ending Oct. 15, 1902, ii, pp. 865–1049; 1903—second annual report of the Secretary of Public Instruction, iii, pp. 667–985; 1900–1903—containing various general reports for those years, and which occur in the preceding volumes, pp. 121–129, 257–272, 399–434, and 685–721; 1904—third annual report, etc., iii, pp. 811–971; 1905—fourth annual report, etc., ending June 30, 1905, iv, pp. 369–652.

In addition to the above much other educational matter will be found scattered through the other volumes for each year. These volumes are also published separately in the Reports of the War Department.

Reports of the Commissioner of Education (Washington). Several of these reports contain matter on the Philippines, as follows:

> 1899–1900—ii, chap. xxix (in part), pp. 1595–1640, "Intellectual attainments and education of the Filipinos"

(contains some Spanish data, act. 74, of the Philippine Commission, a bibliography, and the Tagálog alphabet); 1901—ii, chap. xxix, pp. 1317–1440, "Present educational movement in the Philippines," by Fred W. Atkinson; 1902—ii, chap. i, pp. 2219–2271, "Education in the Philippines;" 1903—chap. xlvi (in part), pp. 2385–2388, "Education in the Philippines" (taken from report of David P. Barrows for the year ending Sept. 30, 1903).

Bulletins of the Bureau of Education (Manila, 1904 and 1905), as follows:

No. 1, Philippine Normal School prospectus for the year 1903-4, (in both English and Spanish); no. 2, Course of study in vocal music (for vacation normal institutes); no. 3, Philippine School of Arts and Trades (1904–1905, in both English and Spanish); no. 4, Philippine Nautical School (prospectus for the year 1904–1905, in both English and Spanish); no. 5, Notes on the treatment of Smallpox (for use of teachers); no. 6, Report of Industrial Exhibits of the Philippine Schools (Louisiana Purchase Exposition); no. 7, Courses of Instruction for the Public Schools of the Philippine Islands; no. 8 (?); no. 9, List of Philippine Baptismal Names; no. 10, Government in the United States (prepared for use in the Philippine public schools); no. 11, Courses in mechanical drawing, woodworking, and ironworking for provincial secondary schools; no. 12, Advanced and postgraduate studies offered by the Philippine Normal School (preparation for entrance to American colleges and universities or to the university of the Philippines; in English and Spanish).

Municipal Code (Manila, 1905). Contains matter on schools, teachers, etc.

Census of the Philippine Islands (Washington, 1905), iii, pp. 638–669, "[Education] under the Americans," by Prescott F. Jernegan, of the Philippine Normal School (a short account through 1903). Also, another division entitled, "Schools: schedule; summary of statistics; classification; buildings; teachers; pupils; sources of revenue; expenditures," pp. 670–694.

Bulletin of the Bureau of Labor. No. 58, May, 1905 (Washington, 1905), pp. 721–905, "Labor Conditions in the Philippines," by Victor S. Clark. Much of this will be found to have a bearing on education.

Books on the Philippines

Atkinson, Fred W.: *The Philippine Islands* (Ginn and Co., 1905); especially chap. xiv, pp. 373–412, "Education."

Freer, William B.: *Philippine experiences of an American teacher* (New York, 1906).

LeRoy, James A.: *Philippine Life in town and country* (New York and London, 1905); especially chap. vii, pp. 202–245, "Education and public opinion." Most of this book has a bearing on educational matters.

Stuntz, Homer C.: *The Philippines and the Far East* (Cincinnati and New York); especially chap. xii, pp. 185–215, "Educating a nation."

Willis, Henry Parker: Our Philippine problem (New York, 1905), especially chap. x, pp. 226–246, "American education in the Philippines." See a criticism of this book by James A. LeRoy, in Political Science Quarterly, for June, 1906.

We shall bring this brief statement regarding American education in the Philippines to a close with a short abstract of the recent address by Dr. T. H. Pardo de Tavera, before the teachers assembled at Manila in order to attend the Summer Institute, founded by the director of Public Instruction, and inaugurated this year, and published in the supplement of the issue of May 17, 1906, of El Renacimiento. His point of view of true civilization and education is in the main that they are the resultant of not one but of many factors, and that those of one race may be debtors to another race and yet not lose their identity. True progress does not consist in exclusiveness but in the admittance of all that is good notwithstanding its source. By adopting Anglo-Saxon civilization and education, Filipinos will not weaken, but strengthen themselves. The viewpoint of a people may change, and must change often in order that they may progress. To speak of special mentalities is vague and misleading. On whatever side the situation of the Philippines be considered, he says, whether political, social, or economic, it is seen that "public instruction is the chief factor, to which we should direct the most vigorous action of our energies." Progress is the direct and necessary result of education, and the Filipinos realizing this desire the extension of schools. It has often been said that the Filipinos need an education in harmony with their customs and traditions, in order that they may preserve their peculiar manner of existence, or "that the conscience called poetically 'the Filipino soul' might not be changed or disfigured." Let those who criticize the American method of education, on the ground that it is destroying the "Filipino soul" define that term, and name the characteristic qualities belonging to it, which will disappear with the new education; and let them propose a system of education. Some wish to preserve the traditional education of Filipinos which is conservative and exclusive. The teaching of Filipinos, since Spain is a Catholic monarchy, where the divine origin of rulers is a tenet, has always been dogmatic, and blind obedience is to be given to the government. Such teaching produces a conservative and exclusive society, which is opposed to change. The Filipinos desire a democratic government, but their traditions and education form in them a mentality quite opposed to democratic ideas. Consequently, they must first change their mental viewpoint before they can become democratic. It must be a work of peaceful evolution, through free instruction. Living as they are now under a democratic form of government, Filipinos should adopt a form of education in accordance with the ideals of democracy. The two forces working in the formation of the character of individuals, and hence peoples, are conservatism and the reforming force, the latter of which means progress and constitutes education. Those peoples who do not progress live under the laws of conservatism, inheritance, and tradition. Those progress who have conquered inherited and traditional traits by means of education. Some races are inferior to others, but that inferiority is not necessarily permanent. Inferiority is purely an historical cause, and inferior races are those that preserve their national soul unchanged through the centuries. The Spanish race is not inferior to the Anglo-Saxon, but its education is under a political and religious dogmatism which has made of Spain a country with a traditional and truly conservative soul. Italy has gone through and is even now going through a period of regeneration. In Spain, men are struggling for better education based on Anglo-Saxon principles.3 Before the Filipino revolution, many Filipinos were sent to Europe to study without any fear of destroying the "Filipino soul;" but now that the civilization that they went to seek has sought them, under the form of Anglo-Saxon public instruction, there is a strange reaction. The Franks and Gauls who submitted to Roman civilization have not lost their peculiar identity. Had they not adopted the Roman civilization, their condition would have been that of the Malays under British domination, who are now inferior. Since they did adopt it they were enabled to raise their coefficient of capacity. The Filipino mentality has been already changed by Spanish education, the customs and life of the two races having been quite distinct. Civilization is the result of the contact of peoples by means of which the victories obtained in all departments of intelligence and morality may be increased, perfected, and transmitted from one to another. Anglo-Saxon education will not cause the Filipinos to lose their desire for independence. The Filipino revolution was started by men who received a Spanish education. The entire Filipinist movement was guided by men educated in Europe and the University, the latter of which was Spanish. They were broader men. The Anglo-Saxon education cannot make submissive peoples. It is destined to form individuals capable of thinking for themselves, and of working according to their own impulses. Those civilizations that mark an epoch in history were the result of other civilizations. The Anglo-Saxon race today bear the torch of civilization formerly borne by the Romans. The Anglo-Saxon civilization will extend, but not Anglo-Saxon domination. The Japanese are an example of a race who have changed their standpoint in regard to civilization. Filipino mentality is composed of good and bad traits. Complete education must be arrived at by conserving the good and eliminating the bad. Complete assimilation cannot take place. The Filipino character cannot entirely change, for the instruction in the schools is not sufficient to cause such a radical change. Happiness does not consist in seeking easeful and unresponsible repose, but in the struggle for existence that entails work. Filipinos must learn that true progress comes through struggle and a show of energy. The Filipinos are intelligent, easy to educate, and prepared by their Spanish education of three centuries for the new education now offered them. Education means advance. The greater means of communication that are to be established will aid in the work by destroying inequalities and composing differences. The various dialects are a great barrier to Filipino homogeneity, and a common language is needed. The Filipino people free and capable of self-government will be formed by the American and Filipino teachers. "Filipino soul"[4] is a poetical expression which reveals a poetical mentality in those who use it. Such mentality is insufficient for the progress of a people along the true path of modern civilization.

[1] In a letter from James A. LeRoy, of June 27, 1906.

[2] J. A. LeRoy: Philippine Life.

[3] Chief among these men may be cited Francisco Giner de los Rios, of the Madrid University, who has established the Free Institution of Teaching in Madrid for the training of teachers. He follows principally American methods. Both Church and State have opposed him, but he has persevered and his institution has had good results.

[4] Apropos of the "Filipino soul," James A. LeRoy says, in the letter cited, ante, note 118, "No Filipino on earth, if pinned down, could tell what the 'Filipino soul' is today, as Tavera hints."